THE
MEXICANS

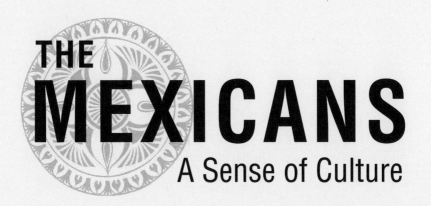

THE MEXICANS

A Sense of Culture

floyd merrell

Purdue University

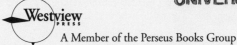

Westview
PRESS

A Member of the Perseus Books Group

Copyright © 2003 by Westview Press, A Member of the Perseus Books Group

Westview Press books are available at special discounts for bulk purchases in the United States by corporations, institutions, and other organizations. For more information, please contact the Special Markets Department at the Perseus Books Group, 11 Cambridge Center, Cambridge MA 02142, or call (617) 252-5298.

Published in 2003 in the United States of America by Westview Press, 5500 Central Avenue, Boulder, Colorado 80301–2877.

Find us on the World Wide Web at www.westviewpress.com

A Cataloging-in-Publication data record for this book is available from the Library of Congress.
ISBN 0-8133-4043-8 (HC)   ISBN 0-8133-4044-6 (Pbk.)

The paper used in this publication meets the requirements of the American National Standard for Permanence of Paper for Printed Library Materials Z39.48–1984.

10   9   8   7   6   5   4   3   2   1—05   04   03

Contents

Preface

Our Big Problem

Knowledge of "Latino" cultures is now more important than ever. During the late 1980s and early 1990s, over 500,000 immigrants arrived annually in the United States, the majority of them from Latin American and Asian countries. That number has increased over the past couple of years. As a consequence, there has been talk of a so-called browning of America. This is in large part due to the influx of Latino immigrants, documented or otherwise, who now reside in the United States. Along with U.S.-born Latinos, immigrants from Latin America make up the growing population of Spanish-speaking people in this country. In fact, among the Spanish-speaking countries in the world, the United States now ranks fifth in population size—after Mexico, Spain, Argentina, and Colombia.

Moreover, the economic malaise throughout much of Latin America from the 1980s to the present caused salaries in the professions to lag behind inflation. Consequently, there is a "brain drain": Many educated professionals are leaving their homelands for job opportunities in the United States, and so Latinos are becoming more visible in white-collar jobs. Additionally, an increasing number of U.S.-born Latinos with college degrees are entering the job market, making it even more crucial for non-Latinos to learn more about their Latino counterparts. Sadly, however, although we eat a bland imitation of Latino food, applaud Latino baseball players, enjoy Latino music and Latino actors, and occasionally laugh at jokes about Latinos, in most cases we remain ignorant of Latin America and its cultures.

My Own Little Problem

For the past quarter century I have yearly taught a course in Latin American cultures and civilizations, in Spanish, to undergraduate students. Most of the students are language majors, and a few are native-speaking students from other departments. During the past decade and a half it has become increasingly important that students in fields such as business administration, restaurant and hotel management, family guidance, education, and indeed the traditional disciplines as well, have some familiarity with cultures south of the United States. The problem is that few of these students study Spanish. For the spring semester of 1999, I was scheduled to teach a new course of my own design, in English, on cultural awareness, focusing specifically on Mexico. I had few expectations. To my surprise, the class was soon filled to capacity with a growing waiting list. I felt apprehensive about the students, who, sealed within their customary ways, would resist my effort to enlighten them with cultural tidbits from a strange foreign land. Wrong again. They were surprisingly open to a form of life other than their own.

As a consequence of this experience, I set myself the project of writing this book about Mexico's diverse cultures. These cultures include Amerindian, African American,[1] European, and other ethnically diverse groups, beginning with the conquest and colonization. I offer a historical overview of Mexico while at every opportunity focusing on what makes Mexico the way it is. Emphasis rests on understanding daily life and its complex artistic, political, economic, and social patterns. This book should be of interest to students who during their professional career expect to come into contact with citizens of Mexican and Latin American origin in the United States. It will also, I expect, be helpful for visitors to Latin America.

Presenting a story with appeal to such a diverse audience from many fields brought challenges at every turn. With these challenges in mind, I attempted to create a convergence of the diverse views readers will bring to this book on the need for (1) greater intercultural awareness and (2) cultivation of an ability to appraise radically distinct cultural conventions. Given this focus, the cultural and intercultural concepts presented in this volume offer the image of a broad panorama, including the origins, history, and contemporary trends of one of the most diverse cultures in Latin America.

A Survey

After a brief introduction, Chapter 1 stresses the importance of communication in intercultural encounters. It offers examples from (1) miscommunication regarding Justice of the Supreme Court Clarence Thomas's hearings and Anita Hill's charge of harassment and (2) interlinguistic, intercultural communication bloopers common in the advertising media and international diplomacy. These examples involve people's inability to comprehend messages across races, ethnicities, and genders, which serves to emphasize the importance of language and cultural awareness.

Chapter 2 introduces the notion of "contact zones" between cultures within which conflicts emerge. Communication, when it is forthcoming within contact zones, consists of a folding over of a cultural field into and onto itself in such a manner that all people involved enter into *interdependent, interrelated*, human *interaction*. Such interdependent, interrelated interaction plays a role in the emergence of Mexico's ethnic mixture, a mixture that began at the time of the conquest. Actually, the process was preordained when Christopher Columbus first dropped anchor in the Caribbean. It led to what historian Edmundo O'Gorman terms the "invention," rather than the "discovery," of America. America was "invented" in that it was foretold in myths, legends, and broad cosmologies that existed in learned societies and in the popular mind at the end of the fifteenth century.

Chapter 3 discusses the Aztecs and Spaniards. This leads in Chapter 4 to the conquest and colonization of New Spain (Mexico). These two chapters serve to usher in Chapter 5, where Mexico's ethnic and racial miscegenation catches the spotlight. This miscegenation has resulted in the emergence of and differences between Spaniards and criollos (Spaniards born in America), African Americans and mulattos (of European and African parents), Amerindians and mestizos (of European and

Amerindian parents), and many other racial mixtures too numerous to list here. This radical *hybridization* of human types and cultures could not avoid conflicts, chief of which occurred at the end of the eighteenth century between Spaniards and criollos. As we see in Chapter 6, this conflict erupted in the movement for Mexican independence at the beginning of the nineteenth century.

These first six chapters set the scene for a survey, in Chapter 7, of some of the chief characteristics of Mexican individual and collective behavior that developed especially during the nineteenth century: *personalismo, machismo, caudillismo*. Chapters 8–9 review Mexico's social-political-economic movements through the nineteenth century and up to mid-twentieth century, including the tumultuous Mexican Revolution from 1910 to 1920. Chapter 10 bears on Mexico's inclination toward *forms*, or *formalities*. Mexican formalities reveal themselves through subtle verbal nuances of the sort that are found in Mexico's particular twists of the Spanish language. Chapter 11 makes use of the material developed in Chapters 7 and 10 to illustrate how Mexico presents on the surface most of the trappings of modernization. Yet Mexico is *both* modern *and* unmodern and at the same time *neither* modern *nor* unmodern. This uniquely Mexican paradox introduces an element of *contradictory complementarity* within Mexican culture.

In Chapters 11–12, the tensions that had been seething under the surface of Mexican society since the revolution finally reveal themselves. There was discontent and political repression in the 1960s. That decade was followed by a wave of populism and abuse of power in the early 1970s, an oil boom in the late 1970s, and a bust when prices fell in the early 1980s. There was economic recession during the 1980s, NAFTA and the rebellion in the state of Chiapas in 1994, and finally the election of President Vicente Fox in 2000 to end Mexico's seventy-one-year single-party rule. Thus Mexico's dream—or illusion as it were—of taking its place among the economic giants of the world remained far from realization. What went wrong? Where could the blame be placed? Is there something within Mexican culture that hinders the country from achieving political, economic, and social development?

Chapter 13 briefly addresses these questions by highlighting the Mexican image of family, friends, and associates. It foregrounds the nation's hierarchical stratification, revealing how Mexico's social, political, and economic means and methods are based on citizens whose sentiments often lie more with authority figures, respected individuals, and cultural heroes, than with abstract and impersonal institutions and their structures. All these characteristics are antithetical to an entirely open society. Nevertheless, they are distinctively Mexican. For sure, Mexico's particular characteristics as developed in Chapter 13 might cast a pallor of gloom. However, Chapter 14 suggests that broad cultural rhythms hold Mexico together in an intimate, warmly human way that would not be possible in mainstream Western societies. Mexico is by no means simply Western, and if it were to become Western, it would already have ceased being Mexico.

In Retrospect

This book, then, offers a nonlinear trajectory requiring your active *coparticipation* along the way. Its chapters oscillate between (1) discussions of the chronological sequences of events leading up to contemporary Mexico and (2) narrative about what makes Mexicans Mexicans. I hope that this alternating pattern will give the reader a certain feel for the Mexican people.

At the end of each chapter I offer a list of suggested readings. These readings are from various disciplines, and they range over a broad diversity of topics. I offer a variety of readings so that readers may pick and choose from them according to their tastes and inclinations (some of the books, I might add, are in Spanish, for the benefit of those who read the language). In addition, at the end of this volume I include an appendix listing Mexico's twentieth-century presidents for quick reference and a brief glossary of key terms.

floyd merrell

Notes

1. In this volume I use the term "African American" to designate people of partly or wholly African heritage throughout the Americas, thus including "Afro-Mexican," "Afro-Caribbean," "Afro-Cuban," "Afro-Brazilian," terms that are often used in English to designate people of African heritage in particular nations of Latin America.

Introduction
Learning Language, Knowing Culture

Why?

We live in a rapidly changing world. The global community is now the arena in which we make our friends and enemies. Obviously, greater knowledge of world cultures is more vital than ever. In order to compete in the global community, we in the United States must be able to appreciate, understand, and work in the framework of other cultures. Some of our competitors already realize the importance of language study and cultural awareness. In Japan, every public school student begins studying English by the seventh grade. Almost all students in the nations of the European community learn two or more foreign languages. We in the United States bring up a distant rear in this race toward global cultural awareness.

Occasionally I hear students at my institution say something like the following: "Why bother with learning another language or coping with another culture? I can go to Europe, Asia, Africa, or Latin America whenever I want, loll on the beaches just as I do in Florida, eat American food, stay in American hotels, and get by with English, since I can always find somebody who speaks my lingo." Well, yes. Hang onto your security blanket. Cling to the "American way." Do Mexico—or whatever country—your way, while enjoying your standard comforts. And while you're at it, take in some Corona beer, piña coladas, a few touristy mariachi bands, and lots of fun and the good life. After all, so the story goes, the almighty dollar rules. So why sweat it?

Why sweat it? Sweat it because, given the current trend toward "globalization," we of the United States will rightly be considered no more than a small percentage of all the citizens of this Planet Earth. Sweat it because globalization brings multicultural trends along with it. To the question, Is the United States itself rapidly becoming more multicultural? the answer is yes and no, depending on what is meant by "multicultural." If we use it to allude to the population mix and ethnic-racial makeup of the workplace, the answer is, Yes, this country is rapidly becoming more multicultural. If by the term we mean our general awareness of distinct ethnic groups in the United States, then the answer is a resounding, No! This country is becoming multicultural at a snail's pace. (See *Culture, Biculturalism,* and *Monoculturalism* in the glossary.)

During recent years we in the United States have found ourselves caught up in vicious debates over what goes by the label "multiculturalism." Unfortunately, these debates are often the product of culture wars. Some of the wars have emerged by natural processes, and some of them are mere fabrications. At times, this country appears to be a collection of monocultural power groups, each with its own agenda. Each group takes refuge in the dark corners of its deeply rooted traditional identity. Each tries to hermetically seal itself from the outer world as a defense against all other groups; each wraps itself in its own rhetoric, a closed rhetoric that stultifies the mind and blinds eyes, deafens ears, and mutes lips. Consequently, open dialogue is becoming rare. Finger pointing is becoming the norm and faultfinding is the name of the game. People avoid taking responsibility for their own actions at all costs; mistakes are always attributed to something else or somebody else. Unfortunate, all this.

So why sweat it? Sweat it because we had better wake up to the music before it's too late.

We'd Best Remember That . . .

We in the good old U.S. of A. are too often content to finger the keys of our well-worn cultural accordion and bellow out "We're Numero Uno," oblivious to our aging accordion and our weary, wheezing voices. We'd best remember that the world is changing more rapidly than we realize and perhaps more rapidly than we would like. We have recently entered a new, profoundly uncertain era rendering us subject to nature's unreasonable whims, unpredictable terrorist strategies, and wild economic swings. We'd best remember that each year many people in other countries are in a better position to challenge us, and that at times we have difficulty rising to the challenge. We remain trapped in our cultural skins, as if we existed in a bubble. Our cultural immune systems have not developed properly; hence, we carefully protect ourselves from any and all possibilities of contamination from outside cultures. Many of us place this plastic bubble around ourselves, preventing other cultures from touching us until they have been properly cleansed from foreign contaminants.

All too often U.S. travelers in Latin America receive stock messages: "Don't drink the water. You know, Montezuma's revenge. Beware of food that has never before touched your delicate gullets. Quick, lock everything up! They're all out to get your money. Never go anywhere alone at night; you'll be taking your life in your hands." Everything must be properly filtered for us through the semipermeable membrane of our cultural prejudices. That is our life support system, the membrane that keeps us at a safe distance from all foreign bodies, human and nonhuman alike.

As a result, we are often ill equipped to cope with the unexpected. We have never learned how to make do with whatever is at hand. We must have everything prepared and packaged and ready for delivery to be paid for with a piece of plastic. We want no surprises; we want to get exactly what the commercial hoopla promised us. If we don't get it, we respond with outrage and demand a replacement or our money back. We've lost the ability to resolve our problems with a little ingenuity. Indeed, our track record regarding our adaptability to foreign settings is pretty dismal. We could have read in an August 1984 article in the *International Herald Tribune* that "more than one-third of all Americans who take up residence in foreign countries return prematurely because they are unable to adapt to day-to-day life." We read in Craig Storti's *The Art of Crossing Cultures* (1990, xiv) that 10–20 percent of Peace Corps volunteers return early; that 68 percent of Americans who take up residence in Saudi Arabia without cultural training fail to complete their contracts; and that even in England, with the same language and a comparable culture, 18 percent of employees without training return home prematurely. If left to luck, the average American's chance of a satisfying experience living abroad is about one in seven (Kohls 1984, 2). In the business world, the Peace Corps and diplomatic offices, and religious missions, this perpetual displacement and replacement of personnel is expensive. It also consumes time and energy, to say nothing of lost productivity. The *Washington Post* (November 22, 1986) reported that "the same bull-in-a-china-shop attitude toward foreign cultures and languages that has always cost American travelers respect overseas is now costing American business billions of dollars a year."

Our isolationism and ethnocentrism keep us at a far remove from other peoples and other cultures. Americans abroad representing the United States often fail to understand the local viewpoint entirely. In order to avoid uncomfortable encounters, they tend to seek out other like-minded and presumably "right-minded" Americans. They are interested in making the proper "contacts" among the "natives" only to further their careers or fill their bank account back home with fatter salaries. Such self-centeredness only serves to perpetuate the problem (see *American* in the glossary).

We'd best remember that people from other cultures are not the same as we are and they don't necessarily want to be like us. If we think we can make them like us, then it's later than we think. Fidel Velázquez, a long-time powerful labor leader in Mexico, once confided to an American journalist, "We're Latins, and our mentality is totally different from yours. We are further removed from material things than from those of the spirit. We are better able to bear poverty than mistreatment. If that were understood in the U.S., we could be closer to you" (Velázquez 1987). But perhaps in recent years we have not been as far removed from the Latinos as Velázquez thought. Have you noticed how many more battered clunkers are on the streets now than in years past? Have you been reading for years about downsizing and early retirements and laid-off employees who can only find jobs for which they are overqualified? Are you aware of the growing disparity between CEO salaries and what the average worker is making? Do you wonder why street people don't disappear at times when newspapers are reporting that the economy is healthy? In fact, the United States is slowly taking on the appearance of what we used to call the "third world," whether we know it or not and whether we like it or not.

North America is becoming increasingly diverse. More than one hundred languages are heard in New York City, Chicago, and Los Angeles schools. The U.S. Census Bureau in 1994 predicted that by the year 2000 "minorities" would be a majority in California, and by 2015 a majority in Texas. "Minorities" are already a majority in Hawaii, New Mexico, and the District of Columbia. By 2020 Maryland, Arizona, New York, Nevada, and New Jersey will have 42–45 percent "minority" peoples. Latinos and African Americans will make up one-third of the population by 2050. We'd best wake up to the music, smell the aroma of the coffee, and learn about cultures other than our own.

By now you're probably asking, What is this book about? A good question. It is about Mexico, of course, and about culture. Thus it begins with a concept of culture, not a survey of Mexico and the Mexicans. With that in mind, we will slide into the importance of understanding Mexico's past, especially regarding the rich mixture of racial and ethnic characteristics it evinces today. We will then survey Mexico's pre-Hispanic heritage, Spanish conquest and colonization, independence, and the Mexican Revolution of 1910–1920. We will learn how its revolutionary past is an indelible part of everyday life in contemporary Mexico. We will see how the official ruling party, PRI, made Herculean efforts until the year 2000 to keep the memory of the revolution alive through rhetorical practices.

But this book does not treat Mexican culture as if it were an isolated shell. It is about interrelations between Mexican and U.S. culture. "Poor Mexico, so close to the United States and so far from God," nineteenth-century dictator Porfirio Díaz once uttered. Nowhere in the world is the disparity between the haves and the have-nots so great as it is along the two-thousand-mile border between the United States and Mexico. The Mexicans have never forgotten that in 1848, after the Mexican-American War, the United States came into possession of slightly over half of their national territory. And today's Mexico cannot escape the presence of the richest country on earth, which dominates her economic, social, cultural, and political life. In this light, we will ask why the United States and Mexico can't get along, and how they somehow get along in spite of themselves.[1]

In the final analysis, I hope to leave you with a few hints regarding how to comprehend the Mexican mind when you come into contact with people from the Other America. I also hope that by the time you finish the last page of this volume, you will nod your head in agreement that we are all in this big wide world together. If the human species manages to survive, it will be due to the cooperative effort of us all. In contrast, if we wish to continue on in dreamy bliss under the assumption that we are the best and can ignore the rest, then a bleak future might be in store for us. In whichever case, the choice is ours.

Further Reading

On the topic of bi-, inter-, and multiculturalism, see: Condon and Yousef 1975, Eddy 1996, Ferraro 1990, Gudykunst and Ting-Toomey 1988, 1995, Kohls and Knight 1994, Seelye 1996, Seelye and Seelye-James 1995, Seelye and Wasilewski 1996.

Notes

1. A brief confession and a qualification might be appropriate at this juncture. Some of my comments about Mexico might appear excessively critical, in particular on the nature of Mexican politics. Please bear in mind that I sincerely love Mexico and its people. However, Mexican society, like societies the world over in our times, is caught up in a number of contradictions, dilemmas, and conflicts that simply cannot be ignored. My revelation of some of these contradictions, dilemmas, and conflicts takes nothing away from what must be admired and applauded in the Mexicans' ability to overcome many of their complex problems.

1

Getting It, Between Cultures

"It," A Difference That Makes a Difference

What exactly do I mean by cultural awareness? In a manner of speaking, cultural awareness enables us to "get it." Get what? "It." What do I mean by "it"? "It," a feel for what needs to be known. And what's that? In this book at least, it is how more effectively to know people of another culture. That is a tall order indeed. Am I up to it? Perhaps. At least let me try, by beginning this way.[1]

Back in 1991, African American Justice Thurgood Marshall retired and left a vacant spot on the Supreme Court. Another African American and a justice of the peace, Anita Hill, accused Ronald Reagan's appointee, a hitherto relatively undistinguished African American, Clarence Thomas, of sexual harassment. This business of an African American woman blowing the whistle on an African American male was something new. The entire idea of sexual harassment became subject to close scrutiny and fine-tuned interpretation. In short order, the Judiciary Committee hearings on the Thomas nomination became the trial of Anita Hill. Both Thomas's behavior and Hill's credibility were suspect. Above all, there was something that penetrated deep into the issues of gender and race. Was a black man being "lynched" (Thomas's word) by white men over his abuse of a black woman?

White congressmen on the investigating committee were uncomfortable as they groped for a way to articulate this strange new situation. Many women soon raised voices: "They (the men) just don't get it. They don't realize that a woman might be given a position at work because she is expected to tolerate harassing behavior; that to reject this behavior might jeopardize her job security; that to sound the warning bell would place her testimony against that of a male coworker who is often her superior." The Thomas-Hill hearings demonstrated that certain circumstances call for discussion of the limitations of male perspectives with respect to the experiences women share: "They just don't get it." The press picked up on the words and made them into a story about how men misunderstand the ethical seriousness of sexual harassment. During the hearings, women in their more daring moments were saying: "You don't get it because, in spite of your good intentions, you can't experience what we experience and feel what we feel."

"Getting it." It's a matter of flowing along the same wavelength, tuning in to the same channel. "Getting it" is a certain feeling, and it applies to all walks of life. "It" is shared by those auto repairmen of years past who could listen to your car and know exactly what was wrong with it while all you heard was a funny sound. The jazz pianist has "it" when his fingers know what to do and they just do it. The master chef has "it" when she knows the moment the sauce touches her tongue what was added to perfection and what additional ingredients should be tossed in the pot. The painter has "it" when she checks her canvas from a distance and then steps up to give it a few final daubs, the significance of which totally eludes us. "It" is sensed by the basketball pro who fakes to the right and switches the ball from his right hand to his left hand behind his back and with a leap deftly stuffs the ball through the hoop. You have "it" when you know what you know and you know that you know "it," with neither pride nor prejudice. You just know "it."

"Getting it" with respect to intercultural awareness can be possible when you let yourself go and forget who you are supposed to be. It's leaving your biases and preconceptions behind (as much as possible) and allowing yourself to imagine what other people experience and how you would feel if you experienced things the way they do. It's a matter of imagining a world other than the one you ordinarily inhabit, of pouring yourself into that world, of just going along with the flow. In the process, you free yourself from yourself, and you begin to see your own world and your culture and yourself through different eyes. Everything becomes topsy-turvy, a world upside down. Your culture becomes something different, something less familiar, and at the same time that other culture is becoming somewhat familiar. What is happening? You and the other culture are merging with each other. You took a slight leave of your own habitual pathways and you began treading another path. You are now somehow beginning to "get it." I hope this book will aid you in beginning to move along that other path. But before we proceed, allow me to take you into a world populated by people who didn't "get it."

Linguistic Bloopers

Problems of translation from one language to another and from one set of cultural conventions to another can lead to misunderstanding and confusion as profound as the male senators' not "getting it" during the Hill-Thomas trial.

Take promotional blunders. Transnational corporations should make every possible attempt to get things right when presenting their products to the public. Mistakes can be damaging. They can defeat the promotional purpose by inviting potential customers to take the advertised items as a joking matter rather than commodities to make life easier and more pleasurable. Some years ago General Motors advertised a new Chevrolet model, the Nova, in Puerto Rico. It was also called the "Nova" in Spanish, which can mean "it doesn't go." Chevy "Novas" obviously became the object of considerable humor. Ford Motor Company once proudly advertised its Pinto in Portugal, where the word "pinto" alludes to small male sex organs. A prominent U.S. firm invited its Mexican employees to a New Year's party. "Year" was spelled *ano* instead of *año*. A big blunder. *Año* is "year," while *ano* is "anus." Chrysler Corporation promoted its Dodge Dart with a translation of the English slogan "Dart Is Power." Unfortunately the translation implied that the drivers might be lacking in sexual vigor. "Come Alive with Pepsi" after faulty translation became the promotional slogan in Asia "Bring your ancestors back from the dead with Pepsi" (Ricks 1983).

Miscommunication through bumbled bits of information to tourists is notorious. A Japanese hotel once informed its patrons: "You are invited to take advantage of the chambermaid." From a Soviet weekly one could once read: "There will be a Moscow Exhibition of Arts by 150,000 Soviet Republic painters and sculptors. These were executed over the past two years." In a Rome laundry there was the invitation: "Ladies, leave your clothes here and spend the afternoon having a good time." A Mexican hotel proudly informed its guests: "The manager has personally passed all the water served." A Copenhagen airline ticket office promised: "We take your bags and send them in all directions." A Hong Kong dentist confidently informed his ailing patients: "Teeth extracted by the latest Methodists." In a Bangkok dry cleaner's shop one could read: "Drop your trousers here for best results." In a Czechoslovakian tourist agency there was the ad: "Take one of our horse-driven city tours—we guarantee no miscarriages."[2] Comparable booboos are countless. I trust the point has been made. If you don't "get it" linguistically, you'll soon stick your foot in your mouth.

Spanish and English are both members of the class of Indo-European languages, yet in some respects they are worlds apart. The Mexican accustomed to Spanish rhythms finds English brusque and curt. The North American who took two years of Spanish in college listening to Mexicans hears little more than a machine-gun staccato of unintelligible consonantal explosions penetrating fluid vowels. Mexicans see North Americans as blunt; North Americans would prefer that Mexicans get to the point and say what's on their mind. North Americans just say hello and get on with business; this is quite impolite for our neighbors to the south. At work, Mexicans sprinkle technical language with a liberal dose of colloquialisms; North Americans would rather keep linguistic practices in their proper place. North Americans stand a yard or more away from each other when carrying on a conversation. This is cold and impersonal for Mexicans, who prefer proximity, a few touches, and perhaps even a hug when a humorous account or some good news is forthcoming (Luce 1992).

In fact, nonverbal communication between North Americans and Mexicans is an entirely different ball of wax. It is terribly subtle and mind-bogglingly complex. If one "gets it" extralinguistically when immersed in a foreign culture, one is aware of nonverbal cues that come to the tune of gestures, body language, and a host of subtle nuances the complexity of which lies outside words and would require a thousand pictures. It's like the person who asked Louis Armstrong, "What is jazz?" He responded: "If you don't know, I can't tell you." Or, as Count Basie once said about music: "If it feels good, it's good."

In the final analysis I can't simply explain my modest knowledge of the extralinguistic, nonverbal aspects of Mexican culture. Ultimately, you'll have to learn for yourself. But by all means, be careful. There's nothing safer than listening intently before you speak, and observing and sensing the general mood of things before you act.

"Getting It" Tacitly

Before proceeding, we need to distinguish between *Culture* with a big *C* and *culture* with a little *c* (see the glossary).[3] When you have a hankering to do something cultural for an evening, your thoughts might turn to art, literature, drama, classical music, or perhaps ballet. That's *Culture*. Culture with a big *C* is chiefly the province of institutionalized practices. More often than not you must dress properly, possess respectable credentials, be willing to shell out some bucks, and use rather sophisticated language when sharing your opinion with others regarding your Cultural experiences. Big *C* Culture is most explicitly studied in university departments of art, languages, history, political science, sociology, anthropology, and even psychology.

Culture written with a small *c* is the implicit and largely subjective side of our everyday living. Little *c culture* includes the shared patterns of values, beliefs, and behaviors that guide people's interaction during their daily comings and goings. In academia, little *c* culture is often dubbed "popular culture" or "mass culture." These terms are problematic, for they often carry elitist implications: a distinction between those who have "real culture" and those whose culture is of the "vulgar" sort. In the most general sense, little *c* culture is what we do without really having to think about it because that is the way things are, and that's that. We've simply "got it." Little *c* culture allows us to know which words to use during our daily activities, how to make and how to take our nonverbal gestures, when to speak and where we sit or stand when doing our speaking, and how to address people at work, at play, in the street, in church, or in the home. Little *c* culture gives us our presuppositions, preconceptions, and prejudices. And that is what gets us into trouble when we just don't "get it" in the company of people from other cultures. We can have considerable classroom knowledge regarding big *C* Culture, but with respect to little *c* culture we may be babes in the woods.

Consider a hypothetical scene. You meet a person of the opposite sex from Colombia at an informal cocktail party. He is friendly, perhaps a little too friendly for comfort. He moves toward you slightly when addressing you, meeting your eyes, a huge smile on his face, nodding while he speaks as if tacitly asking for your approval. You are a little uncomfortable. You shuffle your feet back a few inches. He moves forward. You mumble a few words in response to a question with what seems a wooden face in comparison to his ebullience. You feel stiff and inflexible, but he continues to come on to you. Is he really attracted to you? Should you reciprocate? No. That would be too bold a move. So you smile a little, though nervously. You interject a comment here and there, feeling socially immature in comparison to his outpouring of words. How can he be so relaxed? After all, you just got to know each other. You inch back a little further and touch the wall. Uh-oh, further retreat is out of the question. Now he's pressing in again. You begin averting your eyes, looking around for a possible escape, but there is none. What to do?

The chief problem is that you just don't "get it." You don't understand his small *c* cultural habits: facial gestures, language inflections, body language, and spatial distance during a casual conversation. You are uncomfortable because your cultural practices differ from his. You can't effectively cope with the differences. They catch you off guard. What you don't realize is that he was possibly suffering through a comparable experience, asking himself all the while: "Why doesn't she seem receptive to what I'm saying? Why doesn't she speak more freely? Is she afraid of me? What gives?" The problem is that neither of you really "gets it."

In this imaginary situation neither you nor your Colombian acquaintance were intentionally and explicitly articulating your relations with the other person to yourselves. Your discomfort was sensed and felt tacitly. At nonconscious levels you were slightly disconcerted over this unexpected behavior. Was he excessively forward? Were you too uptight and formal? These are not the questions to ask. He was more likely than not neither forward nor giving you any come on. He was simply interacting with you in the same way he would interact with anyone of the opposite sex at his home base in Colombia. But he is not in Colombia. He may have spent considerable time in the United States, picking up the English language and using it with remarkable dexterity. His problem is that he remains caught within the nonverbal practices of his home culture. Whether he realized it or not, his attitude and behavior seemed to you uncomfortably forward. He might conceivably have placed himself in a quandary in the event that you had decided to "reciprocate" vis-à-vis his advances with a few moves of your own. That strategy might have caught him entirely off guard, and then it would be his turn to feel the heat of misinterpreted cultural cues.

So much for nonverbal cultural misunderstanding.

"Getting It," in Space

We often consider language as little more than a box full of tools for communicating. You want to say something? Take out a few tools and use them, and then they go back to that master toolbox, your brain. Here the tools, there the ideas, and they all create meanings somewhere else. If one tool doesn't work, toss it back in the box and draw out another one.

In a certain sense, it is true that language is a tool for communicating. Language also to a degree predetermines how we perceive and think. It brings a set of verbal categories that guides us in forming our sentiments, desires, ideas, and opinions. It preconditions us to dissect our world according to the ways and means of our cultural conventions. Consequently, language to an extent determines the way we come to understand our cultural world. When you were talking to your peer from Colombia, he was speaking in English but interpreting the North American context much as he would have interpreted it in his native territory. The language was English, yet he created nonverbal messages as if he were a Colombian speaking Spanish. As a result, there was miscommunication.

The idea that language presupposes us to interpret our world in a particular way alerts us to the possibility that our experience of reality could always have been something other than what it is. *Language* and *experience:* the combination of these two commodities creates a confusing mix. Many scholars tell us that learning a culture involves subtle knowledge of conventions that have been developed over the generations through *experience* and *language use*. These conventions with respect to everyday life are for the most part a matter of little *c* culture, that which we know nonconsciously and implicitly. It is just what we do, so we do it. We do it because we've "got it." All this, of course, involves language as a category maker. But language isn't all-important. When we are speaking of culture, language is of relatively little use if we disregard *context* and nonverbal communication. And how can we become familiar with the range of our cultural *contexts*? Through our *experience* in *using* language in conventional ways.

Context accompanies and complements language use. Anthropologist Edward T. Hall places language use along a continuous spectrum from *low-context* (LC) *cultures* to *high-context* (HC) *cultures* (Hall 1966, 1976) (see glossary). When people engage in communication that tends toward HC, the focus of information either is in the physical context or is internalized in the speakers and listeners. If the focus of information lies chiefly in the physical context, there is less need for explicit and exclusively linguistic meanings: the meaning is in the entire context, including the situation that prevails, the conditions present, and nonverbal gestures and body language displayed by the interlocutors. If the focus of information is primarily internalized in the body and mind of the interlocutors, they have expectations as a result of past experience that certain meanings will be forthcoming. Consequently, the success or lack thereof of their ability to communicate will be a matter of how effectively their expectations merge and interact with one another. If LC is the tendency, information is forthcoming chiefly by way of explicit linguistic ways and means. The context is of lesser importance because language is more explicitly used.

For example, recall your imaginary conversation with your acquaintance from Colombia. The person with whom you were talking was liberal with his facial gestures and body language. He might have touched you gently on your shoulder while moving his face uncomfortably close to yours when talking. He moved in too close to you according to *your* cultural conventions, but as far as he was concerned, he was just doing what comes naturally. His culture is more HC than yours; your culture is more LC than his. His body talked more than yours did; your mouth more explicitly communicated than did his. Thus the miscommunication. Thus the failure of both of you to "get it."

Take another scenario. You are preparing to step off the curb and cross a busy street in New York. A car running the red light is bearing down on you and someone screams, "Watch out!" You implicitly and tacitly have certain expectations, given the context of your actions, that this scene might be a possibility among other possibilities in everyday New York life. Your head jerks around, you spot the car and leap back on the curb. That's HC communication for you. Very little explicit information, given the context, was necessary.

Now imagine that within your LC culture you are engaged in a conversation. Someone is speaking and you are listening. She tells you about someone who started crossing the street without looking both ways first. The language is detailed, precise, and explicit. When the story is finished, you know the name of the streets at the intersection, the make and model and year and color of the car, approximately how fast it was going, whether the scene occurred during rush hour or not, how crowded the sidewalks were, and so on. You were told all this in a matter-of-fact way, with little emotion and few facial expressions or movement of the body. That's LC communication.

Now suppose you find yourself in an HC culture, for example, in Colombia with the same Colombian fellow you became acquainted with in the United States. He narrates a similar story about a pedestrian almost creamed by a car. However, in contrast to the calm, cool, and collected demeanor of the previous speaker, you now experience a dramatization of the scene. He acts out the entire event, giving you few details but profusely spicing up his account with the Spanish equivalent of "Wow!" "Good God!" "Jumped back just in time!" "Awesome!" "Close call!" and so on. That's HC communication. LC, I repeat, is linguistically more explicit; HC is less explicit. HC imparts relatively little linguistic information up front; yet the meaning is there, and it can be more impactful because dramatization accompanies linguistic messages. LC imparts a relatively high degree of linguistic information that contains much meaning, the effectiveness of which is gauged by the speaker's ability to express herself well. In general, Mexican culture is relatively HC; our own North American culture is relatively LC (of course, within the United States,

African American, Latino, Italian, Asian, and other minorities are also experts at HC communication).

No culture is exclusively HC or LC. Every culture manifests a tendency toward one end of the spectrum or the other. Cultures from Germany, Switzerland, Sweden, Finland, Denmark, and Holland tend toward LC communication more than most groups in the United States. The countries of southern Europe, Africa, Asia, and Latin America tend more toward HC communication. One might assume that technologically advanced cultures would prefer LC communication. Granted, when solving engineering and mathematical problems, when programming computers, when arguing in the courtroom, when drafting legislation, or when administering a corporation, people should convey information as explicitly as possible, whether the culture tends toward LC or HC communication. However, after work, when they are still talking shop, Latin American professionals, technicians, and business associates engage in intense HC communication to a considerably greater extent than what would be expected in the United States or northern Europe. HC communication is in the nature of their cultures. Why would they wish to communicate otherwise, even when getting down to business? (Hall and Hall 1990).

The moral to this story? Awareness of the distinction between LC and HC cultures and between LC situations and HC situations within the same culture is crucial to proper communication. On the one hand, awareness of body language and nonverbal communication in HC cultures is of utmost importance. If you lack such awareness, you risk missing the boat entirely. On the other hand, proper comprehension of your verbal messages in your LC culture is impaired if your messages are not spelled out properly. Consequently, your listeners may be left in the dark. Messages within HC cultures are often rather vague and ambiguous. This is in the very nature of HC communication. It leads to greater emphasis on human interrelations within specific cultural contexts. Human interrelations according to the situation can take priority over clear and precise language use. LC cultures place greater emphasis on explicit language use. Consequently, human interrelations are usually of somewhat lesser importance. The above "bloopers" might be taken as hardly more than humorous accounts by citizens of a relatively LC culture, while they could be demeaning and even insulting to the person of a relatively HC culture, who places greater priority on human interrelations, social standing, gender, and age.

Please keep the HC/LC distinction in mind as you navigate through and negotiate the pages in this book. It will help you get a feel for Mexican cultural tendencies.

It's About Time

In addition to context, there is another element of culture and communication that complements space: time. Edward T. Hall offers a temporal continuum that serves as a counterpart to his HC/LC spatial continuum.

At one end, Hall places *monochronic time* (MC) and at the other end, *polychronic time* (PC) (see *PC Time-MC Time* in glossary). If you live and breathe in MC culture, you customarily do one thing at a time, and you usually feel compelled to complete the task at hand before beginning another one. If you have assimilated PC culture, you immerse yourself in a mix of activities, flitting from one to the other with a facility that would boggle the MC inhabitant's mind. Time in predominantly MC cultures is *linear*; time in cultures leaning toward PC time is relatively *nonlinear*. Linear time is like an interstate highway in the midwestern region of the United States. It goes on and on in a straight line, until disappearing from sight. This form of time is cut up into regular segments; hence you usually know where you are, since linear time follows clock time. Nonlinear time is like finding yourself in one of a parallel series of roads that at irregular intervals branch off and interconnect with one another. You might discover that you are intermittently veering off along branching lines and into parallel times. It all becomes a confusing mess. But . . . wait a minute! That's not right. I'm assuming that you are from an MC culture; so PC time would place you in a distressful of labyrinthine time lines. Actually, for PCers who have effectively internalized nonlinear time, there might be no confusion at all. They can switch from one task to another, from one topic to another in a daily conversation, and from one subject to another in a term project they are working on with a facility that might appear utterly incomprehensible to MCers.

Relatively explicit learning arbitrarily imposes MC time on us. We learn to govern our activities by the clock. We are told since childhood to finish one activity before we begin another one, to put our toys away before going out to play, to put the CDs strewn around our room in order. We learn that time can be "saved," "wasted," "lost," and "spent," as if it were money or the material commodities money can buy. We are told that "a stitch in time saves nine," that "the idle mind is the devil's workshop," that "haste makes waste," and that "the early bird gets the worm." We learn that we must always be on time. We must keep ourselves busy, plodding along, grinding out our work, wrapping things up and neatly tying them with a linear ribbon, and health and prosperity will smile brightly on us. Yes, indeed. Everything must be in its proper pigeonhole. As a result, we construct a world of segmented compartments that are rationally conceived and logically orchestrated. MC time profoundly affects how we perceive our world and think and act in it.

MC living can be quite convenient within an MC culture. It can have disastrous consequences in a PC culture. Confusion arises when North American businesspeople travel to Mexico with the assumption that MC business is the only way, or when diplomats attempt to force MC thinking on their counterparts from Mexico. The same occurs when university professors invited to teach a course in Latin American institutions expect universities there to function as they do in the United States, and then they get bent out of shape when their expectations are thwarted. Mexicans in business, government, and universities frequently engage in several activities and tasks at once. They often dabble in a host of outside activities that influence the nature of their work. Presidents who are poets, businesspeople who paint, mathematics professors who write novels, lawyers who teach literature, doctors whose knowledge of the Roman Empire is vast, accountants obsessed with Oriental religions, and so on, are nothing out of the ordinary in Mexico. The beauty of it all is that these individuals never quite separate their professional activities from their intellectual pastimes.

It hardly needs saying that Mexican culture is relatively more PC; North American culture is relatively more MC—given obvious exceptions among African American, Hispanic, Italian, and other ethnic groups within the United States. English and Spanish are both Western European languages, and hence there is much overlap in the concept of time as it is expressed through them. However, intercultural awareness, specifically between Mexico and the United States, cannot ignore the tendency toward PC time in Mexico and toward MC time in the United States.

Extralinguistic Communication

Learning a language without adequately learning that language's culture presents a problem. Learning nothing but language is strictly a matter of learning words and rules for putting them into sentences—as if language use within culture were contextless (beyond HC and LC) and timeless (beyond PC time and MC time). In addition to learning language, learning culture has a lot to do with nonverbal expressions. It involves all sorts of sights and sounds, as well as smells and tastes and everything you feel with your hands and body within a particular culture. You could learn a language much like a robot. But during this learning process, you would assimilate very little with respect to the culture and contexts within which that language is spoken. This is because culture is to an extent beyond language. How can we account for this aspect of culture?

Take the Virgin of Guadalupe, considered by many Mexicans to be the patron saint of their nation (according to the legend, this representation of the Mother of Christ appeared to an Amerindian in 1531, a decade after the conquest of Mexico). Suppose in conjunction with my verbal expression, "Why, there's the Virgin of Guadalupe," I point to a visual depiction of the familiar Catholic icon. If you know virtually nothing of the Guadalupe tradition, the words and the image mean very little to you (in your alien and predominantly MC time and from a LC culture). You nod, perhaps shrug, and that's that. For a Mexican peasant raised in the Catholic tradition, in contrast, the words, the image, and my gestures are indeed significant (especially regarding his predominantly PC time and HC space). They evoke a warm feeling in him. They might even compel him to cross himself and, with proper contrition, softly articulate a few words of reverence. In other words, my words and gestures and the physical image cooperate and collaborate with each other to create profound meaning for the peasant. In contrast, were I to use no more than words in an empty room with the peasant, their meaning would be sorely deficient.

Words, gestures, and visual images support each other, and in so doing they augment meaning. Much meaning for the peasant would have been forthcoming had I made no more than a wordless physical gesture toward the Virgin of Guadalupe image. The words pronounced in addition to gestures and images were icing on the cake: they aided and abetted the meaning. Verbal communication without its proper context and nonverbal expressions is deficient; context and nonverbal expressions can be sufficient, though they are rendered more effective when accompanied by their respective verbal messages. As the saying goes, a picture is worth a thousand words. The same could be said of other forms of sight, as well as sounds and smells and tastes and touches. The proof of the pudding is in the taste, they also say. Try to describe a taste precisely in words. You can't. Neither can you effectively account for a Mexican's nonverbal expressions in language. The nonverbal expressions can pretty much stand on their own, without language; yet they are made considerably more effective when accompanied by language. Just as the physical image of the Virgin of Guadalupe brings on that familiar feeling within the Mexican peasant in his HC culture, so also the words, "Virgin of Guadalupe," can be meaningful in the absence of the image. However, put the two forms of communication together, and you have his familiar feeling magnified. All told, words and nonverbal gestures and cultural items within their proper contexts are necessary for effective communication in both HC and LC cultures. On this note, let us consider cultural contact in various forms.

In the Classroom, and Concrete Experience

Suppose a professor gears up to teach a course on a culture with which the students have little familiarity. During the semester, the students read a few texts, listen to a lot of lectures sprinkled with theoretical terms (many of which they never quite comprehend), and see a few dozen slides and a couple of videos. They are expected to imbibe this information by taking pages of notes and then spitting it all out in an exam at the end of the term.

Utterly hopeless. The students learned how to use a few words and retained a few exotic and undoubtedly distorted images, and that's it. What about the subtle distinctions between HC and LC communication? The different worlds within which PCers and MCers live? The communicative nuances illustrated in nonverbal communication? The so-called educational process might have been somewhat like the professor's narrating a vast series of "bloopers" without the students' awareness that they were "bloopers" at all, and they took them for real. For example, you might gawk in wonder over an Amerindian peasant's reverence before a faded image of what you saw as "that strange lady inside a bunch of jagged lines" (the Virgin of Guadalupe). You would gawk because you would have no awareness of the Amerindian's feeling for the image or the reason for which it is pregnant with meaning.

Some years ago our Museum of Art in Lafayette, Indiana, received a grant to hold a few "seminars" on various "exotic" cultures for the general public. I committed myself to one of the "seminars." The participating group was given the task of reading a Mexican novel for each session, and my charge was that of explaining the novel's content. The idea was to "impart culture." Impart culture—in about an hour! Yeah, sure. That was the first problem. The second problem came up in a discussion I had with a colleague when telling her about my impossible task. Her response was: "You, an Anglo male talking about Mexican culture through a few novels? Get real!" Me, an Anglo male, assuming I could teach Mexican culture to citizens of my own culture: the blind leading the blind!

I thought about it. She was right. At least she was partly right about her assumption that only a Mexican would be qualified to talk about Mexican culture and that I was automatically disqualified for the task. I have spent years in Mexico and my wife is from Mexico City. Yet by virtue of my ethnic background I might be considered entirely disqualified. A legitimate guide capable of conducting the local "tourists" through the Mexican novels they had read must be Mexican. The fact that the "tourist readers" had only a few pages of verbiage and perhaps a few visual images was seen as no handicap, as long as the guide—a Mexican but not myself—had the proper credentials. Whether or not the guide had spent enough time in the United States to become familiar with our concoction of cultures for the purpose of comparison and contrast between what the novels said about Mexican culture and the U.S. cultural scene would not be considered a problem. As long as the textual "tourists" had a Mexican guide, that would be sufficient. The guide could point out the important signposts in the novels, and all would be fine. The "tourist readers" would experience culture firsthand from a respectable authority.

All this bothered me for some time. Then I ran into Mary Louise Pratt's (1991) concept of cultural *contact zones* (see glossary). This made sense. Understanding a culture, any culture, one's own culture or that of other people, requires a contact zone. Without the zone there are no cultural differences capable of bringing one's attention to what is most important and what is of lesser importance within each of the two or more cultures in question. In the contact zone, no holds are barred. Within the same culture and between members of different cultures, there is tension, struggle, and negotiation, and then tension and struggle and negotiation all over again, as the cultural processes unfold. The contact zone suggests that there is hardly any value in gazing out of a well-latched window at quaint peoples and strange practices in the distance. There is nothing of value in listening to a lot of lectures and passively viewing slides and videos. There is even less to be derived from thousands of words plastered on a couple of hundred pages. In the contact zone, there is only actual conflict and struggle and sometimes violence and hopefully some negotiation and a little bit of comprehension. During this *process*, the contact zoners' life changes.

That, precisely, is the appropriate word: *process*. Not culture as a fixed product to be captured in slides and videos and books but *process*. Culture as a flux and flow of activity is impossible to fully understand, for when one thinks one has it, it has already moved along down the stream to leave one standing on the bank in consternation. So one enters the cultural flow and reestablishes contact, contact with people, with the coming and going of everyday practices, with language and nonverbal modes of communication. Contact is within the *process*. Such contact, if only for a brief duration, can hardly be deeper than water-skiing on the cultural surface. But at least there has been contact. Perhaps along with the contact there has been some *adaptation* among those who learn how to *accept* and *embrace* the other culture.

I have been in contact with Mexicans and Mexican culture for over forty years. I have spent countless hours with peasants and lower- and middle-class peoples, and with my Mexican wife and her relatives and friends. I have wandered hour after hour in the ghettoes of Mexico City, looking, listening, smelling, tasting the food, feeling the culture, and all the while pondering, contemplating, thinking, and occasionally talking with the people. I did this unaccompanied by anyone from my own culture and without the aid of a local "tourist guide." I just did it, and in the process I believe I gained a certain feel for the contact zone between Mexican culture and my own culture. I just did what I did in Mexico, and I believe I somehow "just got it." If I were asked whether the expenditure of time and energy was worth the effort, I would be at a loss for an answer. But, I would suspect, there is in the final analysis no other way to do it and to feel it and "get it." And now here I am, presumably writing a book about Mexico and a sense of culture. While doing so, I am waging a battle with myself, for I realize that within the contact zone there is only process. How is it possible more effectively to articulate this enigmatic process?

Our Participatory Cultural World

Please engage with me in a moment of mind twisting. Notice that the Möbius strip in Figure 1.1 consists of a band that doubles over and twists itself into itself and reenters its own two-dimensional field within three-dimensional space. Metaphorically speaking, just as the Möbius band twists into itself, so also the mind must contort itself before it can absorb certain aspects of another culture. What initially appears strange within the other culture is in this manner enfolded into what is ordinarily familiar

Figure 1.1 Möbius Strip

within the home culture so that the strangeness may become to a degree familiar. Thus the peasant's familiar Virgin of Guadalupe image can become intelligible to someone of any religious creed because there is something profoundly human about the reverence we all hold toward sacred images. Such a mental warp can create a second, then a third, and many perspectives. Eventually it brings about a fluctuating and flowing awareness of one's culture with respect to another culture. I write "fluctuating and flowing" because all cultures are in a *process* of becoming something other than what they were becoming. By means of this metaphorical image, I would suggest, it is possible to imagine how distinct cultures merge, *interdependently*, *interrelatedly*, and *interactively*, with one another (see *Interdependence* in glossary).

This little exercise in creating mind warps in order to get a feel for other cultures is not a simple game, however. Such a feel requires the ability to create the inversion of one's culture, and even of one's self, at a moment's notice. The person of genuine bicultural spirit capable of folding herself over and into herself to become someone other than who she was becoming manifests three characteristics. First, she is capable of *accepting* and *embracing* diverse perspectives. Second, she is adept at *adaptation* to the cultural world these perspectives imply. She can subtly slither into cultural flows, while altering, to a certain extent, her behavioral patterns, values and attitudes, and predispositions and propensities. Third, she is a master of *submersion* within different cultural flows. She can, so to speak, lose herself in another culture. All this is to indicate that biculturalism is not the yield of one person but, so to speak, of two or more persons in one body. It involves two persons in *interdependent, interrelated interaction* at the cultural contact zone. In a word, culture is a *participatory affair*.

The idea of participatory culture can be illustrated by a variation of that familiar parlor game Twenty Questions. In the customary version of the game, one person leaves the room and the group decides on a particular object in the room that the person must discover upon reentering and asking up to twenty questions. The question asker then comes back into the room and begins her interrogation, to which the answer is either yes or no. By a process of elimination, she is usually able to guess what the item is after a dozen or so questions. In the variation of Twenty Questions, you are asked to leave the room. You do so, and you wait . . . then you hear some giggling . . . and you wait some more. Finally, the door opens and someone asks you to enter. You begin asking questions. At first the answers come at a rapid-fire pace. As the game proceeds, you notice that the responders have to think about your questions too much. What are they doing? Why can't they just give you a simple yes or no? The pauses become longer and longer. You begin to get uncomfortable. You can't seem to narrow down on the object in the room that is presumably the focus of the responses. Why not? Are you just plain stupid? The questions gradually mount. Finally you reach the twentieth question, which is the final one. If you don't get the answer, then you must once again leave the room for another round of questions. You don't know quite what to ask. You blurt out a feeble inquiry. The response is yes, and everybody breaks out laughing.

What was going on here? What happened was that the group did not pick anything at all as the focus of attention. Rather, group members decided to allow your questions to determine the nature of the solution. The only rule was that each player must have something in the room in mind when answering yes or no. Consequently, each response had to match up with all the previous yeses and noes. That's why the responses came with increasing difficulty. Everybody had to keep all the previous responses in mind before answering yes or no to your last question. Then, for your twentieth question, suppose you asked, "Is it a statuette of Don Quixote"—like the one sitting on the piano—to which the response was yes. The yes, coupled with your question, determined what the object was. You, with your questions, had gradually eliminated many of the other things in the room, and you, with your final query, brought the statuette into existence by means of the nature of the whole collection of your questions. What is the lesson here? We, as *participants*, pull our cultures into existence, and we, as *interdependent, interrelated, interactive* subjects within culture keep culture in a flowing, fluctuating, transient *process*. Our queries regarding another culture provoke responses on the part of the people and things and events in that culture. After we have asked a sufficient number of questions, we know, and, smug with our newly discovered knowledge, we go our way.

But what is it that we learned? We learned how culture would respond to the particular questions we decided to ask of it. In that respect, we did not learn about culture as it was in and of itself, but about what culture decided to put forth to us as *participants* when we began our inquisition of its inner secrets. No inner secrets were unfolded and displayed for the benefit of our gaze. Instead, wily culture changed its face somewhat as a result of our *participation* with it in order to satisfy our curiosity. When our questions were answered, we also changed as a result of our *interdependent, interrelated interaction* with culture. All we can know is the result of culture's changing its features when responding to the nature of our questions.

By means of our silently asking questions of culture, it can manifest LC or HC, and MC or PC, and big *C* Cultural as well as little *c* cultural characteristics. In this manner, by our interacting with citizens of another culture, we can hopefully bring about a *submersion* of ourselves within that culture insofar as it may be possible. It is definitely to a greater or lesser degree possible because all cultures and all peoples are interdependently, interrelatedly linked to one another, and through their *interaction*, they can to a degree realize mutual submersion. This book, I repeat, may be a beginning along these diverging and converging lines of cultural entry. In the following chapters, you will be required to engage in mind twisters in order better to understand how Mexican ways are not yours and how the differences can be sensed. After you finish this book, the long, sinuous road beyond this book and into Mexico's cultural flows will be your journey and yours alone, when you begin concretely experiencing, for yourself, the language and culture of our neighbor to the south.

So much for the enigmas of culture. I ask that you keep the preceding pages in mind, for they have a bearing on the chapters that follow.

Further Reading

Berger and Luckmann 1966, Brislin 1993, Carbaugh 1990, Carr-Ruffino 1996, Gudykunst, Ting-Toomey, and Nichida 1996, Hall 1959, 1983, Lu 1996, Lustig and Koester 1993, Rosenfeld and Civikly 1976, Tannen 1990, Trompenaars and Hampden-Turner 1998, Weaver 1998.

Notes

1. I owe a debt to Dennis Fischman (1996) for the following paragraphs.

2. These bloopers appeared anonymously on the Internet, entitled "Signs in English over the World" (July 15, 1995).

3. More detailed definitions of key words, and especially those that are italicized at first mention in the paragraph, can be found in the glossary.

2

The Importance of Mexico's Past

When an Immovable Object Meets an Irresistible Force

Mexican poet and Nobel laureate Octavio Paz (1979) wrote that when he was ambassador to India he marveled at the never ending quarrels between Hindus and Muslims. What accident or misfortune of history caused two religions as irreconcilable as these to coexist yet perpetually clash within the same society? A stubborn form of monotheism collided with one of the most complex polytheisms in the world. Paz sees this clash as testimony of history's indifference toward the perpetuation of paradoxical cultural mixes at a rough-and-tumble *contact zone.*

Paz recalls that back home he was caught up in a no less singular paradox: the twisting, turning relationship between Mexico and the United States. We are neighbors, condemned to live side by side. Yet profound social, economic, political, and even psychological differences separate us. These differences are not simply differences of developed and developing, powerful and weak, dominant and dependent, wealthy and poor. The differences conceal a more fundamental, intangible distinction: the United States and Mexico are two distinct versions of Western civilization. Paz's conclusion hits the mark. But, I would suggest, we must add a qualifier. The United States is a version of Western civilization, for sure. It is a variation of the West as envisioned by Renaissance and Enlightenment and liberal and neoliberal thought, as well as the scientific and industrial revolutions and the rise of Protestantism and capitalism. Mexico is a version

27

of the West, but it also has deeply rooted non-Western strains. Mexico diverges and deviates from virtually all Western norms, and it often inverts and sometimes even subverts them entirely.

It would seem quite obvious that tangible differences between U.S. and Mexican cultures can in part be explained through social, political, economic, and historical determinations—in addition to the PC and MC and HC and LC distinctions discussed in Chapter 1. When addressing ourselves to civilizations, we customarily focus on differences with respect to institutions and modes of organization, the sciences and the arts, styles and morals, beliefs and values, and fashions and fads. These determinations are for the most part visible. They revolve around the material aspects of big *C* Culture. There is also that other aspect of culture, the occult, ordinarily nonconscious, unspoken culture—little *c* culture. It is chiefly this culture that splits the United States and Mexico into two faces that belong to the same person. These two faces are like those of that Greek mythical figure, Janus, one face looking forward to the future and the other face, on the back side of Janus's head, looking to the past. The two faces portray two visions of the world, two senses of time and space. One is perpetually optimistic, inordinately self-confident. The other face, remaining fixed on the past, is caught up with doubt and suspicion; it is always uncertain and hesitating, laden with an enormous load of historical baggage that has become increasingly burdensome.

Before the European invasion of the Americas, the northern part of the North American continent was inhabited principally by nomads. To the south, there were agricultural civilizations: the Olmecs, the Toltecs, the Aztecs (or Mexicas), and the Mayans. These relatively advanced civilizations were organized around sophisticated social and political institutions. They were dominated by tightly knit religious practices; they produced magnificent art and complex philosophies; in many respects they rivaled and surpassed anything Europe could offer. The capital of the Aztec empire, Tenochtitlán, was at the time of the conquest possibly the largest city in the world. Constructed on an island in Lake Texcoco, with three broad causeways leading to it from the shores, Tenochtitlán was a beauty to behold—Bernal Díaz del Castillo, author of *Conquest of New Spain* (1963), compared it to Venice.

Mexico at that time was quite diverse. There were cultures that lived from hunting and cultures that cultivated the soil. There were people who could pick up and leave at a moment's notice and people who were tied to their vast city-state. There were communities that could be either pushed aside or exterminated and cities that had to be conquered and dominated. There were human beings who could not be assimilated into the dominant culture of the Spanish conquest and human beings who, having seen the material aspects of their civilization destroyed, had hardly any alternative but to adopt the Spanish civilization imposed on them. And they did so, however reluctantly.

This tells us much about U.S.-Mexican distinctions. In Mexico the Spaniards imposed their culture on the Amerindians, while at the same time adapting themselves to many facets of the Amerindian cultures. In the United States, the Amerindians and their cultures were shoved aside, and if they did not move out of the way, they were often virtually exterminated. Consequently, in relative terms, the United States is today somewhat more exclusivist than Mexico; Mexico is more inclusivist than the United States. The Spanish idea of conquest and control involves conversion to Catholicism accompanied by a relatively large degree of mutual adoption and adaptation and merging of cultures. The English and Anglo-American concept of conquest and control is guided by segregation, with conversion to Protestantism added when it became convenient. Inclusivist cultures like Mexico's are more hierarchical and centralist, and they allow for a considerable degree of individual expression. There is division of classes and ethnicities, for sure, but mobility up and down the ladder allows for vague rather than precise distinctions between races and ethnic groups. In the Mexico of today, a rich *mestizo* (of European and Amerindian parents) might be given considerable respect, while a poor mestizo is treated much as if he were Amerindian. Exclusivist cultures like U.S. culture maintain strictly defined racial and ethnic lines, while within the same racial and ethnic group there is considerably more equality, especially if the members of the community are in general like-minded.

The English generally fled Europe and came to America to organize their activities and worship as they saw fit. The Spaniards, in contrast, were attracted to America in the name of God, king, and Spain, yet with sugarplums of gold and fame and prestige dancing in their heads. In England, the Reformation triumphed and Protestantism became defiant. Spain remained Catholic and championed the Counter-Reformation. The Spaniards finally threw out the Islamic Moors in 1492, ending their domination of most of the peninsula, which began with the invasion of A.D. 711. They expelled the Jews in the same year. Inebriated with their recent success, they set out as a corporate body to take on anybody and gather up everything they could get their hands on, all in the name of the only true religion: Catholicism. The Protestant Reformation finally led to independence for the United States and Anglo-American style democracy. Spain, in contrast, remained profoundly influenced by Muslim culture and the Catholic form of Christianity and kept alive the idea of a holy war against all infidels. This idea could not help affecting the nature of the conquest, which was largely an extension of the "reconquest" of Spain during the prolonged and bitter wars against the Moors. When independence finally arrived in Mexico, much of the Spanish influence remained, even though there was a great effort to repudiate everything Spanish.

In sum, Mexico (a relatively HC and PC *culture*) has a rich past from which it cannot free itself. The United States (a relatively LC and MC culture; see *HC Culture–MC Culture*; *PC Time–MC Time* in glossary), in contrast, is intent on getting beyond its past and forging ahead toward a perpetually new future. Mexico often resists change of traditions with a passion, although there is change. The Mexicans' push to modernize their country has wrought massive transformations. During this modernization, the "North American way of life" has exercised a great deal of influence. Moreover, Mexico's economic ups and downs have enriched some people while compelling others to tighten their belts, and the ensuing unrest has provoked new government programs and hence more change. Yet the more the surface of Mexico's culture changes, the more its interior resists change. In contrast to Mexico, the United States to all appearances welcomes many changes with open arms. These changes alter traditions in the United States to a greater extent than Mexico's surface changes. However, the United States, living perpetually in the present and for the future, creates change that is often hardly more than change for change's sake.

How do these profound differences between the United States and Mexico have a bearing on misunderstandings between the two countries?

Here's an example. News correspondent Patrick Oster (1989, 285–287) tells the story of a U.S. intelligence report in the 1980s on Mexico. It listed urban and rural unrest, a flight of Mexican pesos into the United States and Europe, a foreign debt so large that the government was facing total collapse, widespread corruption, and rising violence. Listening to the report, one might think that Mexico would soon go the way of Iran, Libya, Nicaragua, and other areas where the United States was greeted with increasing hostility. The assumption, Oster writes, is that under the same conditions, other countries, and even the United States, would erupt in outrage and rebellion. In other words, the Mexicans should be expected to react to a downturn in their country's political and economic situations in much the same way citizens of the United States and most other countries would. Erroneous thinking. Mexicans are not like North Americans. They are Mexicans, and Mexicans they will remain. They have respect for and pride in their past and their traditions, and they would not trade them for any other collection of traditions. They complain about their lot in life, they criticize their leaders, and they seem to squabble endlessly with each other; yet they would not trade their national life for any other one.

The Mexicans' glass may be half-empty, and hence they are never satisfied with it. But as far as they are concerned, their glass is also half-full. This gives them pride and the will to go on. They have endured many hardships, they now endure them, and they will continue to endure them into the future. In a word, they know how to *aguantar* (to resist, remain steadfast, endure, be patient and tolerant, to put up with whatever life throws at them, to shove toil or fatigue aside, to remain unmoved and unchanged against all odds).

Aguantar: There is a certain fatalism in the word. The Western way of modernity is to control nature and take from it what you can, all the while using and abusing it with neither remorse nor regret. She who has a certain tendency to harmonize with nature and the nature of other human beings is outside the straight-ahead, banging rhythm of modern Western societies. She who bends to the swings and swerves of culture—many Mexicans who have not effectively embraced Western ways, for example—is often considered by mainstream Westerners to be like the traditional and now justifiably maligned image of a woman: *subservient.* The U.S. way, by contrast, is to *dominate*, often in a damn-the-torpedoes-and-full-speed-ahead way (Pike 1992).

Traditionally, the Mexican has a tendency to acquiesce when confronting his presumed superiors. Thus he is able to *aguantar* whatever comes his way. Nature and the nature of culture, community, and individuals set limits. These limits are often accepted and endured, with few questions asked. This makes for a charming, courteous, friendly, and often docile community that unfortunately leaves itself open to abuses by another community intent on domination and control. As a consequence, Mexico's road to "modernization" has by no means been a one-way street. Confrontation with hardcore Western society, obsessed with materialistic visions of linear progress, has bred a tendency toward either (1) adaptation to the "modern" ways, (2) passive acquiescence, or (3) an exaggerated form of Mexican-style *machismo* (discussed below) as a denial and defensive measure. The more Mexicans succeed in adapting to modernity, the more often they take on their own form of macho aggressiveness. Nevertheless, the disposition to *aguantar* whatever life doles out lingers on. It offers a lesson in living: take what comes, *aguantar*, and make the best of it. More often than not, the Mexicans find life quite enjoyable, in contrast to the "North American way of life" bent on control that often ends in frustration and bitterness (Shorris 1992, 105–110).

In short, the Mexicans generally know how to *aguantar*. Sometimes they do it while becoming increasingly entrenched in their past to the extent that they almost become immobile. I must repeat. Mexicans are steeped in their past; they have more faith in their myths of the past, where imagination is more valid than any ephemeral truth. North Americans, in contrast, take nothing for granted and frantically push on, sometimes blindly, toward a horizon in the distance that promises an unambiguous answer to every question and a rational method for every operation. For the Mexicans, the community's past is the measure of all things; for the North Americans, the individual is the measure of all things. This is to say, once again, that Mexico is an HC spatial and PC temporal culture through and through. Thus the power of the contact zone at the U.S.-Mexican border and elsewhere. Thus the difficulty of the U.S. citizen's adaptation to and submersion within Mexican culture. A difficulty, but not an impossibility, I would suggest, for it *is* possible to get a feel for Mexican ways.

Enough preliminaries. We will do more justice to this theme in some of the following chapters. The task at hand is to set the stage for a view of what makes Mexico Mexico and the Mexicans Mexicans.

An Overview

Geographically speaking, Mexico is a land of contrasts, a mosaic of distinct units that run the gamut from tropical to temperate to virtually glacial. There are majestic mountains, jungles, deserts, valleys, lakes, and beaches. The country also enjoys abundant coastlines. It is met by the Gulf of Mexico to the east and the Pacific Ocean on the west. The peninsulas of Baja California and Yucatan provide additional coastline, with some of the most spectacular beaches in the Caribbean found on the eastern side of the Yucatan Peninsula, where tourists spend their leisure time at Cancún and elsewhere. The central part of the country, from the north to the Guatemalan border, consists of a high plateau, ranging in elevation from almost eight thousand feet above sea level around Mexico City to less than four thousand feet at the U.S. border. Rainfall varies from the center, where peasants engage in dry farming, to the desert north, sprinkled with cattle ranches and irrigated farms. These highlands are dissected by two mountain ranges, the Sierra Madre Oriental and the Sierra Madre Occidental, which come together south of Mexico City, reaching elevations of 18,701 feet (Pico de Orizaba) and 17,887 feet (Popocatepetl) in a volcanic region of impressive peaks.

Minerals are abundant in the mountain regions. Silver at Guanajuato, Zacatecas, and San Luis Potosí played an important role in the economy of colonial Mexico (then called New Spain) from the sixteenth century to the beginning of the nineteenth century. Mexico is still the world's leading producer of silver. Copper, lead, zinc, sulfur, and iron are also important, although these minerals are now overshadowed by oil production in the Gulf offshore fields, developed since the latter 1970s and early 1980s.

Mexico City, once Tenochtitlán, capital of the Aztec empire, dominates the human geography of the country. This city boasted of an estimated population of 17 million in 1990, and it probably had over 20 million by the turn of the century. It sprawls far beyond the lake margins where it originated, creating vast problems of housing, traffic congestion, pollution, water supply, and drainage. An industrial-urban complex has emerged in the volcanic axis extending from Puebla to Guadalajara, with Mexico City as its central focus. The chief industrial area and the backbone of Mexico's economy, however, is Monterrey to the north. Although pockets of poverty exist even in the most prosperous areas, in general the North and the central plateau are relatively wealthy, while the South, with a high proportion of Amerindian population, is the poorest. As a rule of thumb, the peoples of the north tend to be mestizo and European. In the central area, there is a larger proportion of *Amerindian* mixture in the mestizos and a greater population of Amerindians. To the south, the mestizos range from almost exclusively Amerindian to a small minority of people with predominantly European features. Here there is an even larger proportion of Amerindians than in the central area.

The Mexican nation had a population of 28,012,000 in 1950, 88,598,000 in 1990, and 90,420,000 in 1993. It had an estimated 107,223,000 people in 2000 and will have some 125,166,000 by 2020. In another way of putting this in perspective, Mexico's population grew at about 1 percent per year early in this century, 1.7 percent per year in the 1930s, and 3.4 percent in the 1960s. It became one of the fastest growing countries in the world. Since during the 1960s roughly one in two Mexicans was under fifteen years of age, rapid population increase was virtually inevitable, at least for another generation. Fortunately, increase in the number of people in Mexico has recently stabilized at about 1.9 percent per year.

As in most Latin American countries, urbanization was the central theme during the last half of the twentieth century. In 1950, 43 percent of the population was urban. In 1990, the number rose to 73 percent, and in 2000, it was 77 percent; an estimated 81 percent of the people will live in the cities by 2020. In ethnic terms, about 85 percent of Mexicans are mestizos, with some African Mexican mixture, 5 percent are Europeans, and the remaining 10 percent are Amerindians. The statistics vary according to how the Mexicans see themselves and who is doing the study. Mexicans tend to emphasize their "lightness" of skin, often proclaiming themselves Europeans rather than mestizos. Scholars wishing to present a "lightened" view of Mexico tend to skew the figures in favor of greater European and mestizo proportions.

The vast majority of Mexicans are neither Europeans nor Amerindians. They are mestizos and often have trouble accepting their racially mixed culture. In part for this reason, from the conquest by Hernán Cortés (1519–1521) to independence (1810–1821) to the revolution (1910–1920) to the present, Mexicans have engaged in a self-perpetuating quest for identity. Are they chiefly traditional or modern? Developed or developing or hopelessly undeveloped? Where are their cultural roots? In Spain or among the Aztecs or Mayans? What about the Arabic influence among the Spaniards, and the African roots along the coasts where slavery abounded? Or the impact of Enlightenment thought at the end of the colonial period and shortly after independence? Or the fascination with French culture during the nineteenth century? Or the powerful influence of the United States? Actually, it is in the collision and fusion of the sum of these roots and these influences that the complexity of the Mexican peoples resides.

Thus Mexicans are unique and defy the foreigner's comprehending the hows and the whys of the way they feel and think, love and hate, believe and doubt, act and react. Their special attitudes toward themselves, toward others, toward life and death, and their enigmatic cynicism, their ironic humor, their rigid formalities, the male's relationships with women and the female's relationships with men, the subtle relations between ethnic groups, social classes, people from the capital city and people from the provinces, and urban people and peasants: the sum of these characteristics defies the inquisitive mind trying to figure Mexicans out. Yet Mexicans somehow manage to understand themselves. They understand themselves on an intuitive basis, quite often without the ability to articulate their understanding clearly and distinctly. During childhood they assimilate an elaborately complex set of customs, language patterns (sprinkled with "Nahuatlisms," from the language of the Aztecs, Nahuatl), and gestures. They come to accept the paradoxes of their vague sense of identity and their culture. They repeat, over and over again, the consistency of their myriad cultural inconsistencies. It is their way of life. It's the way things are. Yet Mexicans often stutter and stumble when asked to explain themselves to the inquisitive outsider. They know who they are, deep down.

They sense it in their guts. At the same time, they have trouble articulating it. This inarticulability reveals their melancholic, contemplative, introspective nature. For the Mexicans, feeling and sensing and believing often take priority over explicitly analyzing, saying, and knowing. Analyzing, saying, and knowing are just so many necessary adjuncts. What one feels, senses, and believes is all-important. In short, Mexicans are chiefly HC people.

Mexicans are different from other Latin Americans as well as North Americans. During the early 1950s a number of small but penetrating studies in a series called México y lo Mexicano (Mexico and Mexicanness) emerged. Among them was the original version of Octavio Paz's international acclaimed *Labyrinth of Solitude* (1961). In México y lo Mexicano, poets, essayists, philosophers, psychologists, anthropologists, and linguists collaborated in trying to come to grips with what it is to be Mexican. Since that time the outpouring of books on the subject has continued unabated. There is still no consensus, and most likely there will be none in the near future. The problem is not simply that Mexicans can't figure themselves out. The problem is that their complexity defies human imagination and conceptualization. This complexity patterns not one culture but a concoction of cultures.

The enigma but also the beauty of Mexican cultures is that Mexico for centuries has been experiencing what Europe, the United States, Canada, and other regions of the world are only beginning to experience: collisions and confusions of cultural contact zones resulting from massive migration and immigration. This process of multiple cultures merging into one another is a process far from completion. This process toward completion that has characterized Mexican cultures for centuries helps one get a feel for the Mexicans' melancholy, their contemplative, introspective nature. There is a sense of the Mexicans' difference, with neither their capacity nor the outsider's capacity to specify the difference because it is a process of becoming different. Mexico is a complex racial, ethnic, social, economic, and political process that is perpetually becoming something other than what it was. Yet, I repeat, during this process Mexico has somehow remained the same. This makes it one of the most puzzling cultures imaginable. One's response to the Mexican puzzle can only flow toward the melancholy, contemplation, and introspection that in large part qualify the Mexicans themselves. Any attempt to explain Mexico outright can be hardly more than artificial.

The enigmatic process of many cultures flowing into a fluctuating Mexican culture is further along than in most other Latin American countries. In the Caribbean, the Amerindian population was virtually decimated a few decades after Christopher Columbus (1451–1506) put anchor in 1492. In Brazil, most of the Portuguese colonists were content to remain on the coast, trading and occasionally cohabiting with the natives instead of conquering or exterminating them. In Argentina and Uruguay, the Amerindians were primarily nomadic and did not take to the idea of becoming Catholics or adopting Spanish ways. As a consequence, their destiny was much like the plains Amerindians of the United States. In Paraguay, the Jesuits put up a jungle curtain around the nation of Guaraní Amerindians. It was as if they were declaring, "These Amerindians are ours to bring up in the Catholic faith our way, and everybody else, out." They taught the natives European ways, or at least the Jesuits' interpretation of what ideally should be European ways, until the Order was considered too powerful and expelled by the Spanish Crown in 1767. As a result, much of Paraguay is *bicultural* today, but without the complex mixture found in Mexico. In Central America and the Andes, where large Amerindian populations survive, Europeans still make up the ruling classes, while maintaining relatively clear racial, social, and cultural distinctions.

In part since racial mixture is further along in Mexico than in any other Latin American country, in Mexico there is also a political and economic system that has some of its roots in pre-Hispanic traditions. Thus Mexico, we see anew, is in certain respects non-Western as well as Western. The history of the country is mirrored in the faces of the people. This collection of faces is like the masks that are as popular in Mexican folk traditions. In the words of Octavio Paz, Mexicans find themselves compelled to don a different "mask" for every occasion. Given the myriad complexity of their culture, for every situation, a different "mask" becomes convenient, and even necessary. But what is a given Mexican individual's genuine "mask"? Who knows? The collection of "masks" has become the "reality," the only "reality" that exists. Yet that "reality" is somehow mirrored in the faces of the people. To know the people is to know the "masks," a difficult but perhaps not impossible task.

In this respect also, the most important key to Mexico lies in the past, where the masks have their origin. The past remains alive as an ongoing process in the inner workings of each and every Mexican mind today. It is a vibrant past. It is also in many respects a cruel past, a past of conquerors and conquered, exploiters and exploited, favoritism and discrimination, corruption and violence. By this I do not wish to imply that there is merely a struggle of opposing forces. Rather, there is *interdependent, interrelated interaction* (see *Interdependence* in glossary) between everybody and everybody else, as there should be in all human cultures. Mexicans speak Spanish and glorify their pre-Hispanic past. Yet while doing so they might hold actual Amerindians selling a few items or begging on the streets of the cities in contempt. Mexicans are obsessed with the idea of modernizing their country, of becoming a full-fledged member of the so-called developed world. Yet they love their Mexican cuisine along with their hamburgers; their wardrobe sports ancient Amerindian colors and shapes along with European looks; their manners remain personal and traditional when among family and friends, although they can become increasingly businesslike in the Western fashion when at work. Enigmatic, all this.

Invented Cultures

Enigmatic, for sure. Nevertheless, perhaps Mexico gives us a suggestion of things to come in the Western world at large when one takes into account the present collision and convergence of cultures in Europe, the Middle East, the United States, and Canada.

Speaking of cultures, anthropologist Roy Wagner (1975) has a provocative hypothesis. The anthropologist, he writes, "invents" the culture she studies (I use "culture" as a combination of big *C* and the little *c* here). Wagner's invention of the term "invention" does not allude to freewheeling fantasy, unbridled imagination. The idea of invention is the yield of the anthropologist's experiencing a new culture by lurking around at the contact zone. As a result of her experiences, she realizes that there are different possibilities for living life, different possible perspectives of the world, different cultural alternatives. Consequently, she becomes aware that her home culture from which she traveled to this strange new land was only one among a myriad array of possible cultures. In due time, she may experience a personality change, as she becomes aware of, adapts herself to, and submerges herself in these new ways. The strange culture gradually becomes "visible," and she comes to "believe" it. Thus she comprehends for the first time, through her mistakes and triumphs, what anthropologists speak of when they use the word "culture." Before this breakthrough of comprehension, the anthropologist really had no culture, since the culture in which she grew up was never really visible to her. Like the alien culture she studies, it had to be invented. Only in this way, according to Wagner, can the abstract significance of culture be grasped. In the act of inventing another culture, the anthropologist reinvents her own culture, and in fact she reinvents the very notion of culture.

Mexican historian Edmundo O'Gorman (1961) also uses the term "invention," regarding entry of the idea of *America* into the European mind. O'Gorman boldly proclaims that America was from the very beginning "invented" rather than "discovered." That is to say, America as it was conceived was a mental construct as much as it was the object seen. Following O'Gorman, Spanish intellectual Fernando Ainsa (1993) points out that in this respect the word "invention" can be understood in four ways. It can imply (1) "discovering" something that was unexpected. This was certainly the case regarding the Americas, for until the day of his death Columbus insisted that he had arrived at the Indies. There can be "invention" in the form of (2) "producing" something new, as in the case of inventing the wheel, the lightbulb, the internal combustion engine, or the hula-hoop—we find no Columbus here. In addition, "invention" can be taken as "imagining" something and either (3) "fabricating" it (a lie, a con artist's scheme) or (4) "creating" it (like a folk tale, a legend, novel, a poem, a cubist painting). It is in (4) that we find the most telling story about the invention of America. America became an idea, a concept, a hope, a utopian dream, and a chance to recreate human society and get it right once and for all.

In order to encapsulate O'Gorman's story as briefly as possible for the purpose of my story of Mexico, let us go directly to Christopher Columbus. Columbus was obviously in possession of a keen sense of observation. The catalyst that set him to the task of finding an alternative route to the Indies was endowed in him by virtue of his nature as a headstrong visionary. Whenever he confronted some unexpected features of the "reality" that spread itself before him, he was hardly ever deterred a whit. He harnessed his visions and rode them roughshod through the empirical labyrinth he had entered, refashioning them to fit his needs. Thus in the "marvelously real" new panorama before him in what was to be known as America, he saw one-eyed men, men with dog faces, women in the form of mermaids, men and women who engaged in cannibalistic practices. In fact, he saw an entire menagerie of strange nonhuman and subhuman beings and beasts (Arens 1979).

Columbus, like many other voyagers during his time, was unable, or at least did not wish, to separate "reality" from fantasy. Fantasy brought with it a world constructed with considerably more than mere rational knowledge: it created its own "reality." Merlin the Magician and the tales of Amadís of Gaul were as "real" to them as the material landscape they contemplated. Thus "they felt a desperate need to test their imagination, one formed by fables and books of chivalry" (Alvar 1992, 167). Indeed, Columbus had not yet attained that presumably enlightened "disenchantment of the world" his Renaissance successors of the West were later to enjoy and employ in their obsession with using and abusing nature.

The phrase "disenchantment of the world" comes from sociologist Max Weber (1958). Weber argued that the "secularization" of society with the rise of Protestantism, the scientific revolution, and industrial development, moved minds away from the "enchanted" sense of being at one with nature's ways toward the "disenchanted" attitude. The "disenchanted" posture assumes that nature is there to be brought under control and used for the sake of human progress. Columbus was definitely not of the disenchanted worldview. His observations were the outcome of his mind-set and his mind-set alone, and his mind-set was aided and abetted by his observations: his world looked sympathetically upon him just as he was in sympathetic attunement with his world. Yes indeed. Columbus's enchanted world was at the outset not the Indies at all, but a New World in the full sense of the term.[1]

Columbus's encounter with this "enchanting" New World had a profound impact on European life and thought. The idea of a New World eventually shattered the reigning conception of the world. Edmundo O'Gorman argues that neither Columbus nor other Europeans of the time could have *discovered* America because they could not fathom the idea of another continent and another collection of human souls. The general notion had it that God created the world and endowed "man" with its stewardship, and that was that. The world as the Europeans knew it was all there was and all there could possibly be. Consequently, America had to be *invented;* it had to be conceived as something where nothing was supposed to have existed. As an *invented, dreamed,* and *intersubjectively constructed* something, it could then gain its rightful status in the world of observed somethings. In a manner of speaking, the *invented* map would become coterminous with the territory.

Columbus, consequently, twisted and warped what he saw in order to jam-pack it into his original idea of things. He once proclaimed that Cuba was part of the mainland of Cipango (Japan), and he proceeded to cajole his crew into signing a statement swearing that they were at the shores of the Orient. During his third voyage he reached the coast of Venezuela at the Orinoco River delta. He found the water fresh rather than salty, which would have accounted for a large body of land and played havoc with his newly formed theory that this area was populated by many small islands and that there was no continental mass at all. In order to support his notion that this strange new land was no continent, Columbus postulated by use of biblical evidence that this river poured forth from a large fountain in the center of the Garden of Eden. Blindly insisting that the garden was in the Orient, he had no qualms about a recomputation of the Earth's circumference so as to render it considerably smaller than previously believed. Thus Columbus simply erased America, and the vast distance across the Atlantic and Pacific was drastically reduced.

Moreover, Columbus claimed that instead of being round, the Earth was pear-shaped, with the garden at the uppermost point—desperation can lead to what during later times could be taken as naive rhetorical manipulations. In the final analysis, however, and in spite of Columbus's efforts, the existence of a new continent, as well as its population of new peoples, was forced upon the European mind. But before this concession could be forthcoming, the medieval image of the world had to be revised, with many appendages and accommodations and deletions. The amended image was not reality precisely as it had been observed, but reality according to the newly invented model: America had been fashioned and mentally fabricated rather than simply found.

Reality could not hope to cope with the subtle machinations of the human mind. Wagner's "invention of culture" hypothesis pales at the side of Columbus's and the European mind's invention of an entire continent. As a consequence of the invention, America became conceived as a utopia in embryo. It is not mere coincidence that Thomas More's classical work, *Utopia*, emerged shortly after the invention of America. This work stimulated utopian projects throughout the continent. Bartolomé de las Casas (1474–1568) dreamed of founding the ideal society among Amerindians in Guatemala and Venezuela. Father Vasco de Quiroga's (1470–1565) created a grand project in the state of Michoacan, Mexico, along utopian lines. And Portuguese Father Antonio de Vieira (1608–1697) saw the Amazon region of Brazil virtually as a biblical paradise.

Invented worlds, enchanted worlds, worlds of fantasy, marvelous realities: what does all this mean? It means that Mexico and Latin America had their beginning in a human cultural sphere that was radically *Other* than the cultural sphere to the north, where the English colonies found a precarious existence on the rocky shores of New England and elsewhere. In Spanish and Portuguese America, everything was colored with utopian visions in myriad realities that were destined to become radically HC cultures within PC time and manifesting culture with a big *C* in the most sublime fashion. These were the invented cultural worlds that the most magnificent dreams are made of. They are worlds fabricated without a shadow of a doubt, in defense of traditional Catholic dogma and in denial of what was spread before the Europeans' eyes. With respect to the idea of America as invention, there was no mere acceptance of what there was, but rather an attempt to impose what was preconceived onto American reality.

Quite understandably, the relatively drab LC Anglo-American culture with its linear, step at a time PC march, has trouble coping with the subtleties of Mexico as an invented reality. When the Spaniards' preconceived and invented reality was imposed on the Amerindians' world, and when in spite of this attempted imposition there was, as we shall see, a hybrid fusion of these realities, in addition to a dose of African American influence, the result is, I repeat, a cultural complexity that does a slam dunk in the face of logic and reason and intimidates all efforts to articulate it.

How to Talk About Invented Worlds

O'Gorman's idea might be labeled idealism. However, idealism can't get far unless there is some collective give-and-take between minds. Otherwise, every mind would be the inventor of its own world.

The meeting of minds between Columbus and Europeans at the turn of the fifteenth century, whose hands were put to work refashioning the world, entailed practical interaction between citizens of the community and between them and their world. Rather than merely the work of individuals and small groups, the New World was an effort of the entire Spanish and Portuguese communities. The citizens of these communities interacted in their talk and in their interrelations with each other and with their environment. Above all, it was a matter of the community's fashioning its world according to presentiments of what the future possibly held in store. And presentiments there certainly were prior to and during the time of Columbus. There were purportedly signs of the existence of a fourth region or continent with a fourth race of people. This particular presentiment came in the form of the ideal space of a golden age, of a pagan or Christian paradise, of a promised land. The ideal was born out of nostalgia for a mythical space where the trials and tribulations of the present would be alleviated, and the good life would be waiting for all.

In this respect, Mexican intellectual Alfonso Reyes (1960, 29) wrote that America was "desired before it was found." Europe discovered America because she needed to. Consequently,

> this desire and necessity turned the spirit of invention from its classical origin toward the construction of spaces that were essentially the *counter-image*, the inverse of European reality. . . . On this virgin soil without history, even though millenary civilizations ostensibly proved the contrary, one *could* (or better, *should*) remake the western world. As soon as America was integrated into universal history, its future was colored with the nostalgia of the European past. (Ainsa 1989, 103, 106)

The "ideal" and the "objective" complemented the "real" such that a New World was born. What was in the mind brought about the doing and what was done was done in large part because the doing was in the mind. Invention is intrinsic to humankind's very thinking and doing. Put the ideal and the objective and the real into one package, and we have invention. Invented America was the product of a community effort to reconstruct what was presented (as an act of presentment), thus bringing about the emergence of a New World, America.

Mexican novelist Carlos Fuentes sees the spirit of invention deeply rooted in Miguel de Cervantes's (1547–1616) timeless masterpiece, *Don Quixote de la Mancha*. The problem is that Quixote's fabricated rather than found world was of individual rather than collective effort. Quixote, as an individual out of tune with his community, believed what he wanted to believe, saw what he wanted to see, and during his initial adventures he said what he believed and saw (Fuentes 1976). Let us not feel so smug, however. It might well be that we are hardly any better off regarding invented worlds than were Don Quixote or Columbus. One of our greatest physicists ever, Isaac Newton, was not as connected to reality as we might wish to assume. He was not far removed from the Don's reality concoctions. Newton, John Maynard Keynes writes, was actually the "last of the magicians" (in Dobbs 1975, 13–14). He remained with a foot caught in the doorway of his "enchantment of the world" (he dabbled in alchemy and believed in the magic of numerology). In comparable fashion, the Don remained firmly embedded in a world that corresponded to the novels of chivalry he had voraciously consumed, and his creator, Cervantes, is one of the first to perceive the fallacy of the grand idea of words that are capable of representing the world. The master builder of the machine age, Newton, and a demented old man, the Don, lived out their wildest dreams: each in his own way told an intriguing tale. In this manner the Don, like Newton, retained his enchantment of the world. At the same time, as an individual, he divorced himself from it, when he entered that know-it-all universe of disenchantment. Don Quixote and Isaac Newton: an intriguing odd couple.

Newton's scientific story about the world out of another pen at another place could have been written off as outlandish and absurd, and he could well have passed his days in an asylum. The Don's spoken world was equally outlandish, and, unlike Newton, during his day he was subjected to scorn and ridicule. Both Newton and Quixote invented their worlds and found a way to relate them to what they saw. If the Don's enchantment with his world lingered, there was also some premonition of the West's waning enchantment; if Newton's partial and lingering enchantment was conveniently hidden away in the closet, he was so much the wiser for it, since thanks to his rhetorical sleight of hand, he was destined to be regarded as a giant among giants in what later became a thoroughly disenchanted world.

America was invented at a time when the enchantment of the world still reigned supreme, especially through the eyes and at the hands and pens of the likes of Columbus. If Newton was the last of the magicians and if the Don's enchantment patterned a lingering tendency in Spain, how could America have escaped enchantment? America wasn't, nor has it ever been entirely, disenchanted. It still retains a certain aura of enchantment: its magical, mythical, mysterious, even mystical character endures, timelessly, within an imaginary space. Invented America was first constructed as a result of European longings and later was reconstructed when a New World presented itself in such fantastic, magical dress that it couldn't help lending itself to the most incredible flights of the imagination motivated by dreamy desires for some other place: utopia. As enchantment, invented America was a symbol of nostalgia realized.

At this juncture somebody is surely wondering why I bring all this up. What does it have to do with gaining cultural awareness? I bring it up because, as suggested above, Mexicans live more in the past than do North Americans. They live *in* it, they live *it;* it is *with* them and they are *with* it; they *are* it and it *is* them. This rootedness in the past might seem strange to those cultures that remain to a large degree "disenchanted," cultures that look to the future to a considerably greater extent than to the past. But for the Mexicans, the past is real: it lives in the present. I would expect we now know why it is important to know something about Mexico's past before we can expect to know something about her present. A past-present interrelationship between Mexico and the United States takes place in the contact zone, along with HC-LC space and MC-PC time. That is where the focus must lie if we are to come to grips with what it is that makes Mexico Mexico.

The next move is toward Spain, land of the conquerors.

Further Reading

Baudet 1965, Berkhofer 1978, Fuentes 1992, Gerbi 1985, Gibson 1964, 1966, Hanke 1959, 1965, Haring 1947, Leonard 1964, 1966, Morse 1989, Nuñez Cabeza de Vaca 1961, Rabasa 1993, Sale 1990.

Notes

1. See Tzvetan Todorov's *The Conquest of America* (1984). For a critique of Todorov, see Jara and Spadaccini (1992). For "disenchantment" and recent "reenchantment" in the West, see Berman (1981).

3

This New World, Spanish Style

An Unexpected Encounter with the Expected

Some years before the conquest of Mexico, explorers along the coast of mainland Mexico and Central America had heard from the *Amerindians* about fabulous riches to be found in marvelous cities to the east.

At least to Spanish ears and eyes, the account was of riches on the order of gold and precious stones, which were for the Amerindians so much ornamentation and far removed from European concept of monetary and material wealth. These accounts given to the Spaniards by the soon to be conquered natives were for the most part gross exaggerations. The Amerindians might have had in mind a response something like: "Very sorry, sir. We have no gold here. But if you continue on down the road you will find fabulous cities with more gold than they know what to do with." This would be a contrived attempt to get rid of these strange and frightening foreigners with their awful fire-belching sticks and terrifying monsters, which some of them straddled (according to certain reports, at the outset some Amerindians believed horse and man were one). In such cases the Amerindians were certainly "fabricating" and the Spaniards were looking to "invent-discover" the expected. But, as we shall note, the Spaniards were quite disappointed when they found considerably less than they had hoped for. (We see here, then, not miscommunication through bloopers but rather miscommunication through the Amerindians' contrived images of reality that became for the Spaniards more "real" than what they actually saw.)

Hernán Cortés (1485–1547) and his small army landed on the Gulf Coast of what is now Mexico in 1519. They soon found evidence of an advanced civilization in the interior. The population of the Aztec empire and the surrounding environs has been estimated at approximately 25 million. (France during the same time had around 20 million and Spain and the United Kingdom each had approximately 6 million.) Some of the largest cities the world had ever seen were found in this area. Tikal, in northern Guatemala, had reached a population of some 100,000 by A.D. 600. Teotihuacán, twenty miles northwest of Mexico City, had approximately the same number of people around A.D. 300. And Tenochtitlán, the capital city of the Aztecs, had an estimated 200,000 to 250,000 population when Cortés set foot on the continent, making it larger than Paris and twice the size of Seville, Spain's most populous city. The Aztec and Mayan empires were highly developed. Their agricultural system was for the Europeans a technological marvel, their architecture and art were remarkable, and their astronomy and medicine were well in advance of anything in Europe.

The Aztecs had a rigidly stratified class system, with rulers chosen from noble families, a priestly class, government workers making up the precursor of a modern bureaucracy, a professional military force, a class of trained artisans, and at the bottom of the pyramid, the peasant class. The society was imperialistic, maintaining order through military might. The outlying city-states and cultures were the source of tributes of up to one-third of all that was produced, and of slaves to provide labor in the Aztec capital. The city of Tenochtitlán, as we might expect, was the center of bustling activity. The markets were remarkably large, yet clean and organized. The market at Tlatelolco, slightly north of the island city, served 60,000 buyers and sellers daily, making it twice as large as the Salamanca market in Spain. The chief exception to Aztec control of the smaller city-states surrounding the capital city was Tlaxcala, northwest of Tenochtitlán, which the Aztecs never subdued. There was an ongoing war between the Tlaxcalans and the Aztecs called the *guerra florida* (war of the flowers), the sole purpose of which was reportedly for the acquisition of prisoners for human sacrifice to the Aztecs' insatiable gods.

All told, the culture that met the Spaniards in many respects did not take a backseat to Europe. So who were these conquerors? And how could a handful of them subdue the entire Aztec nation?

The Spaniards

There have been and there are various "Spains": Castile, Aragon, Galicia, Asturias, Andalucia, Catalonia, and the Basque region, to name the principal areas.[1] The majority of the provinces were independent kingdoms before their unification into what is now known as Spain, while some provinces (e.g., Andalucia) were never political entities on their own. In and of themselves, the independent kingdoms were loosely held together by loyalty to local lords and rulers on the part of the people who fiercely resisted any form of unification into a nation-state in the modern sense. When unification finally began to take place, one of the older provinces, Portugal, became an independent state, and two others, Catalonia and the Basque provinces, remained and continued to manifest insurrectionist and independentist tendencies.

The Spaniards were a conglomerate of various peoples. The original Iberians suffered through invasions by the Visigoths and Romans (202 B.C.–A.D. 711), as well as the Moors (711–1492), who were of Arabian stock and Islamic religion. These invasions contributed minor details to what eventually made up the diverse Spanish character. The Spaniards customarily adopted some cultural traits from the invaders, rejected others, and totally transformed yet others to yield an original product. In many respects, during the Roman dominance, the Spaniards became as Roman as the Romans. When the Moors made their presence felt, the southern Spaniards became quite Arabic, yet they retained their Roman characteristics, especially the religion they had embraced: Catholicism. The result was subtle and profound, giving rise to a unique Spanish vision of the world, a singular mode of everyday living, and to an extent even a distinct religion, though it was never anything but Catholic. Nevertheless, the Spaniards remained a breed apart. Their particular character traits, their eccentricities, distinguish them from the rest of Europe. The Europeans tend to take the Spaniards for what they are. They enjoy trips to Spain, the relatively inexpensive goods, the delicious cuisine, the enticing Spanish Mediterranean coast, and leave it at that. As far as they are concerned, it's like traveling to an exotic land.[2]

Perhaps due to the nature of the Spanish spirit, as something other than European, there exists a tension, an interior conflict, that inexorably draws the Spaniard within himself. This tension emerges in art, especially evident in that Spanish classic and perhaps the first genuine prose work that can legitimately be called a novel in the modern sense, the above mentioned *Don Quixote de la Mancha* (1605, 1615). The Spaniard reveals, within himself, the incongruent coexistence of two personalities: an everyday sense of *realism* found in Don Quixote's squire, Sancho Panza, and Don Quixote's own radically idiosyncratic, intransigently individualistic *idealism*. It is the practical and the impractical, mundane and visionary, sensible and irrational, reasonable and illogical, collective and individual, conventional and personal nature of the Spaniard that splits him into two and then into many. The Spaniard takes on his idealistic or realistic side in concert with each situation. He is now one thing, now another, now something else according to the context. Whatever he may be at a given moment, for him everything is perfectly normal, although from the outsider's vantage point things may seem to go awry.

Some examples of Spanish idiosyncrasies are in order. (1) On the coast of today's Veracruz and shortly before the conquest, Hernán Cortés's men became mutinous, and he had his ships burned. In so doing Cortés prevented the rebellious troops from returning to Cuba. At the same time he risked all, since retreat was now impossible in case the Spaniards were unsuccessful in their conquest. This was a supremely daring act by Cortés, though he took it as a matter of course. (2) After Gonzalo Jiménez de Quesada (1499–1579) conquered present-day Colombia and founded the city of Bogotá in 1535, he could have been expected to live the comfortable and prestigious life of a lord. Not so, as far as the restless Spaniard was concerned. He embarked on an apparently insane adventure in search of the mythical El Dorado, a civilization of unlimited gold. (3) Francisco Pizarro (1475?–1541), with a minuscule army of 180, was surrounded by thousands of Inca warriors. He took Atahuallpa, their commander in chief, prisoner and boldly declared that he would keep him under custody until the Incas filled a few chambers to the ceiling with gold and other metals and precious stones. The Incas did so. Then Pizarro had Atahuallpa executed as a usurper and polygamist—during a civil war prior to the arrival of the Spaniards he had killed Huáscar, who was the legitimate heir to the throne. This was certainly one of the most intrepid maneuvers in the entire history of human conquests. For Pizarro, however, it was apparently just business as usual.

Such acts of bravery in the face of danger, impetuous activity when a cool head would be expected, and daring behavior in place of calculated moves gives a faithful picture of the Spaniards' inner tension between idealism and realism.

Realism Predominates?

In spite of this tension within the Spanish soul, idealism can surface. But, I must emphasize, the Spaniard is more often than not an idealist with her feet firmly planted on solid ground. She definitely has a vision regarding the nature of the world as it should be, and she conducts her life accordingly. Of course, this characteristic is common to all humans in all cultures, to a certain degree. Yet it takes on a unique flavor in the Spaniard.

One of the supreme examples of Spanish idealism is the so-called *Requerimiento* (Requirement), a document drawn up in order to justify morally and legally the conquest of America. The *Requerimiento* gave a summary of the entire history of Christianity, beginning with the creation from Genesis of the Bible and ending with the Spanish expansion in the name of God, king, and country. Before the Spaniards were allowed to commence with their invasion of new territory in the American continent, they had to read the document before the incredulous eyes and ears of the natives. It was read, preferably in translation, and if no interpreters were available, in Spanish. The *Requerimiento* demanded that the local inhabitants lay down their arms and submit to the Spanish monarchy. The natives, branded "heretics," must embrace Catholicism, the pope, and the Christian God, and forget their evil practices. If they declined the offer, the Christians asserted through the document that they would not be held accountable for the plunder, rape, and slaughter that might ensue. Obviously the Amerindians understood virtually nothing of the message they received, and the consequences were dire. If the natives were villagers, the document was often read to empty houses, for the inhabitants had fled into the forest. Then the "conquest" was appropriately carried out with little bloodshed. If the people remained in their village in awe of these strange creatures, they were properly subdued. Dominican priest and "defender of the Amerindians," Bartolomé de las Casas, wrote in his *Brief History of the Destruction of the Indies* that when he read the document he didn't know whether to weep or to cry, given the absurdities in it.

Another noteworthy case of Spanish idealism is that of Bartolomé de las Casas himself, an incorrigible visionary. With a group of priests and a minimum of military protection, he entered a zone of bellicose Amerindians in Guatemala and Venezuela. These indigenous peoples had effectively resisted Spanish military forays in the past. Now they were caught by surprise when confronted by these strange frocked figures who claimed the right of God instead of the might of the sword. Actually, de las Casas envisioned a "City of Man" made over into the image of the "City of God," a utopia on earth, the ideal society that never existed in Europe. Here in America, de las Casas thought, the natives were like innocent, uncorrupted children, whose hearts and minds could be molded in the ways of the Christian God. To make a long story short, de las Casas encountered multiple problems in Guatemala, and he barely escaped with his life in Venezuela. It seems that the ungrateful heathen were content to remain in darkness and didn't take to the ways of that strange light-skinned, frail, and somewhat effeminate-looking atoning God nailed to a cross. So much for utopian dreams.

These and many other adventures of epic proportions give us an idea of the grand projects and the disillusionment, the visions and the illusions of the Spaniards in this "enchanted" new world. The Spaniards were and are inveterate dreamers, but always with an eye attuned to "reality," that is, what in their conception reality should be—recall the nature of "invented" worlds. Behind these multiple and multiply colored dreams lies a long-standing effort to win over any and all obstacles life might present. It is a good recipe for survival, and the Spaniards in all but a few instances survived. They survived magnificently, not simply through exercising their will on their environment but also by adopting and adapting themselves to their circumstances and becoming one with them. In this sense their circumstances were bent slightly to their will and at the same time they bent their will to their circumstances.

Once again, we see the emphasis on big *C* Culture, that of visionary ideals over the natural emergence of culture from within everyday living.

This is Culture as an intended imposition on the indigenous peoples of Mexico. However, in the final analysis the conquered peoples conquered the conquerors in the sense that they both accepted and resisted the Spanish imposition. In the process the conquered adapted themselves to the Culture of their new masters and in turn transformed that Culture. On the other hand, the Spaniards' imposition of their Culture on the conquered people included their own adaptation to the new circumstances, and hence a transformation of their Spanish Culture. What emerged was a radically complex *hybrid culture:* present-day Mexico.

Me and My Circumstances

People like the Spaniards, who are relatively unconcerned about the material aspects of life and remain more interested in ethical-moral and spiritual values, occasionally end up exalting the individual over the community. In today's jargon there is always a special place in the heart of the people for a "role model," a charismatic individual whose words are noble but whose actions are even greater than his words, at least in the mind of the community. Thus in Spain, the Virgin and the saints, the king and queen, the landlord and the local priest occupy a special position and play a key role to a greater extent than almost anywhere else in Europe.

This is not to imply that the common person is of any lesser worth. Exalting the importance of the ideal individual and those in society who in the collective imagination approximate that ideal is to exalt the individuality of every member of the community, whose principal dream in life is to become the spitting image of that ideal. Spanish *yo-ismo* ("I-ism") is unique. During the time of the discovery and conquest, it was the prime ambition of every Spaniard to become a hidalgo, a "son *(hijo)* of someone *(de algo, alguien)*," someone of importance, a lord. The conquerors were given grants of land by the Crown as a reward for their efforts. Cortés's grant sprawled from the central valley of Mexico south to the state of Chiapas. He was now a lord, not merely over the land but over lives as well, Amerindian lives. Land grants to the conquerors from the Crown, called *encomiendas,* gave the Spaniard sole dominion over the area and over the natives who happened to reside there (see glossary). But the *encomiendas* did not come without strings attached. The *encomenderos* (recipients of the grant) were sworn to responsibility. They had to see that the material and spiritual welfare of the native residents were taken care of. The Amerindians had to have the means to feed their families, and a priest was needed for Mass, baptisms, marriages, deaths, and other ceremonies.

Cortés and other lesser *encomenderos* at times lived up to their responsibilities. At other times they did not, and the Amerindians suffered physically and mentally as a consequence. In either case, the coveted result was that these conquerors were now hidalgos. In Spain during the same time, gold and other riches came in and then went out just as quickly to other areas of Europe that were beginning to experience the rise of science, industry, and early capitalistic enterprises, thus producing goods the Spaniards wanted. Spain was obviously destined to suffer from poverty as a consequence of its newly discovered wealth. In addition, the Crown had spent itself into bankruptcy as a result of its military struggle against the Protestant Reformation and its effort to defend its vast overseas holdings. Meanwhile, would-be hidalgos roamed the country, taking on airs of importance even though they could hardly put threads on their backs. The point is that *hidalguismo* (the unwritten and unorganized order of hidalgos) stresses *who* you are, not *what* you're worth. For the Spaniard, material worth often takes a backseat to personal worth in terms of how you can fit the image of the lord, the charismatic individual, the person whose will to acquire nobility takes precedence over his physical well-being.

Hence the exaltation of the *yo* ("I") might often bring pain and physical depravity. But to the Spanish mind, possession of a good and noble heart and mind and soul more than offset the loss of physical comforts. Moreover, it enabled the individual to put up with or endure *(aguantar)* hardships and injustices that would break the spirit of lesser people. This particular nature of the Spaniard, and hence also of the Mexican, equipped him to accept whatever life had to offer and suffer in silence. He knew how to *aguantar*. At the same time, the nascent mercantile class in the countries north of Spain offered the promise of material comforts. If one happened to have money in addition to nobility, why not spend it all on foreign goods? Thus a constant flow of riches proceeded from the Americas to Spain and into the developing urban centers of Europe.

Nevertheless, the manifestation of "I-ism" in confidence of one's own capacity, despite the rampant egocentrism that might ensue, gave rise to many innovations and services to the community, both then and now. For example, between today's Mexico and the rest of Latin America, there is evidence of an intercontinental solidarity that cannot be found between, say, the United States and Canada, and much less between these countries and New Zealand and Australia, all previous colonies of the British Empire. This difference is in part the result of different functions between Spanish settlers and English settlers. The Spaniards were chiefly adventurers (searching for *hidalguismo*), soldiers, government functionaries, ecclesiastics, and lords of land and Amerindians. The settlers to the north from England were primarily farmers, artisans, and merchants. They were economically active and relatively independent. The Spaniards, in contrast, depended on land privileges, government positions, or religious orders. Their "I-ism" stemmed from *who* they were more than on *what* they were and *what* they could do.

The Spaniards conquered territory by force or by a "spiritual" conquest on the part of the religious orders. Then they colonized it. The English, who did not need to wage wars of conquest in most cases, were in the beginning for the most part peaceful colonizers. Spanish soldiers of fortune and a few nobles were ambitious for prestige and the honor—as well as the power—it would afford them. They at first reduced the Amerindians to slaves in order that they, the Spaniards, could live as masters, exploiting land and mines as they saw fit. English settlers, more often than not of humble origin, worked the soil, using whatever resources they happened to have at hand. They defended what was theirs at all cost, for it was all they had. The Spaniards were inseparable from their *hidalguismo*, and whatever material possessions were implied by that title, so much the better; the English, in contrast, were inseparable from their relatively meager material possessions.

Those who left England for America did so because of religious and economic oppression. They wanted to forget the past and get on with life. They came not in search of personal prestige and nobility of the nature of the landed gentry back in England, but with a will to work. This will forged a strong, independent character. Since the settlers did not wish to return to their native country, their colonizing efforts implied long-range planning: they were here to stay. The first Spaniards, in contrast, brought few women—hence there was a liberal mixture of European men and Amerindian women—and in many cases the intent was to make a name for themselves, return to Spain, and lead a life of lordship. (The ratio of men to women in the Spanish colonies as opposed to the English colonies is revealing. Among the early Spaniards in New Spain, it has been estimated that there were ten men to each woman, while in Massachusetts the ration was 1.5 to 1 [Harrison 1997, 178]. The English came as yeoman farmers and merchants to settle with their families, while the Spaniards came chiefly as individuals in search of adventure, wealth, and above all, notoriety, fame, importance, and *hidalguismo*.) Unlike the relatively homogeneous society that grew up in the English colonies, the Spanish colonies soon became a heterogeneous mix that produced social stratification placing classes of peoples in perpetual separation. That is the downside. The upside is that from this social stratification there arose a vigorous mestizo class that is today the bedrock of Mexico.

As a result of the differences between Spanish settlers and English settlers, evolution of customs, life patterns, and political convictions diverged sharply. The Anglo-Americans were more community oriented regarding civil action. They supported laws that tended to strengthen the community, while disregarding the laws they believed to be unjust. They believed in social equality in fact and in right. They also believed—however erroneously—that they were authors of their own destiny, captains of their own ship. The rugged, industrious, and hardworking individual thus counted above all. The community existed to back him. Yet there was community orientation. The community backed the individual because of *what* he was worth and *what* he could do. The individual worthy of community backing was the individual who stood out in terms of personal achievements, quite often gauged in terms of material wealth.

From the very beginning, inequality emerged in the Spanish colonies. It was everybody out for himself with respect to how effectively he could become somebody of importance. The underprivileged classes—Amerindians, African Americans, mulattos, and mestizos—were often abused in the process. The individual was exalted in terms of his individual value in spite of any legal and social rights of the masses. The community existed to back the individual, for sure. But this backing was not simply economic. It was to a great extent moral, ethical, social, even aesthetic. The individual deserved backing because of *who* he was, a person of worth, a hidalgo. The backing was relatively nonmaterial, and as a result it had to do with the person as and ideal role model of *hidalguismo*, the sort of person everyone would like to be. The concept of community in the Anglo-American society was predicated on the idea that virtually everybody, if talented and industrious, could become like the best of individuals within the community. The concept of community in the Spanish colonies applied to those outstanding individuals whose example was to be emulated but could never be equaled. The Spanish Americans were obviously aware that only a few among them stood a chance of becoming genuine hidalgos, while the Anglo-Americans seemed to think that everybody could become rich and powerful—the so-called American myth that stands hardly a chance of becoming reality.

The relative indifference of the Spaniard with respect to the material life was also due in part to the serenity and tranquillity with which she organized her life, following the particular manner in which she conceived of her Catholic faith. On the one hand, this philosophical quietude of mind and spirit gave the Spaniard solace vis-à-vis the northern Europeans, who were somewhat stressed out by the rapid changes occurring in their own society, given the incipient industrial revolution's gaining a head of steam. This transition took place in northern Europe during the Reformation accompanied by the rise of Protestantism—which motivated the Catholic Counter-Reformation, vehemently defended in Spain. Indifference was noteworthy in the Spaniard's resignation in face of the inhospitable conditions of her life and in the manner in which she resisted conformity to them (this rendered the Spanish character one of the most culturally conservative of all Europe). The occasional criticism of the Spaniard on the grounds that this indifference bred a spirit antipathetic toward material progress seems to have affected her very little. Her likely response might be, "So what?" or "It's really of no importance," and she would leave it at that.

In sum, the Spaniard maintains a stoic view of life. At the same time, there is an obsession for remaining in control of life situations by maintaining the role of *caballero* or *dama* (gentleman or lady), without revealing a self-destructive spirit of anguish when confronted with personal or collective tragedies. In this manner the Spaniard has usually been able to perpetuate her cultural particularities remarkably well. One of the chief goals in life is to keep the upper hand regarding whatever situation may arise, while remaining relatively unperturbed in the process. At the same time, the Spanish motto seemed to be: By all means, assert "I-ism." That's what makes the individual an individual. (Thus we note in the Spaniards the makings of the Mexicans' hierarchical culture, and their inclination toward HC space and PC time, in contrast to the tendency in the United States toward LC space and MC time. On the one hand, the particular Spanish "I-ism" demands emphasis on circumstances, the entire cultural setting, before complex human interrelations can be properly understood. On the other hand, the lower importance placed on intricate human interrelations in the United States diminishes the importance of context.)

More on "I-ism" in the Form of Personalismo

The notorious Spanish individualism is one of the keys to the Spaniard's elusive nature. For the Spaniard, the individual exists as if she were the center of the universe, her universe.

"Center of the universe" does not refer to the concept of the individual as a "human being" endowed with some sort of permanent "essence" or fixed identity. The individual is a concrete, living and breathing, perpetually in the process of changing organism. She enjoys personal dignity and collective pride. From the viewpoint of the "I" as center of the universe, the zone of influence of the individual as "center" expands to include other individuals in *interrelated, interdependent,* and *interactive* rhythmic concert swinging and swaying to the cultural beat of the general symphony playing itself out. This circle of influence includes *interrelations* by way of friendship, family relations, work, recreation. The individual, as her own "center" of these interrelations, maintains vigilance in order to avoid penetration by outside spheres of influence and thus maintain her individualism.

Those who are not members of the circle of influence are out, and out they must remain until given the nod by the collective whole of or some subgroup within the circle. Spanish philosopher José Ortega y Gasset

(1883–1955) considers the central "I" a matter of "me and my circum-stances," and as those circumstances go, so go I (Ortega 1957). As they put it in Spanish, *Cada cabeza es un mundo* ("For every mind, a different world"). And so it is, culturally speaking. Every I, every mind, is in and of itself a world. Put all the minds of a community to gyrating about a cen-tral individual, the I of presumably greatest personal worth (*who* she is, not *what* she is), and you have a circle. Belong to this circle, and you are the member of a community. It is not you against the world in the sense of "rugged individualism," North American style, but I and my commu-nity, and as the community goes, so go I. It's not simply a matter of "What's in it for me?" but more a matter of "How does it benefit me and my community?" Not a matter of "I and all the others," but rather, "I within my community and all others within their own communities." The difference is crucial.

Take, for example, Hispanic political life. A given individual, let us call her María, bears allegiance to her political party, and she defines it in her own way. She remains firm in her position, come what may. In a heated discussion of politics, she may listen to one of her friends while impa-tiently awaiting her turn. Then the opportunity comes, whether the other person has finished or not. She begins, enthusiastically, energetically, and apparently with no fear of equivocation. She tells it like it is, that is, from her point of view. She is hardly willing to accept concession or concilia-tion because that would be like confessing to her own shortcomings. She defends her opinion tooth and nail. It is her point of view and nobody else's. Her point of view is in fact inseparable from her "I." Her "I" is her way of thinking and feeling and believing that her way of thinking and feeling and believing is her "I." There is simply no line of demarcation be-tween her community, her world, and herself in the sense of the Anglo-American who defines herself in terms of her car, house, diploma on the wall, job, clothes, and such, all material commodities easily separated from the person.

It is chiefly for this reason that in Spain and to even a greater extent in Mexico, *personalismo* rules (see glossary). In the national political scene, sooner or later politics becomes a matter of personalities that become comprehensible through the dominant individual's "I." Political factions, members of the party, the rulers themselves, become defined as a matter of *who* one is more than *what* one has. One's pride in one's community and in one's birth, background, cultural heritage, and ethnic make-up, take precedence over pride in *what*, precisely, one can do and what one has right here and now. In a real sense, then, the past is more important than the present. And the future? Look at *who* is doing the talking, and if that person is of admirable qualities, then the future will take care of itself. That is to say, in *personalista* politics, legitimacy is endowed in the *person* (a concrete living and breathing human) more than in the *position* (i.e., the "presidency," the "priesthood," the "manager," all abstract categories) the person happens to occupy. In Latin America a novelist or a successful ex-president's wife stands a good chance of being elected because he is a famous novelist and she is the ex-president's wife, not simply because of their qualifications or *what* they have or what they can do. (In this manner, as we shall note below, in Mexico, interhuman *interrelations* take on more value than abstract political, ecclesiastic, or commercial or manufacturing *positions*.)

Pride, Spanish Style

Another characteristic of the Hispanic soul that must be foregrounded is *orgullo* ("pride"). In the collective mind of the people, pride in the community is virtually taken for granted.

But here, one must distinguish between the Spanish feature of pride in contrast to predominantly Mexican-mestizo traits.[3] Mestizo nature can at times be as vacillating as Spanish nature is gregarious. The Spaniard is bold and confident in comparison to the mestizo's frequent hesitation, doubt, uncertainty, indecision. Whatever doubts the Iberian might have, he tends to hide it behind his characteristic pride. His delight in honors, adulation, praise or acclaim that might come his way, is living proof of his success and further merit of his pride. It is great for confidence building. Unfortunately, as with all members of the human species, such pride threatens to degenerate into vanity, arrogance, and envy of others. At times the difference between a valid opinion and one constructed out of vanity, arrogance, and envy, becomes well-nigh imperceptible. Of course, there are occasions when this attitude has served the Iberian well, especially in maintaining the hierarchical colonial structure intact. The

Spaniard might need to do no more than remind those of mixed ethnicities and Amerindians and African Americans who they are, in order to reestablish rigid social lines. However, circumstances that demand more moderation and less ostentatious comportment can go against the Spaniard's favor. Writing on the Spaniards' penchant for envy as a distinct character trait, Spanish intellectual Ramón Ménendez Pidal (1957) asserts that the Spanish individual is hardly ever favorably disposed to value the work of his compatriots. This is because the Spaniard believes that to applaud the work of his competitors is tantamount to devaluation of his own work.

In such a battlefield of sentiments, objective criticism and friendly dialogue seem impossible. Provoked emotions remain bared to the bone and open for all to see. It might even appear that one tends either to love or hate one's friend or associate; there often seems to be no middle ground. Nevertheless, when Spaniards—and Mexicans as well in this regard—are confronted with a crisis, all people within reach may be capable of putting their shoulder to the wheel and in a gallant community effort resolve the problem at hand, of whatever stripe it may be. A case in point: the devastating earthquake in Mexico City, 1985. Ignoring a paralyzed government that apparently was incapable of proper action, thousands of citizens gave of their time and resources in the aid of their fellow compatriots. In other words, the Iberians and Mexicans are neither excessively emotional nor sentimental, neither detachedly impersonal nor exactly neutral, but rather, both characteristics of all poles of opposition are folded into the same heart and mind.

The Spaniards' exaggerated concept of *honor* has been throughout history a basic expression of their pride and independence and one of the supreme expressions of their "I-ism." This deeply entrenched personality trait is noteworthy in the theatrical work of Pedro Calderón de la Barca (1600–81), *The Alcalde de Zalamea* (The Magistrate of Zalamea). De la Barca writes that one's worldly possessions legitimately belong to the King, but *honor* is the patrimony of the soul, and the soul is the property of God and God alone. Honor, like *hidalguismo*, is the shield that protects one. It is one's defense and that which builds a moat around one's personality. Honor implies a certain code of conduct that one must follow, and if one follows it faithfully, nobody and nothing can permanently damage one's "I." Honor extends outward and spreads an umbrella over one's entire family and intimate friends. When social *interrelations* emerge and bring up the matter of *pundonor* (point of honor, something that affects one's honor or reputation), unmitigated vengeance can be the sanctioned response. When one *caballero* offends another *caballero*, jeopardizing his honor, reprisal and justice may not come through legal channels but at the hands of the offended party, who is obligated to humiliate, or otherwise reap punishment of one form or another, on the offender.

Bear in mind in light of this chapter that the confrontation between the Spaniards and the Aztecs involved an indigenous people whose worldview was fatalistic, in contrast to the Europeans, whose demeanor was one of almost unbridled confidence. The Aztecs viewed themselves as buffeted about by the forces of nature and the wrath of their gods, and there was not much they could do about their destiny. According to their cosmology, this destiny was slated to play itself out over and over again in a self-repeating cycle of destruction, regeneration, destruction, and so on. The Spaniards, in contrast, bold and brash after their successful campaign against the Moors, were positive of mind. As far as they were concerned, there was nothing they couldn't do: conquer whatever human societies they might encounter, loot and rape as they pleased, establish an empire by the force of their own will. As we shall see, these two characteristics combine into the Mexican-Mestizo soul to create a group of people and a set of cultures that are genuinely unique.

Further Reading

Bradford 1962, Brading 1986, Brenan 1943, Crow 1985, Elliott 1989, Keen 1971, León-Portilla 1990, Michener 1969, Pitt-Rivers 1961, Pritchett 1965, Souchère 1964, Stone 1990, Wolf 1959, Zavala 1955.

Notes

1. Here as elsewhere, in order to discuss the nature of the Mexican mind-set, I must use generalities. Please bear in mind, however, that for every generality there are numerous exceptions; yet generalities are a way to get a handle, however slippery, on complex cultural traits.

2. I must point out, however, that since the fall of Spanish dictator Francisco Franco in 1975, Spain has been rapidly transforming itself into a society more akin to those of the rest of Europe, for better or for worse.

3. I do so by resorting to general attitudes and behavioral traits, while asking you to keep in mind that nobody coincides to the letter with these generalities; they are simply a means by which we can hope to get a handle on the problem.

4

Conquest and Colony

The Aztecs: A Military Society

Tenochtitlán was founded in 1325, when the Mexicas—more commonly known as the Aztecs—finally discovered the eagle on a nopal cactus ready to consume a snake, the sign their god of war, Huitzilopochtli, had given them as the site where they were to set down roots.

From that point onward, the Mexicas began appropriating religious and artistic commodities and cultural conventions and customs from the outlying nations. As a token of appreciation, they subdued their neighboring communities. By 1340, through bullying tactics, threats, coercion, and alliances, they began spreading in all directions, especially south. They took control of the area southwest of present-day Guerrero to Colima, east into Veracruz and Tabasco, and south into the Mixtec and Zapotec territory of Oaxaca. By the sixteenth century the Aztecs reached the zenith of their expansion. In fact, they were spread too thin. When Moctezuma II became emperor, a control crisis was afoot. As a makeshift measure, Moctezuma arrogantly claimed to possess qualities akin to those of a god, obviously an attempt to centralize power.

From 1517 to 1519 reports reached Moctezuma's ears that off the eastern coasts were huge canoes with great white wings. Moctezuma feared that the fair-haired god, Quetzalcoatl, had returned to put an end to the empire. This would be the era of the fifth sun. Time, for the Aztecs, was cyclical. It doubled back on itself each fifty-two years. At the end of each cycle, one epoch ended and everything began anew. All vestiges of culture were destroyed, and all fires put out. Then they could greet a new epoch, relight the fires, and begin reconstructing culture as they knew it. Four fifty-two-year periods (or suns) had transpired, and now it was time for the end of the fifth sun. According to Aztec legends, the great god, Quetzalcoatl, had been deceived by other members of the pantheon of gods. In shame he went into self-exile to the east, but not without the warning that at the termination of the fifth sun he would return and wreak havoc on the empire. The date of his return was marked on the Aztec calendar as *ce acatl*, which on the Gregorian calendar the Spaniards used was 1519. In that year Cortés dropped anchor in the harbor of Veracruz. Moctezuma had reason to be worried.

The Aztecs' worldview, as already mentioned, was fatalistic. They were buffeted about by the will and the wrath of the gods. Immersed in a dark form of existential anguish, they felt that what was to happen would happen, and there was nothing they could do to change it. In contrast, having successfully expelled the Jews and "reconquered" Spain for God, king, and country, the Spaniards considered themselves the defenders of the Catholic way and the only way according to all good Spaniards. A new continent supposedly inhabited by infidels, America was seen as an extension of the "reconquest." Thus the wars of conquest took on religious connotations. The intrepid, self-confident Spaniards planted the cross and the sword on American soil with the surety that might made right, and that everything was theirs and theirs alone.

To put the Aztec-Spanish distinction in a nutshell, the Aztecs remained thoroughly within a mystical-magical attitude toward themselves, their gods, and nature. The Spaniards, in contrast, saw that new world as something to be dominated.

Conquest of Paradise?

Hernán Cortés left Cuba for the mainland with 550 soldiers to seek gold and silver. Of course there was that other side of the conquest, the "religious conquest." But initially at least, it was secondary to the object of plunder. The Spaniards first made a stop in Yucatán, where by chance Cortés happened to run into Jerónimo de Aguilar, who had taken up residence with a community of Mayans after a shipwreck. Aguilar knew the native language and later served as a valuable interpreter.

By another stroke of luck, during a stop in the Tabasco area, Cortés and his soldiers were offered food, a little gold, and twenty attractive young maidens. Among the maidens was a certain Malintzín, or Malinche according to the Spaniards' mispronunciation of her name. Malinche, reportedly the daughter of an Aztec *cacique* (see glossary), spoke both Mayan and Nahuatl, the language of the Aztecs. Cortés took a liking to her, apparently for both her interpretative ability and her physical charms. She was properly baptized with the name of Doña Marina. Now the Europeans could communicate with the natives, from Cortés in Spanish to Aguilar, Aguilar in Mayan to Malinche, Malinche in Nahuatl to the Aztec emperor, and then back again. Most likely, a lot was lost in the process and considerable miscommunication occurred.

The Spaniards could not have defeated the Aztecs without allies— Totonacans from Veracruz and Tlaxcalans from the central highlands, who at the time were forced to pay tribute and provide human sacrifices to the Aztec empire. With over 100,000 allied warriors, the Spaniards marched to Cholula close to the present city of Puebla, where Malinche got word of a plot against the invaders. The Spaniards launched a surprise attack, killing four thousand armed Cholulans, including women and children. From that time on, the invaders were called *popolucas,* "barbarians." Unruffled by their deteriorating reputation, the conquerors pushed on to Tenochtitlán. The series of epic battles cannot be recounted here. Suffice it to say that Moctezuma greeted Cortés with open arms, apparently fearing him as he would have feared the wrathful Quetzalcoatl. Moctezuma was later branded a traitor and reportedly killed by his own people. Cuauhtémoc then became their leader and immediately waged ruthless battle against the invaders. All was to no avail, however. He was eventually taken prisoner and tortured in the Spaniards' effort to find out where the Aztecs had concealed their gold and other treasures—they refused to believe there was no more wealth than what had met their eyes. After many hits and misses, and aided by the Spaniards' greatest ally—smallpox, measles, influenza, and other diseases against which the Aztecs had no immunity—the impressive city of Tenochtitlán was finally defeated and razed to the ground. Stones from the ruins of the great temple dedicated to Huitzilopochtli and the rain god

Tlaloc were used to begin construction of the first Catholic cathedral in the Americas. The Aztecs' fifth sun had burned itself out.

Governing Independent Colonists and a Broken People

The Aztecs and other Amerindian groups were put to work tearing down their whole empire. Ancient temples were reduced to rubble and Roman Catholic churches were constructed in their place. Along with this destruction, missionaries came to convert the masses.

The missionaries and the Church set out to systematically destroy all vestiges of the indigenous religion. The codices on which the Amerindian priests had recorded their history, science, and arts were burned. Juan de Zumárraga boasted in a report to the Crown that his religious crusade had managed to disappear five hundred temples and 20,000 religious idols. Bishop Diego de Landa of Yucatán burned heaps of Mayan manuscripts. Today, a mere three Mayan codices remain, along with thirteen from the Mixtecs and nine from the Aztecs. The history of Mesoamerica virtually passed into oblivion. In contrast to the history of Rome, Greece, or Egypt, very little is known of any of the equally great empires of the Americas. Yet the conquered still managed to have their say. On December 12, 1531, a dark-skinned Virgin Mary appeared to the Amerindian Juan Diego at the temple in Tepeyac dedicated to Tonantzín, a "god mother" like Mary.

A shrine was constructed at the site in the name of the Virgin of Guadalupe, who was destined to become the "mother" of the Mexican nation. To all outward appearances, one religion replaced another religion. But not really. Guadalupe's features were Amerindian, and she began inspiring the Amerindians in a manner comparable to their traditional Tonantzín. Over the years, as a consequence, among people of Amerindian ethnicity, Mexican Catholicism has become a *hybrid* religion. The conquered brought about a subtle conquest of the conquerors. So much for the spiritual aspect of the conquest.

With respect to the material transformation of the land, tragedy was in store for the Amerindians. Shortly after the conquest, mining expanded in Zacatecas, Guanajuato, Taxco, Pachuca, and elsewhere. So did agriculture, with increased production of cacao and tobacco, and the introduction of sugar, wheat, and cotton. Stock raising increased dramatically after the first horses, cattle, and sheep made the trip across the Atlantic. In fact, the livestock ate almost everything in sight, depriving the peasants of their livelihood. While the Amerindian population of Mexico according to some reports was reduced from 25.2 million in 1519 to 1.4 million by 1605, the livestock population increased by an inversely dramatic rate. (It is estimated that the population of the Valley of Mexico alone decreased from approximately 3 million inhabitants in 1519 to a mere 70,000 by the middle of the seventeenth century. The years following the destruction of Tenochtitlán must by whatever standard be considered the most brutal demographic catastrophe in history.)

In addition to European diseases, the population was decimated by intensive, unbearable work in the fields and especially in the mines, where the back-breaking labor was sheer torture. A laborer who could no longer produce what was demanded often was brutally beaten to death. Faced with this subhuman existence, the Amerindians lost their will to live, and death from self-inflicted torture was common.

Colonial Administration

Problems of governing the American colonies were virtually insurmountable, given the vast distances between colony and colony and between colonies and colonizers. From the very beginning, control was established, as much as possible, by monopolization of political, ecclesiastical, and commercial affairs. There were two chief administrative institutions: the Casa de Contratación (House of Trade), founded in 1503, and the Consejo de las Indias (Council of the Indies), set up in 1524. The Casa regulated commerce, while the Consejo advised the king regarding the administrative affairs of the colonies. Things were never simple, however. Due to the distances and problems of communication, administration of the colonies was far less structured than desirable.

There was another problem. We have seen the Spaniard's idealistic side, say, as illustrated in the so-called Requirement. Let us carry this idea a little further. At first there were abuses of the Amerindians. The abuses were made manifest early on by the Dominicans, especially Bartolomé de las Casas. According to the protests, the *encomiendas* should be abolished altogether, since they brought nothing but misery to the Amerindians. The appalling slaughter of the New World natives weighed heavily on the Crown's conscience. The pope had charged Spain with converting the Amerindians, not exterminating them. The king called his learned individuals for advice, and according to their recommendations, the Laws of Burgos were drawn up in 1512–1513—almost a decade before the conquest of Mexico. These laws established a more stringent code of conduct regarding relations between Spaniards and Amerindians. They sanctioned the *encomiendas*, provided that the Amerindians were neither enslaved nor mistreated and were converted to Christianity.

The laws were carefully drafted and sent to the colonies. But the Crown lacked the means to enforce them. Due to vast distances, lack of personnel, and communication problems, governors functioned without effective power. They were unable to exact punishment on the *encomenderos* who violated the king's edicts. It is really doubtful whether any *encomendero* in the Caribbean paid more than passing attention to the laws. The royal government's initial effort to establish control was well intentioned, though idealistic, and led to increasing frustration for the Crown and the would-be enforcers in the colonies. This was one of the first of a prolonged series of idealistic laws that simply couldn't be put into practice. They were like the so-called Blue Laws of the English colonies: laws so out of keeping with everyday practices in the colonies that they were considered absurd and simply ignored. The difference is that this practice became customary in the Spanish colonies. In fact, Charles Gibson (1966, 53) writes that "the Laws of Burgos stand as one of the many instances in Spanish colonial history of the ineffectiveness of law."

Another noteworthy instance of the Crown's idealism as opposed to the reality of everyday affairs in the colonies—echoes of Don Quixote and Sancho Panza—is that of the New Laws. The time was 1542 and King Charles V was in power. The task was once again to stop mistreatment of the Amerindians and create in the New World a class of nobles comparable to that of fifteenth-century Spain prior to Ferdinand and Isabella. The idea was that only a conscientious and humanitarian nobility could create the proper relationship with the indigenous peoples. The New Laws were expressed not in terms of a struggle for power but for a more humanitarian policy. They prohibited Amerindian enslavement—

once again—and forbade the granting of new *encomiendas*—the principal instruments of abuse. Also, the tributes taken from the Amerindians were to be regulated. The New Laws were far more stringent than those of 1512–1513, and it is to Charles's credit that they met with at least limited success.

But they were only partially successful. There was an outcry from the *encomenderos* and threats of rebellion. When cooler heads prevailed, the Crown conceded to more moderate goals: tighter control over existing *encomiendas*, limited creation of new *encomiendas*, and restrictions of the landowners' power. Yet the threat of insurrection remained, seething below the surface. A characteristic attitude had by this time become entrenched, incorporated in a customary saying during colonial times: *Obedezco pero no cumplo* (I obey but I do not comply), meaning roughly, "I render homage to the king and Spain, but I fudge on the laws because the existing circumstances do not warrant their strict execution." Consequently, there was a superficial loyalty, but with a slight nod and sly wink the laws were undercut. The Crown's idealistic laws and policies, in the context of the reality of everyday practices in the colonies, often came out second best. As far as the Crown was concerned, the laws were obeyed. But they were not actually obeyed. The Crown consistently drew up new legislation in order to bring greater justice to the Americas. In that respect it is to be congratulated, for it was the first of all colonial empires to create such a set of altruistic, generous, and humane documents. But the colonial form of life proved to be another story. In this respect, chalk one up for the colonists, since lesser humans might not have been able to hold such dispersed colonies together as effectively as did the Spanish colonists.

Spanish Colonialism: Three Centuries and Three Themes

The three centuries of the Spanish colonial period were characterized by (1) expansion, (2) contraction and defense, and (3) reforms. During the sixteenth century, the Spaniards assumed divine providence had endowed them with the responsibility of taking possession of all territory within their grasp for the benefit of God, king, and Spain—and, of course, the "I" of Spanish individualism did not trail far behind. It was not a question of whether they considered their divine charge right or wrong, but the belief that what they were doing needed to be done. Aiding and abetting this belief were (1) the "reconquest" of Spain and expulsion of the Moors, (2) the "invention" of America, (3) the conquest and colonization of America, (4) initial encounters with the Protestant Reformation in Europe, and (5) initial measures taken to defend the colonies against intervention by the English, Dutch, and French, among others. After so much success during the sixteenth century, it was only natural that the Spaniard might begin to feel invincible.

Expansion during the first century took place in three phases. The first was *military:* conquest and exploration. The second was *economic:* a search for wealth among the pre-Hispanic civilizations, and when this possibility had been exhausted, exploitation of mineral deposits by Amerindian and African Mexican labor. The third phase consisted of the *religious conquest,* which in large part took up most of the seventeenth century as well. A missionary zeal in the Americas was partly the result of the Catholic Counter-Reformation: a struggle against the Protestant Reform in northern Europe initiated by Martin Luther in 1517. The Counter-Reformation included a reformation of Catholicism itself. This reformation went against the tide of opulence and luxury that the clergy enjoyed. There was a return to simple, austere forms of life, with concomitant development of programs for the purpose of benefiting humanity, according to the teachings of San Francisco de Assisi (1182–1226), founder of the Franciscan Order.

By the seventeenth century, Spain's maritime and military might was in decline, the supposedly invincible Spanish Armada having been defeated in 1588. The loss profoundly damaged Spain's prestige. At the same time, England, Holland, and France were expanding their maritime activity. However, territorial expansion in the Americas by these countries was minimal. A few islands in the Caribbean were lost, as well as Belice and the Guianas, and that was about it. In short, during the seventeenth century Spain saw fit to moderate her expansionist policy and her accelerated exploitation of mineral wealth and agricultural production. This moderation was due to (1) natural effects of the decline of Spain's power and the exhaustion of her human and monetary resources and (2) aggression from other European nations, which became bolder with each move. Nevertheless, in light of Spain's increasing weakness, it is remarkable that the country didn't lose more territory by the end of the century. This is a tribute to

Spain's perseverance, tenacity, stubbornness, and the Spaniards' capacity to adapt themselves to the demands of a changing social-political-economic milieu in Europe. People less liberally endowed with vital forces would not have been able to survive as effectively against such insurmountable odds.

In 1701, Felipe V took over the Spanish throne as the first of the Bourbon kings. The French Bourbon family replaced the Austrian Habsburg family, which had ruled since the time of Carlos V (1519–1556). Bourbon politics—often referred to as "illustrated despotism," in reference to Enlightenment thought—involved a centralization of the colonies' political and economic affairs. Centralization of power, the Bourbons thought, was the only way to reverse Spain's road to decadence. The Bourbon reforms entailed liberalization of commercial restrictions, allowing the colonists the opportunity to enter into relations with other countries. Taxes were modified or abolished, and forced labor was strictly prohibited. Commercial activity was notably invigorated, and a new commercial class began challenging the old aristocratic class. In the provinces, new agricultural and mining methods appeared, and the administration of social, political, and economic affairs was buttressed and made more efficient. Governors, justices, and magistrates of the old system were removed and replaced by younger, more vigorous administrators. The bureaucratic force, having grown fat and ineffective during the Habsburg reign, was reduced considerably. The new officials were given a respectable salary, which reduced corruption somewhat. All in all, the affairs of the colonies took a definite upswing.

However, things were not all rosy. Although the infusion of Bourbon vigor was effective, new problems arose. First, in spite of the reforms, Spain realized few gains in her military struggle against other European nations. Second, French liberalism of the Enlightenment mold was a swim against the current of age-old Spanish traditions, and it simply didn't take. Discontent boiled up, occasionally spewing forth in open rebellion. Third, and what disturbed the colonial system to the greatest extent, many of the administrative and bureaucratic posts were taken away from the criollos (Spaniards born in Mexico) and given to *peninsulares* (Spaniards born in Spain), recently arrived from Europe. This practice served to aggravate criollo resentment against the Crown. This resentment eventually culminated in the Wars of Independence.

But before we turn to the independence movement, let's take a look at the radically changing ethnic and racial makeup of the colonies.

Further Reading

Alvas 1996, Burkholder and Johnson 1994, Carrasco 1992, Coe 1994, Cypess 1991, Florescano 1994, Fuentes, 1992, Fuentes, 1993, Gibson 1964, Gossen and León-Portilla 1993, Graham 1990, Grieder 1983, Hanke 1965, Haring 1947, Johnson 1983, Kicza 1983, Laurin 1978, León-Portilla 1962, 1990, Lockart 1992, MacLachlan and Rodríguez 1980, Madariaga 1947, Mörner 1967, Nicholson and Quiñones Keber 1983, O'Gorman 1961, Ricard 1966, Rubert de Ventos 1991, Schurz 1964, Sokolov 1991, Soustelle 1961, Thomas 1995, Varner and Varner 1983, Wolf 1959, Zamora 1993, Zorita 1963.

5

Cultural Hybridity Emerging

The Amerindian Disaster

From the very beginning the Spaniards established a system of exploiting land and minerals, with the Amerindians providing forced labor. In fact, during the entire colonial period there were institutional artifices for extracting maximum labor from the Amerindians at a minimum of cost and effort.

As mentioned in Chapter 4, the Laws of Burgos, well-meaning though they were, didn't help much. Neither did the New Laws. The idea was to improve the treatment of the underprivileged. This was a remarkable example of the utopian visions of the Crown, but it simply didn't fly. The colonists were too practical, and at times even cynical, with respect to the Crown's measures, even though they never ceased to pay their due respects to God, king, and Spain.

One of the pitfalls of the Laws of Burgos was that they contained a few ludicrous articles that could not help but color the whole document: prohibitions against forcing Amerindians to dig up their ancestors in order to work the land, demanding that they carry their masters in hammocks, and ordering them to bring ice from the snow-capped peaks in order to give their lords some relief from the burning sun. There was even a stipulation that crimes committed against the native people must be subject to less severe punishment than crimes against any other ethnic group—

under the assumption that the privileged groups were plenty capable of protecting themselves, unlike the Amerindians.

Here we have some of the most blatant examples of elusive tactics on the part of the colonists, following the notorious maxim, "I obey but I do not comply," in the face of laws taken to be so absurd that they deserved little notice. It's the same old story: idealistic measures confront practical realities. The desire to strike a happy medium between the two conflicting forces produced social tension, political discord, and economic contradictions that prevented the emergence of human interrelationships.

Another case in point. The status of the Amerindians declined as they lost their lands. The Jesuits, inspired with utopian ideals, were not alone in their efforts to create genuine Christian communities in this new American wilderness. But the European landowners usually got the upper hand. Amerindians were customarily relegated to subordinate positions, even though after the sixteenth century few were enslaved. The Amerindians' lack of natural resistance to European diseases might have saved many an indigenous soul from undue hardship and death, since, as fate would have it, African slaves were soon imported in large numbers throughout much of Latin America. Although in Mexico importation of African slaves was practically abandoned well before the end of the colonial period, by 1810 Africans numbered roughly 25,000. Over the years countless Africans mixed with other ethnic groups to become African Europeans (mulattos) and African Amerindians (*Cambujos, Zambos*). Today, tens of thousands of African Mexicans are found in areas along the Pacific Coast in the states of Oaxaca and Guerrero, and considerably more in the state of Veracruz. Although the exact number is indeterminable, it is safe to say that a few million Mexicans are of mixed African, Amerindian, and European heritage.

The racial, ethnic, and cultural differences that began with the union of Cortés and Malinche and other conquerors and their mistresses, rape victims, and occasionally legal wives, soon became exceedingly complex. Sorting out the threads of this grand racial-ethnic mix is well-nigh impossible. As a general rule, it can be said that in today's Mexico the cultural matrix is basically fourfold: race, language, social class, education. Those at the bottom rungs of the social ladder usually have darker skin, speak one of the over one hundred Amerindian dialects, and have an education that is usually well below average. Many middle- and upper-class Mexicans swear that there is no

U.S.-style racial discrimination in their country. They are in a manner of speaking correct. Racial discrimination *like* that in the United States is hardly evident in Mexico, not that there is an absence of discrimination, however. Discrimination is everywhere, based on social standing more than racial heritage. Consequently, lower social standing is usually accompanied by skin of a darker hue, fewer years of education, and often a language barrier. The fact remains, however, that Amerindians can become mestizos, and mestizos can become virtual Europeans by upgrading their education, social, and economic standing, and speaking Spanish like people of the dominant culture. An Amerindian who takes on a mestizo lifestyle may be considered a mestizo, and a mestizo who by hook or by crook has managed to enrich himself might in certain social circles take on the status of a criollo.

There is a fusion of racial types quite unlike the relatively clear-cut lines of demarcation in the United States. This fusion is a process that has been occurring from the colonial period to the present. In the beginning, there were attempts to categorize this process, thanks, once again, to the Crown's obsession for putting things in their proper place. One of the Crown's more interesting efforts to pigeonhole race and ethnicity is the following:

1. Spaniard + Amerindian = Mestizo
2. Mestizo + Spanish woman = Castizo
3. Castizo woman + Spaniard = Spaniard (a move back up the hierarchy)
4. Spanish woman + African = Mulatto (derived from *mula* [mule])
5. Spaniard + Mulatto woman = Morisco
6. Morisco woman + Spaniard = Albino
7. Spaniard + Albino woman = Torna atrás (a step down)
8. Amerindian + Torna Atrás = Lobo
9. Lobo + Amerindian woman = Zambaigo
10. Zambaigo + Amerindian woman = Cambujo
11. Cambujo + Mulatto woman = Albarazado
12. Albarazado + Mulatto woman = Barcino
13. Barcino + Mulatto woman = Coyote
14. Coyote woman + Amerindian = Chamizo
15. Chamizo woman + Mestizo = Coyote mestizo
16. Coyote mestizo + Mulatto woman = Ahí te estás ("There you are," and keep your distance)

This hierarchy of racial and ethnic mixes and values reveals the importance of HC considerations within culture. It also reveals remarkable regional differences and variations in the colonies, especially in view of the fact that this classification by no means exhausts the complex field of miscegenation. It hardly needs saying that racial mixture eventually became so utterly confusing that any and all efforts to classify it were absurd. Outside the Spaniards (and criollos), mestizos, mulattos, and so-called Indios, few of the terms cited above were actually in wide use after a few generations of racial miscegenation.

Overwhelmed by the Laws

The colonists usually considered the dictum "I obey but I do not comply" to be in line with the practical demands of everyday life in the colonies. As a counterpart to this dictum, the Crown and the Church were obliged to hand down their own assertion: "This is how the colonies will be administered in order to honor inalienable human rights." An eternal conflict, an infinite regress, followed, in the order of: "You must comply. I'll 'obey,' but I won't 'comply.' But you must. But I won't. But you should. Yet I'll not." And so on. The laws merited respect insofar as they originated from God, king, and Spain. At the same time, they were partially ignored or simply forgotten during the coming and going of daily affairs. They were conceived as noble but impractical.

The problem was one of partly incompatible perspectives. What the Crown dictated was from the viewpoint that reigned in the peninsula, while the manner of what was dictated was misinterpreted from the viewpoint that held sway in the Americas. One hand tries to force the other hand; the other hand, well greased and slippery, slithers and slides free. Miscommunication became the norm. There was mutual respect, but with a wink and a little bureaucratic shuffling here and there, things got done the "good old boy" way—which is another way of saying the "paternalistic," "personalistic" way. There was little open dialogue between Crown and colonists. Rather, there were two sides irremediably separated in time and space: they couldn't understand each other because their perspectives were distinct, and on many points incompatible.

A prime example of this clash of viewpoints occurred at the very outset of a series of debates between Bartolomé de las Casas, "defender of the

Amerindians," and Juan Ginés de Sepúlveda (1490–1573). De las Casas seemed to have his feet on solid ground, since he had firsthand familiarity with the American condition. Sepúlveda, in contrast, was of a scholastic mind. He followed Church dogma to the letter, and he was an Aristotelian insofar as he believed the state of affairs that existed should be perpetuated, since that was the "natural order." In other words, it was the order of things as presumably dictated by God. De las Casas maintained that the Amerindians should have the same rights as those enjoyed by the conquerors; Sepúlveda responded that their subjugation and even enslavement was natural and proper. De las Casas eventually convinced the Crown of his point of view, and consequently the New Laws of 1542 were put into effect. Unfortunately the colonists considered these laws impractical and inapplicable: "I obey but I do not comply."

Consequently, de las Casas was not really as attuned to reality as he might have appeared. He likely believed that simply putting the New Laws into effect improved the conditions of the Amerindians. But American reality was another matter, and it implied something else: business as usual. Sepúlveda's argument, based not on the Amerindian condition as it actually was but on abstract ideals, ironically was closer to the colonists' view of their world. The miscommunication seemed to be the consequence of two "languages" within the same language. Crown and colonists didn't see eye to eye but talked past each other, and the Amerindians were much the poorer in spite of the efforts of de las Casas.

In view of these colonial conditions, conflicts were inevitable. On the one hand, there were large landowners and miners who believed that the land and minerals belonged to the Spaniards as fruits of the conquest; hence the Amerindians were duty-bound to serve their new masters. On the other hand, we have the clergy and certain representatives of the Crown according to whom the Amerindians had rights to their due share of the land, since they were vassals of the king and should be of virtually equal standing. Although the laws favored the Amerindians, in some cases actually putting them in the same category as the colonists, the colonists tended to relegate them to an inferior position. In many cases the native inhabitants had lower social standing than African American slaves.

There might have been no solution to this dilemma. Perhaps the only way of administering the colonies was through a *duality*—an inevitable duality, in view of the *dual* nature of the colonial administration. We have seen the duality among the colonists, caught as they were between their pragmatic *reality* and the Crown's *ideal* measures as illustrated by the "I obey but I do not comply" maxim. There was another duality, this one existing between the representatives of the Crown and the Amerindian caciques, on the one hand, and the Amerindian people on the other. This duality owed its existence in large part to the *double* role of the Amerindians. They were obliged to provide a source of manual labor for their Spanish masters, and at the same time they had to pay tribute in the form of work and goods to their local Amerindian caciques whenever they did not fall under the jurisdiction of the Spanish colonists. At the local level, many of the Amerindian communities were permitted to retain their traditional social and political organizations. The appointed officials of the Spanish administration were almost exclusively from the peninsula. The "foreign" colonial magistrates and the local caciques formed a type of alliance in extracting labor and tribute from the Amerindian underdogs. The fact remains, nevertheless, that this particular colonial system was about as efficient as could be expected. It might have been the only method by which the colonies could have produced the wealth of cargo that left the colonial ports for the motherland.

(In this light, "I obey but I do not comply" is one of the supreme examples of HC space and PC time. It marvelously illustrates both intracultural and intercultural contact zones. On the part of colonists and Amerindians, there was an outward show of acceptance ["I obey"]. At the same time slippery and implicitly subversive practices gave a false picture of what might otherwise be viewed as subversion of the ways dictated by the Crown ["But I do not comply"]. As we shall see below, variations of the maxim have contributed to violence, corruption, and general injustice that are in large part the result of contemporary Mexico's colonial heritage.)

Coping in Spite of It All

As a rule, interrelations between the various ethnic groups during the colonial period evolved: the Amerindian/peninsular dichotomy was gradually replaced by the *encomendero*/servant split, and then by a comparable distinction after Mexican independence from Spain in 1821. First there were Spaniards and non-Spaniards. After the conquest, the *encomenderos* and servants were quite distinguishable as well. However, the offspring of the Spaniards were criollos, and some of the servants were mestizos. Then on the coasts African Mexicans made their entry, and soon mulattos were in evidence. By independence, a confusing concoction of racial and cultural *hybridity* was well on its way.

With respect to the plight of the Amerindians, this evolution is notable in the transformations from the *encomienda* to a system for distributing Amerindian laborers among the landowners called the *repartimiento*, then from the *repartimiento* to *free labor* contracts, and finally, from free labor contracts to the *hacienda* system after independence in 1821 (see glossary). By the middle of the sixteenth century, the *encomienda* had lost much of its importance, and the *repartimiento*, only beginning to emerge here and there, became dominant during the seventeenth century. Free labor saw its beginning at the opening of the eighteenth century with the *Bourbon reforms* (see glossary). An increasing number of Amerindians began entering into work agreements with the European landed gentry under the assumption that they were free to come and go as they saw fit. These workers, labeled *gañanes* (Amerindians free to choose for whom they work for a wage), at the outset continued residing in their traditional communities. They maintained a more or less pre-Hispanic form of life but remained subject to the jurisdiction of the Spanish municipal authorities. Tribute was demanded of them, and as long as they had not paid in full, they could not leave the vicinity. On the surface that seems easy enough: pay the tribute and leave whenever you wish.

Reality presented another face entirely, however. In many cases the Spanish authorities and landed gentry saw to it that the Amerindians' debt always exceeded their ability to liquidate it. So they were in essence trapped; their plight was little better than slavery. Many caciques in the villages argued for a reduction of the tribute and the demands on labor, but their efforts were in vain. The colonists resisted any change in the system because this appeared to be the only means by which they could be assured of a sufficiently large labor force, thanks to the diminishing Amerindian population.

Toward the middle of the eighteenth century, many potential Amerindian laborers were still living in their own communities. They had no desire to lend their services to their European lords. They preferred their austere life, cultivating the small plots of land they still had. This land was some of the poorest around, since the Europeans had confiscated the most fertile expanses for their own use. The Europeans, as a last-ditch effort, began depriving the Amerindians of their last parcels of land in order to integrate them forcibly into the system—an indirect measure to reenact the system of forced labor. The method in most instances worked. The Amerindians were pushed off their poor lands and pulled into the only place where they could eke out some semblance of a living. Thus the birth of the *hacienda* after independence, with their sprawling mansions and collections of Amerindian huts scattered here and there.

During the early years of the nineteenth century many Amerindians could be found wandering about, without land and apparently without direction or purpose. They now had no place in society: their ancient cosmos had disintegrated, and a secure spot in the traditional community was no longer available to them. This loss of security was supposed to have been prevented by the Bourbon reforms of the eighteenth century. The reforms were enacted to provide for more efficient colonial administration, which they did. Logically speaking, then, the Amerindians' welfare should have been provided. But increased efficiency accompanied decreased concrete human interrelationships between those who had money and power and influence and those who did not. Whenever focus rested on expediency, some people or some social group usually paid the consequences. Those who paid were most often those at the bottom of the totem pole: the Amerindians.

It might appear that the Amerindians' best bet was to move onto the haciendas or into the cities. In this manner, they might at least be able to accommodate themselves to the dominant society, learn to speak Spanish, toss off their huaraches (peasant sandals), buy a pair of shoes, eat with a knife and fork and spoon, and join the mestizo crowd. Some of the Native Americans did just that. As noted above, they might find that they were no longer considered merely Indios (Amerindians) but had moved up the social scale a notch to become mestizos. Many of them found that this transformation opened doors to new possibilities of bettering themselves socially and economically. The trade-off, however, was a loss of their traditional way of life, which left a vacuum that could never be satisfactorily filled. And in many ways, this vacuum remains unfilled to the present day. Thus the fruits of the well-intentioned Bourbon reforms never ripened, and the condition of the Amerindians continued to degenerate. The supposed solution to the Amerindians at the time of the reforms was actually no solution at all. It was in the very nature of the indigenous peoples to resist assimilation into the dominant and alien culture. They maintained themselves a breed apart, as a foreign, mute element, as the Other.

Yet the human element, consisting of interrelations between cultures, was considerably more benign in the Spanish and Portuguese colonies than in the colonies of France, England, and Holland. In spite of the rift between the king's ideals and what actually occurred in the Americas, and notwithstanding the injustices, the fact remains that no colonial empire had made such a concerted effort to provide just, and Christian, tolerance and management for the people inevitably dispossessed by conquest. The so-called *Black Legend* (see glossary) is in an ironic way evidence that the Spanish were not as ruthless as their competitors. The very existence of a Bartolomé de las Casas and the fact that his argument was heeded is proof that there was tolerance and a concerted effort to correct injustice. This sort of "proof" does not exist, at least to the same extent, among other colonial empires of the times. Moreover, the very possibility that there can be a Black Legend testifies to the fact that to a certain extent there was a greater degree of "free speech" in Spain and the colonies than elsewhere.

In spite of the apparent dualities that ruled during the Mexican colonial period, there was a process of mutual acceptance and fusion of cultural practices that culminated in a complex form of cultural *hybridity* (see glossary).

The African Mexicans and Mulattos

A couple of decades after Columbus's adventures, the Amerindian population had been virtually demolished in the Caribbean islands. A few Dominican friars, most notably Bartolomé de las Casas, raised their voice in protest. De las Casas himself suggested in a moment of despair that perhaps another race, the Africans, who seemed more fit for long, hard toil under the tropical sun, would be more suitable than the Amerindians. As destiny would have it, the Crown took him up on his "recommendation," and the unprecedented exploitation and slaughter of humans by humans began. In 1517, Spain granted transportation of four thousand slaves per year to Mexico and the rest of the New World. Of this number, one-third could be women, for procreation of the labor force. Thus originated the African element in present-day Mexican culture.

The African Mexicans were able to adapt remarkably well to their new environment, all things considered. They had been brutally uprooted from their native land, transported under intolerable conditions to the Americas, sold in the market, and branded and immediately put to work under the whip, with the threat of dogs and guns when deemed necessary by the slave owners. This series of traumatic experiences might have caused the Africans to fall into a state of inescapable melancholy. Indeed, suicides were frequent, and loss of the will to carry on was prevalent. Yet the African Mexicans' elastic spirit survived, and they were able to accommodate themselves quite remarkably to life's new rhythm. In fact, they were able to exploit the relationship with their new masters to their own advantage. They were changed by the new setting, and their subtle adaptation exercised a reverberation in the society at large to change the lifestyle of the dominant culture as well.

As a result of the mutual adaptation of Africans to European ways and vice versa, African music, dance, folklore, religious beliefs, and lyrics enlivened an otherwise monotonous existence in the colonies. During colonial times the condition of the African Americans was decrepit. Yet, quite understandably, the slaves never ceased nurturing their desire to escape from bondage. Nevertheless, while they remained in captivity, they did the best with what they had. As in the Amerindian-European hybridity, the African Mexicans and Europeans consequently realized mutual adaptation to yield a complex cultural mixture along the coasts of contemporary Mexico.

Available evidence suggests that with the exception of instances of criollo and mestizo cruelty, abuse of slaves was not as severe in Latin America as in the United States. Of the Latin American colonies, the Spanish American treatment of slaves seems to have been, at times and according to the conditions, somewhat more extreme than in Brazil. In the Spanish colonies there was more emphasis on *casticismo* ("purity" of "blood") and allegiance to a Catholicism unblemished by practices brought over from Africa, than in the Portuguese colony (though the Spanish Caribbean, where African influence is most pronounced, is an exception in this regard). Moreover, specific conditions in the Mexican and South American Spanish colonies brought about a type of slavery unlike that of the Portuguese colony.

In the first place, throughout the colonial period in Mexico and elsewhere in Spanish America, African slaves were used more extensively in the pit mines, along with Amerindian labor, than in Brazil. This work was physically more demanding than labor in the fields. Later, when gold and diamonds were discovered in Brazil, the conditions there became somewhat comparable to those in the Spanish colonies. In the second place, the presence of Amerindian masses, who were generally of more docile temperament than the Africans, complicated interpersonal relations in Mexico and elsewhere. The Amerindians always provided a source of labor in case there might be a scarcity of African labor. Consequently, there was a certain tendency to more rigorously exact labor from the blacks, since it would be possible to fall back on the other "beasts of burden" in the event that sickness, exhaustion, or death overtook them. However, the Amerindians often enjoyed at least a modicum of security within their community in its traditional environment, while the Africans had been brutally displaced from their homeland and thrown in an entirely new setting. Thus the Africans, by nature, tended to become somewhat more open to assimilation and accommodation to the dominant culture than the Amerindians. This to a degree buffered severe treatment of the Africans.

In areas where African Mexicans came into contact and conflict with Amerindians, racial mixture gave rise to *Zambos* and *Cambujos*, or African mestizos. People of African and European parentage became mulattos. These mixtures reflect interaction of values, cultures, and customs typical of Mexico; those of the colonizer tended to dominate. Over the long haul, however, hybridization emerged to give a fusion and confusion to the colonial form of life. As a result, today's Mexico, like Brazil and the rest of Spanish America, sports a form of cultural *hybridity* that is more extensive than that in the United States and in the British, Dutch, and French colonies of the Caribbean.

Numerous slave rebellions occurred throughout the Mexican colony during the eighteenth and nineteenth centuries. At times these revolts caused profound disturbances in the entire area. In the middle of the eighteenth century, rebellious African Americans in Guatemala—then part of New Spain or Mexico—brought about such terror in the colonists that they feared even their most faithful domestic servants. In Mexico City subversive activities during the same period led to the policy of randomly selecting slaves and executing them as an example to those who were contemplating subversive activities. Even ex-slaves and mulattos were viewed as a threat to the Europeans. Nevertheless, evidence points to surprisingly few organized revolutions against the dominant society. Basically all the slaves wanted was their freedom and to be left in peace. For example, between Mexico City and Veracruz on the coast, a group of *cimarrones* (escaped slaves) established a village they called San Lorenzo de los Negros. To all appearances, it was a peaceful, industrious community that simply wanted to go its own way.

The Mestizos

In New Spain, the most common ethnic mixture was Amerindian and Spanish to yield mestizo culture. Today, it cannot be overemphasized that Mexico is primarily a mestizo society.

The mestizos, from the very beginning, were neither Europeans nor Amerindians, and they were caught up in a tension that placed them in a sort of cultural limbo. By the nineteenth century in many areas of New Spain the mestizos were considered violent, possessing evil intent, and lacking purpose or direction. Ethnologist Eric Wolf writes in *Sons of the Shaking Earth* (1959) that the mestizos were social as well as cultural pariahs. They became the antithesis of the Amerindians, who were intimately tied to the land. Although the Amerindians could identify with their community and their geographical locale, the mestizos remained on the periphery of both peninsular and Amerindian cultures. Whereas the Amerindians preferred life in the countryside, the mestizos found the city environment to their liking. The Amerindians were comfortable tilling the land to which they had deep spiritual roots; the mestizos found their place in the ever changing market in the cities among people and caught up in commercial activity, where exchanges of money, goods, ideas, and language were given priority.

Whereas the Amerindians maintained contact with their physical world, recognizing that by the sweat of their brow they deserved a decent living, the mestizos often became cultural boundary hoppers between contact zones in the urban areas. Placing themselves at the margin of society, Eric Wolf writes, they also placed themselves at the margin of "reality." Their reality became the reality of their imaginative mind. They lived out their dreams, that is, they wanted to "realize" their dreams, make their dreams "real." The grand dream of their dreams was to transform their dream into reality, to inject their world with their dream. In order to survive on the margins of society, then, the mestizos were forced to learn how to alter their behavior according to the circumstances with the facility of a person changing masks, like a chameleon changing colors. They had to live by virtue of their cultivating linguistic diversity as the occasion demanded, through quick wit and keen sense of humor, and an astute ability to get the upper hand in social interactions. They often took on the characteristics of the prototypical *pícaro* (rogue, rascal, knave, picaresque person).[1]

In this manner, the mestizos' very alienation became the source of their strength. The mestizos gradually came to occupy the middle ground between masters and servants (made up chiefly of Amerindians and African Americans and mulattos). They often dedicated themselves to commerce in the marketplace. To a certain extent, in some regions they became the backbone of colonial society. In the process, many of them lifted themselves by their own bootstraps, moving up the social ladder by acquiring money and cultivating contacts with powerful and prestigious people. Whereas the Amerindians valued the land, the mestizos saw property as the means to an end; while the Amerindians as individuals merged into their community, the mestizos remained apart from their community with the idea that the individual must take advantage of every opportunity. In this respect the mestizos were also the mirror image of the Amerindians, whose nature was more communal than individual. The characteristics that most specifically characterize the mestizos continued through the colonial period and into the national period and to the present day. Since the mestizos emphasized their ability to express themselves through the

word, the power of their will, their charisma, and their personal and physical attractiveness, their psychological makeup lent itself remarkably well
to the role of *caudillo* (see glossary) during the heyday of strongman politics in Mexico.

Throughout the colonial period, some of the mestizos, endowed with
aggressive tendencies from their school of hard knocks in the cities, began
migrating to the countryside. This time they began more actively inter-
vening in the affairs of the Amerindians. In many areas mestizos migrated
to the Amerindian communities to exploit them and take what they
could from their counterparts, who showed relatively little interest in acquiring individual power, wealth, and possessions. The usual tack was the
following. The mestizo joined an Amerindian community with a show of
friendship, but his real motive was to procure a source of labor whenever
he needed it on his newly acquired land or in the marketplace. At the
same time, the Amerindians paid their respects—as had been drilled into
them for generations—to the mestizo as a *terrateniente* (large landholder).
This newly acquired respect brings with it a certain degree of power and
prestige, and the mestizo eventually despoils the Amerindians of whatever
land they have been able to keep.

Although mestizos now existed among Amerindians, the Amerindian
community often remained under the jurisdiction of the local caciques.
In this sense, the same paradox raised its ugly head: on the one hand, local
authorities dictated protection for the Amerindian (the idealistic side of
the story), and on the other hand, the mestizos exploited the Amerindians
for their own interests, their insatiable desire for land and the power and
prestige it afforded them (the realistic side of the story). Conflicts were inevitable between Amerindians and mestizos. Nevertheless, relationships
between the two groups were often surprisingly harmonious. This bears
witness to the passive suffering, and often the resort to no more than passive resistance, of the Amerindians vis-à-vis the mestizos.

The thirst for wealth, prestige, and power is perhaps the chief general
characteristic of the mestizos (acknowledging, of course, that for any gen-
eralization there are exceptions). As far as the mestizos were concerned,
power, especially political power typical of the caudillo mentality, was the
royal road to prestige. The lust for power is at least in part due to conditions created during the colonial period. Since the Jews were expelled

from Spain in 1492, and since they were occupied with what the Spaniards considered "filthy lucre"—the exchange of money and goods in the marketplace—a vacuum now existed. This vacuum was especially acute in the colonies, since Jews, even those who had nominally converted to Catholicism but continued to engage in commerce, were barred from taking up residence in the New World. Somebody had to fill this social and economic vacuum. There were just so many Spaniards and criollos outside the administrative and bureaucratic systems in the colonies to do the trading. So, enter the mestizos. Engaging in business affairs, primarily colonial capitalistic enterprises on a relatively small scale, offered them a ladder leading to wealth, prestige, and power. Eventually the mestizos found their role in society.

To recap, in the Spanish colonial system the *peninsulares* enjoyed full privileges granted them by the Crown, and the criollos, although relegated to an "inferior" position with respect to the *peninsulares,* had a reasonably comfortable existence. Doors for the most part remained open to them until the final decades of the colonial period. Although their own culture had been largely destroyed during and shortly after the conquest, the Amerindians at least found a place in the cosmos among their own kind in the community. The African Mexicans, violently uprooted from their homeland and thrown into an entirely new cultural environment, had hardly any remedy but gradually to take up life in close proximity to the *peninsular* and criollo centers of power and authority and become more or less integrated in the dominant society. In contrast, the mestizos, who had no home they could really call their own, began filling the empty spaces in the social hierarchy, particularly with the commercial class.

Individual mestizo dynamism owes a debt to the mestizo's Spanish heritage. In the mestizo's self-assertive yet occasionally contemplative nature, there is some of the Amerindian. He cannot be genuinely *either* Amerindian *or* Spaniard, and at the same time, although he is *neither* the one *nor* the other, he is *both* the one *and* the other. This creates a particular, and unique, racial and ethnic and cultural mix making up the Mexican nation, a nation that exemplifies the theme of cultural hybridity. Given this hybridity, a certain mestizo tension pervades Mexico. It affords a picture of what the future might hold in store for the highly industrialized countries of the world that over the past couple of decades have experienced an increasing influx of immigrants from Africa, Asia, the Caribbean, and Latin America.

Yet the "mestizo personality" is well-nigh impossible to comprehend. Whatever definition of the mestizo we may draw, it will be a misdefinition. In spite of the problems inherent in attempting to account for what makes the mestizo mestizo, it is probably safe to say that mestizo culture evinces a confusing dualism of tendencies and tensions. Yet it is more than mere dualism. It is always becoming something different, something new. Above all, mestizo culture is shot through with contact zones that confront us at every turn.

Further Reading

Arrom 1985, Bartra 1992, Carroll 1991, Chance 1978, Degler 1971, Fowler-Salamini and Vaughan 1994, Franco 1991, García Canclini 1993, 1995, Israel 1975, Kicza 1993, Meier and Ribera 1993, Mirandé and Enríquez 1979, Naggar and Ritchin 1996, Oboler 1995, Ruiz and Tiano 1987, Schroeder 1997, Simpson 1967, Smith 1983, Soto 1990.

Notes

1. The nature of the *pícaro* is revealed in a subgenre of the novel, the "picaresque novel" of Spain, classical examples of which we can find in *Lazarillo de Tormes* (1554), and *Guzmán de Alfarache* (1599). The "picaresque novel" characteristically has a protagonist from marginalized groups of society. He is an antihero that presents himself in first-person narrative. Born into an environment populated by the dregs of society, the sole avenue remaining for him is to survive by his wits, astuteness, and acumen, and a gift of gab that more often than not allows him to get the upper hand in social situations.

6

Making Today's Mexico:
Criollos, Independence, and Caudillos

Criollo Resentment

We have observed that the enormous distance between Europe and the Americas conspired against the intentions of the Crown to efficiently administer the affairs of the colonies and bring about just and humanitarian treatment of all ethnic groups. As time went on, the dichotomy between the Crown's *idealistic* programs drifted further and further away from the colonists' practical affairs that American *reality* presented.

From the beginning, the conquerors and colonists wanted to become aristocrats, enjoying all rights and privileges coveted by the Spanish upper crust back home. The monarchs, however, had their own agenda. They certainly didn't want a high-stepping, relatively autonomous nobility in the colonies. In order to establish effective control, the Crown became increasingly dependent on the administrative and bureaucratic body in the colonies. Bureaucracies and official administrative corps as enforcers of rules and regulations, perpetuators of proper means and methods of organization, and all-around paper pushers are by no means the most creative, progressive, and dynamic element in a society. Yet Spain wanted to run a tight ship and avoid internal conflict. The yield was an increasingly stultified colony and blocked communication. This fossilization contradicted the dynamics of the emerging Mexican cultures. Amerindians kept to themselves as much as possible, yet they merged their practices with those of the dominant culture. African Mexicans submerged their ethnic practices into the whole. Mestizos in growing numbers began to assert themselves. Criollos soon outnumbered the *peninsulares* by a dramatically increasing margin. "I obey but I do not comply," as a consequence, was gradually becoming standard practice. It revealed an outward allegiance to the Crown and an inward tendency toward rebellion. During the Bourbon reforms of the eighteenth century, when administration became dynamic and bureaucratic protocol changed drastically, these practices became more pronounced.

The chief perpetrators of the "I obey but I do not comply" mentality were the criollos: they were the most outwardly resentful and were often rebellious regarding the strictures placed on them. Born of Spanish parents in the colonies instead of the peninsula, they were unwilling to cede privileges to the *peninsulares,* who were of the same racial and ethnic heritage. Criollo resentment was on the rise, up to and including the independence movement. As the difference between criollo and *peninsulare* population increased, the number of lucrative minor administrative and bureaucratic posts continued to diminish in relative terms, which only aggravated the resentment. The criollos wanted their own privileged place in the order of things, but it seemed that more and more doors were being closed to them. It was these criollos, rather than the Amerindians, African Mexicans, and mestizos, that the Crown should have watched out for but generally didn't.

This conflict had its beginning in the beginning. Although the Crown endowed Cortés and Francisco Pizarro—conqueror of Peru—with the title of *duke* as just reward for their services, few prestigious and enriching titles were granted in comparison to the number of conquerors who coveted such honors. By 1680, only six dukes were created in Mexico, five Spaniards and surprisingly one mestizo, the descendant of a royal Aztec family. In Peru at the outset the situation had been slightly different, most likely due to the promise of greater riches there than in the colony of New Spain. By 1750, more than eighty-five titles had been granted in Peru, in comparison to twenty-seven in Mexico. As a rule, titles went to those who had played key roles in the conquest—often individuals who financed their own venture—and to prominent administrators. There was another custom that became increasingly pronounced: titles could be bought if the offer was so large that it couldn't be refused. Over the years, those who received titles in one way or another were with few exceptions *peninsulares*.

At the very outset *peninsulares* and criollos engaged in distinct activities. Many criollos became the commercial giants in the cities; less lucrative commerce was usually the domain of the emerging mestizo class. They also took up important positions in the mines, agricultural production, and, toward the end of the colonial period, minor bureaucratic slots. These positions were seen as the most viable alternatives, since major administrative posts remained barred to them. The Crown feared that criollo loyalty would be weaker than that of the *peninsulares*. This might have been a critical miscalculation. Had the criollos been warmly embraced by the monarchs and given the same privileges and rights as the *peninsulares,* the seething discontent that culminated in open rebellion might have been prolonged for generations to come. Hindsight, of course, is a simple matter when compared to foresight.

All Spaniards, criollos and *peninsulares* alike, had a hankering for titles, honors, and lucrative positions. As much as possible, they avoided manual labor. Since the *peninsulares* were offered the most coveted titles, honors, and administrative and bureaucratic occupations, the criollos came to view them, whether justifiably or not, as arrogant, fat-headed, and snobbish. Thus the criollos gave them the derogatory label *gachupines* (literally, "wearer of spurs"). Criollo resentment against the *peninsulares* intensified as the years went by. However, there is a contradiction within this criollo resentment. Quite often, when criollos dealt with members of "inferior" social, racial, and ethnic status, their comportment resembled their conception of the *peninsulares'* attitude toward the criollo, as of "inferior" status. It was a matter of "do unto those under you as those above you do unto you." Consequently, social circles and cultural organizations dominated by criollos took on this "criollo psychology." It was neither much more nor much less than a semblance of "*peninsular* psychology" from the higher echelons of society.

Criollo-*peninsular* antagonism was seething by the end of the eighteenth century. Some criollo families, especially those who built commercial empires, had actually become wealthier than many of the peninsular families. Yet doors to the upper aristocracy remained closed and resentment increased. Fathers of rich criollo families often gave their daughters fat dowries in an effort to entice a *peninsular* suitor. As a rule, *peninsulares* preferred that their offspring marry *peninsulares*. Nevertheless, marriages between criollos and *peninsulares* became more common due to the diminishing numbers of the latter as the criollo population increased. This produced a "mixed aristocracy" that became almost as confusing as the racial and ethnic mixture developed throughout the colonial period. But the tension continued and culminated in the movement for independence at the beginning of the nineteenth century.

The Rise of the Criollos

The Bourbon reforms awakened a society that had ossified regarding colonial administrative and bureaucratic matters but was becoming dynamic regarding increasingly hybridized cultural matters. Bourbon emphasis on efficiency, organization of the provinces, increased taxation, and the expulsion of the Jesuits induced disruptions and created conditions that served to motivate the disgruntled criollos.

The reforms played few favorites. Demands on Amerindians and mestizos and other ethnic groups included harder work and more productivity. The 1767 expulsion of the Jesuits, who had controlled much of the economy, left a vacuum that was filled with a new breed of cutthroat merchants and *hacendados*, most of them criollos and mestizos. Criollo discontent continued to increase, as more Spanish officials were imported from the peninsula. Criollos saw their possibilities for upward mobility increasingly curtailed, and the distinction between themselves and the *peninsulares* became even greater. Did the economic and social discontent of the criollos cause independence? A positive answer is difficult to validate. Almost three centuries of envy, jealousy, and antagonism rose to the surface in 1810, when the criollos stepped onto center stage to take advantage of the revolt and claim what they saw as rightfully theirs. Bourbon Spain collapsed when the monarchy came under the control of Napoleon in 1808. Pandemonium broke loose in the colony. Conservatives were pitted against liberals, clericals against anticlericals, criollos against *peninsulares,* and all of them against Amerindians and mestizos and African Mexicans and mulattos.

However, there is another side of the criollo picture: their growing sense of love for and pride in their birthplace. There was an intensifying national spirit among the criollo class. Many felt a separate and distinct sense of identity, a consciousness of being "Mexican" and pride in it. The area's natural beauty and prestige as a colony became a common theme in criollo poetry and prose, essays and political rhetoric. There was much praise for the land and people as a unique society with captivating charm and culture. There was also Mexico's fabled treasure. Silver at Zacatecas, Taxco, and elsewhere had placed millions in the royal coffers of Spain, in the name of Spain and the king. This was truly a source of pride. But the central focus of their sense of national identity was the Virgin of Guadalupe image.

The apparition of the dark-skinned Virgin to a humble Amerindian, Juan Diego, December 12, 1531, was a marvelous event that helped bring multitudes of indigenous peoples into the Catholic fold. The charming tale of Juan Diego and Guadalupe eventually culminated in what was later called the *Guadalupana* cult (see glossary). By the end of the eighteenth century, Juan Diego and the Brown Madonna had never ceased to strike a resonant chord among the Amerindians and mestizos. But more importantly with respect to Mexico's social, political, and economic history, the Virgin was taken up by the fair-haired criollos in defiance of the *gachupines* and their light-skinned peninsular Virgin of Remedios. Guadalupe was in the process of her own conversion into the premier symbol of emerging Mexican nationalism. This process culminated in 1737, when Guadalupe became the official "mother" of the people of New Spain.

The hybridization of peninsular, African Mexican, and Amerindian cultures is perhaps nowhere more evident than in the Guadalupe image. The appearance of the Amerindian-featured Virgin of Guadalupe to Juan Diego served to integrate Christian and indigenous beliefs and by the end of the colonial period emerged as a significant icon representing Mexican nationalism. The important point is that this icon was not held solely by the Amerindian contingency. The criollos took it up and transformed it into a cultural institution, the Guadalupana, a Marianist cult of profound implications. Indeed, Guadalupana can no longer be separated from Mexico as a social, political, and cultural entity. Guadalupe is so much a national symbol of Mexico that the nation would suffer an irreparable diminution without it. The border between Mexican nationalism and Guadalupana has become so diffuse as to be rendered indiscernible.

The annealment of the two symbols was solidified shortly before independence. In the annual homage to the Virgin of Guadalupe at Tepeyac in 1794, criollo priest Fr. Servando Teresa de Mier suggested that the *piedra de sol* (Aztec calendar stone) bore living proof that the image of the Virgin had been indelibly pressed on the poncho of Amerindian Juan Diego by Saint Thomas, who had once visited the New World to preach the gospel to the Amerindian inhabitants. While there, Saint Thomas had presumably revealed the importance of the Virgin Mary. The saint's revelation soon fell into the interstices of the pagan Amerindian religions that eventually took hold. The message was later revealed once again by Saint Thomas through the Amerindian mediary, Juan Diego. This was proof that Saint Thomas's sermons had not been entirely forgotten, since the Amerindians incorporated his presence in the Americas with the legend of their god with clear eyes, light skin, and a beard, Quetzalcoatl ("plumed serpent" in Nahuatl, language of the Aztecs). Eventually Quetzalcoatl was fused and confused with Guadalupe in the minds of the native inhabitants' religions to become a hybrid form of worship.

Such fusion has been labeled "syncretism," and it is often left at that. *Syncretism* means the combination or reconciliation of variant to virtually mutually exclusive beliefs, of distinct cultural artifacts, practices or traits, or in linguistics the fusion of two different inflectional terms (see longer definition in glossary). This notion of syncretism doesn't quite do the trick, however. Phenomena such as the Guadalupe-Quetzalcoatl and Thomas-Quetzalcoatl connections imply at one and the same time a *translation* and *transculturation* (*trans-* = spreading across, over) of images. But neither is this qualification adequately faithful to the cultural practice in question. There is also an *interrelatedness*, a *codependent emergence*, of all tendencies within the contact zone. During this process, the elements *interacting* at the contact zone become elusive—elusive because they may be *felt*, though they are neither exactly *seen* nor *said*.

For example, Amerindians in a local parish in Mexico may see the Virgin of Guadalupe, yet she is not really the same figure seen by the priest, who was properly instructed in Catholic doctrine in the city. The Amerindian believers know that what they see is not really what they profess it to be. Yet they believe what they see; yet they do not really believe it, at least not in the same way devout criollo Catholics in the cities believe in the precepts of the Church. There is no dishonesty here, but rather a lingering "enchantment of the world" as handed down generation after generation from their ancestors in contrast to the creeping "disenchantment" represented by customary Western religious and rational secular practices (recall Chapter 3 on Columbus's lingering "enchantment").

This hybridization shoves classical *logic* aside (see glossary). Mexican Amerindians in rural villages may believe in the images of pre-Hispanic idols they conjure up in their minds. At the same time, they believe in the Catholic images that are before them in the chapel. Both beliefs are for them equally valid. If certain aspects of Mexican Amerindian culture manifest both one tendency and another, then the classical prohibition of any and all *contradictions* can hardly hold water. Mexican Amerindian hybrid culture can embrace contradictory images and beliefs without undue concern, in contrast to citizens of the world imbued with their Western hang-up for clear and precise categories. Moreover, if certain aspects of Mexican Amerindian hybrid culture is neither one thing nor another, then the classical *excluded middle* between two ordinary opposite values opens its door to other alternatives such that new values can always stand a chance of emerging into the light of day. What, then, does this rape of logical principles do to Mexican *identity*, when Mexicans are engaged in radically diverse cultural practices? Perhaps the only response is that there is no one-and-only Mexican identity, at least in the fixed, rock-hard sense of identity in traditional reason and logic and entrenched linguistic practices. The idea of identity, with respect to Mexico, especially, is caught up in the flux and flow of cultural processes.[1]

Thus in today's Mexico, fluid racial and ethnic cultural processes create a tidal wave of tensions and tendencies and propensities and practices that cause breaks and then leave things as they were, but not quite. One can enjoy no possible escape from these processes, for one is within the whole of the cultural milieu. In this sense the cultural hybridity gives a better picture than syncretism. Now back to the story at hand.

On the Eve of Independence

By the end of the eighteenth century Spain had been battered into exhaustion as a result of conflicts in Europe, her efforts to defend her colonies, and the energy expended during the Bourbon reforms. At the same time, the reforms had injected New Spain with a renewed dose of vitality. Her population had more than doubled during that century, reaching 6 million by 1810.

The Amerindians made up roughly 70 percent of the population and the mestizos and mulattos, 20 percent. The remainder consisted of around 20,000 or so white Spaniards and about 10,000 upper-class criollos, a few of whom were somewhat questionably "tanned." Then came the lower echelon criollos, and at the bottom of the heap, below the mestizos and at about the same level of disrespect, came the African Mexicans and mulattos. An eyewitness report by Alexander von Humboldt reveals that New Spain was one of the richest areas in the Western world at that time, and one of the poorest.

The vast majority of the Amerindians contributed to the wealth of the colony with back-breaking toil. They usually worked on large estates, taking up life in miserable huts within walking distance from the landowner's mansion. They were permanently indebted to the local store, later called the *tienda de raya* ("store of the mark"), while growing corn, chile, beans, and squash in tiny plots of land they rented. They couldn't leave the land without paying off their debt, and they couldn't pay off their debt because their *patrón* made sure they weren't paid enough to do so. It was a vicious circle. Amerindian labor also brought opulence to mining towns that in turn made Spain temporarily rich—temporarily, since the riches passed from Spain into the European countries to the east. In addition, Amerindians and poorer mestizos made up the *obrajes* (workers in the newly developed small factories or sweat shops that supplied metal and woodwork and textiles to the colony).

These humble souls—the Amerindians, mestizos, African Mexicans, and mulattos—could hardly have brought about a revolution against their oppressors. Citizens who are brutalized by excruciating toil from sunrise to sunset have neither time nor energy to dream dreams, hope hopes, and realize revolutions. The task of rebellion was in the hands of the criollos, who were fortunate enough to have been born into the leisure class. It was between the criollos and *peninsulares* that the most dynamic, effervescent contact zones existed—today, as already noted, contact zones exist chiefly among the mestizo majority and other ethnicities of Mexico.

The criollo advocates of radical change, inspired by the French Revolution and especially by the North American movement for independence, were nonetheless a mixed bag. The conservatives called for reforms but failed to question the role of the Church and the very idea of centralized government. They wanted to improve the economic condition of their own social class once they threw out the Spaniards, and little else. They joined not-too-subversive societies, founded newspapers, and fought to improve education. They remained true-believing Catholics, often supported monarchy, and wished to govern Mexico much as the Spaniards had done, just substituting criollo rule for *gachupín* rule. They certainly sensed no need for equality with what they considered the dark-skinned rabble.

The more radical criollos, who became the liberals after independence, followed Enlightenment ideals more closely. Intellectuals such as John Locke, Charles de Montesquieu, Jean Jacques Rousseau, and François Maria Arouet (Voltaire) found their way into the colonies in spite of book banning by the Spanish Inquisition. These criollos propagated elimination of the caste system, greater equality, a division of powers, and curtailment of the Church—the richest entrepreneur in the land. Radically anti-clerical, some liberals (chiefly those who had taken up membership in one of the Masonic orders) actually advocated repression of the Church. Somewhat ironically, however, it was initially two priests who actively took up the movement for independence, fifty-seven-year-old Miguel Hidalgo (1753–1811), a criollo, and José María Morelos (1765–1815), a mestizo with a tinge of mulatto heritage.

Hidalgo rose to prominence with a criollo organization that conspired to expel the Spaniards from New Spain. Spaniards got wind of the plot and, instead of fleeing, at daybreak on September 16, 1810, Hildalgo put the church bells to ringing. A group of Amerindians and mestizos entered the church, and Hildalgo rose to the pulpit and briefly addressed his congregation. He then gave the battle cry: "Long live Mexico! Death to the *gachupines!*" There were no allusions to independence, only to the Spaniards' confiscation of the Amerindians' land, three hundred years of bondage, and an embrace of a "new dispensation" with the implication that it was ordained by God. The bloody wars of independence, which lasted eleven years and took over a half million lives, had begun.

A ragtag band of 20,000 peasants armed with machetes, hoes, and pitchforks soon gathered, and a banner of Our Lady of Guadalupe appeared as a motivating force. Led by their aging priest, the peasants stormed San Miguel, Celaya, Salamanca, and Guanajuato. With almost racial vengeance, they burned homes, looted stores, and slaughtered women and children. The mass of peasants in the meantime grew to approximately 100,000 and marched toward Mexico City. Before entering the city, the charismatic Father Hidalgo unexpectedly ordered the unruly mob to withdraw, perhaps fearing the virtually uncontrollable force he had unleashed. The band moved northwest. Many of the peasants soon lost their lust for violence and returned to their homes to take up residence on the recently appropriated lands. Hidalgo's luck soon ran out, and he was defeated and executed. He was then decapitated, and his white-maned head was displayed at the granary at Guanajuato as a symbol of triumph for the Spaniards and a warning to the swarms of rebellious peasants. Overkill on the part of the initial revolutionary push had backfired.

Now it was the Royal Army's turn to reap vengeance. It swept through the countryside like a scythe, burning fields and entire villages and murdering any non-Spaniards who got in its way. Morelos rose to the occasion with a peasant guerrilla band some two-thousand strong. The small army marched through Michoacan, Guerrero, and Oaxaca, while confiscating Spanish lands and wealth and abolishing slavery. In Veracruz, Vicente Guerrero (1783–1831), son of black slaves, waged guerrilla warfare against the hated white oppressors in the area. The battle tactics had changed, and now the revolutionaries began gaining the upper hand. In 1813 Morelos called the Congress of Chilpancingo, where a French-inspired declaration of independence was drawn up. But Morelos was captured and shot in 1815. There seemed to be no end to the chaos.

The movement, born of racial strife, now did an about-face. The criollos under Agustín de Iturbide (1783–1824), previously of the Royal Army, struck a bargain with the remaining peasant revolutionaries. The bargain was ratified in 1820 with the Plan of Iguala. It called for independence and established Catholicism as the religion and monarchy as the political system. This implied that whites, now in the guise of the criollos, were to remain at the top of the heap, and the peasants were to return to their charred huts to work for them much as they had worked for the Spaniards.

Shortly thereafter, Iturbide, in a fit of narcissistic passion, declared himself emperor for life. Independence, they asked? Independence for whom? The dark-skinned Mexicans had their say, but the day belonged to the fair-haired crowd.

Picking Up the Pieces

Now enter that actor in the tragic, comic, farcical, or absurd (however you wish to view it) theater that lasted over three decades under the intermittent domination of the paranoiac, exorbitantly self-centered, first caudillo of Mexico, Antonio López de Santa Anna (1790–1877). Of the numerous governments Mexico experienced during the first decades of independence, eleven were led by Santa Anna, and each time he either resigned or was thrown out.

Iturbide's reign ended in 1824. After a rebellion and his exile he returned in counterrebellion, and he was arrested, tried, and executed. The Mexican treasury was empty, the mines were either closed or destroyed, many of the haciendas had been abandoned, and the countryside was plagued with banditry and killing. In the cities there was little food, the shops and small factories were closed, and the Amerindian and mestizo laborers experienced new levels of poverty. The mining, manufacturing, and commercial know-how of the *peninsulares* no longer existed, since they had filled their bags with whatever money they could gather up and left for greener pastures in Europe. The criollos had inherited power with little or no experience in self-government. Military leaders exercised control however they desired. Local caciques took their turn at playing the role of strong-arm bosses and tyrants. Conservatives longed for a wedding between theocratic Catholicism and centralist monarchy. Liberals wanted retaliation against the church fathers and a disguised decentralized government under the control of an educated minority.

Santa Anna gained control of this chaotic situation and proclaimed himself "liberator of the republic" and "redeemer of Mexico," and, as if this were not enough, "His Serene Highness." He pushed and shoved to keep himself in power, like few caudillos of nineteenth-century Latin America. Yet as an administrator, he did little more than create havoc. Until 1855 he emptied the treasury every time he became president; after that public administration bored him to tears. He was simply incapable of running a decent government. Nevertheless, since he was such an overbearing caudillo, nobody else stood a chance of taking the reins and organizing the chaotic affairs of Mexican politics. What had happened to the idea of independence? Mexico's leaders were admirably versed in the ideals and zeals of liberty, equality, and fraternity. So why couldn't they put them into practice?

The answer is not easy for those who wish to understand the cultural makeup of the Mexicans. The Mexican view of leaders and of the very idea of leadership, interrelated with the concept of family and friends and indeed of human interrelationships in general, is intimately tied to the reasons for Mexico's failure during the early years of independence to establish a stable political system. To explore these reasons, let's go back in history to the Napoleonic invasion of Spain in 1808. Immediately after the invasion, the Spaniards rose in rebellion against the French troops in the name of King Fernando VII, whom they considered the legitimate heir to the monarchy.

Why did they reject the French so vehemently and why did they long for monarchical rule, which many Europeans saw as decadent and archaic? In establishing a secular center of power in Spain, Napoleon broke with a long-standing tradition that included what we might call an "implicit" or a "tacit" pact, an unwritten, generally unspoken, agreement—a sort of unconsciously developed social contract—between the people and the Crown. The agreement was taken for granted without the necessity of its being made explicit in the form of a document. The implicit pact, incorporating a common sentiment, was profoundly rooted in the minds of the Spanish and Mexican people. It entailed acknowledgment that the king is "our king, by the divine grace of God." Consequently, it symbolized the inextricable union of Church and Crown; it constituted the unifying thread of Spanish culture that carried over into the colony. At the same time, it embodied a form of government by the will of the people. This was a democracy of sorts but was unlike the democracy to which people in the United States aspire. This democracy was not the result of campaigns and polls and voting booths but a tacitly acknowledged agreement among the people. If a king sat on the throne and ruled in an acceptable manner, all was more or less well. If not, then the will of the people might prevail, and the king could find himself checkmated. This uniquely Hispanic way found expression in the philosophy of Francisco Suárez (1548–1617).

Consequently, when tacitly acknowledged and venerated King Fernando VII was deposed, a *legitimacy vacuum* (see glossary) remained: there was no authority figure. Who, in the minds of the people, could become the embodiment of Church and authority and *Supreme Patrón*? Joseph Bonapart? Of course not. The junta (council, provisional government) that had been left in Spain by Bonapart? Hardly. Any other ruler outside the Royal Family? Very doubtful. The truth of the matter is that there was nobody capable of filling the legitimacy vacuum. Nobody could embody ecclesiastical and secular authority in the hearts and minds of the Spanish and Mexican people in the genuine sense, "By the Divine Grace of God." This lack of legitimacy was especially crucial in the colony. Now that there was no sacred-secular authority figure in Spain, could the viceroys take over where Fernando VII left off? No, because it would be too radical a break with tradition. Perhaps some charismatic criollo caudillo might be able to assume the people's confidence in the absence of the deposed king. A possibility. But this move would be dangerous because it implied rebellion against the Crown.

Nevertheless, the criollos wished to take advantage of the situation. For the first time in the history of the colonies, they saw the opportunity to wrest control from the *gachupines*. The equivalent of town meetings popped up throughout New Spain. Juntas were organized with the idea of following the juntas that had been called in Spain for the purpose of declaring their loyalty to their fallen monarch, Fernando. The will of the people was making itself evident. Quite conveniently, in the absence of the king, there appeared to be no alternative in the colonies, separated by so much time and space from mainland Europe, but to assume the authority that had been exercised by Fernando. And so it was. The criollos perceived in their declaration of support for Fernando a pretext for separating themselves from the French usurpers and, indirectly, from the Spanish Crown. A masterful stroke, it might seem.

By the year 1810, after three centuries of colonial rule, independence was at hand. Ironically, the French invaded Spain with the idea of "liberating" the Spaniards from the clutches of a decadent and corrupt monarchical system. But the Spanish battle cry was: "Long live our monarchical chains!" The criollos organized their own rebellion in the name of their absent monarch. But they ended up in rebellion against him with the undercover idea: "Neither Napoleon nor the king!" However, in the final analysis, those same criollos remained in a sort of political and cultural limbo. Alienated from the Catholic monarchy, they now found themselves in a sea of confusion consisting of political tension, social intrigues, economic crises, religious sentiments pulling toward the past, and desires for sovereignty pushing toward the future. There was no predefined route to guide the criollos' tumultuous navigation in the riotous waters of social unrest. Nevertheless, the umbilical cord was broken, and there was no alternative but to forge ahead.

Putting the Pieces Together Again

There was still the problem of authority, that is, of legitimacy. Who, after independence, would be capable of occupying the sacred-secular image that had been created around the concept of the Spanish monarch?

Political power, in part due to the legitimacy vacuum, tended more and more toward centralization and away from the idea of government of the people, by the people, and for the people. Unfortunately, often the conclusion was that the recently liberated Mexican republic was not yet ready for full-fledged democracy and required central control as a means of combating the ever present threat of anarchy. Actually, Mexico had inherited many colonial practices that over the centuries had become sedimented within the minds of the colonists. The fact is that, upon throwing off the yolk of the Spanish monarchy, the Mexicans had in mind a repudiation of all things Spanish. After getting rid of their peninsular heritage, they wanted to adopt distinct cultural values and practices. What would be the source of their cultural and political models? The cultural model was primarily France, and the political models were France and the recently emancipated United States. However, it is impossible for any nation to shake off all vestiges of its cultural heritage and begin anew. Consequently, a wide, deep, black and bleak, yawning gap opened itself in Mexico.

Mexico, in the final analysis, did not become a republic guided by heads of state in the contemporary sense of the term, but rather a republic led by the caudillos most capable of responding to the particular conditions that happened to present themselves. Understanding the caudillo will aid in our gaining an understanding of leaders like Santa Anna, who made a caricature of the ancient Hispanic idea of a legitimate monarch by the "grace of God" and the "will of the people." However, in order to understand the caudillo, we need a "feel" for some basic Mexican characteristics, described in Chapter 7.

Further Reading

Alba 1967, Bazant 1977, Hale 1990, Johnson 1980, Ladd 1978, Lafaye 1976, Lomnitz 2001, Lynch 1992, Madariaga 1947, Morse 1989, Rodríguez 1994, Rodríguez O. 1989, Taylor 1987, Whitaker 1961, 1962.

Notes

1. This "rape of logic," I would suggest, is common to all human cultural practices and to the notion of cultural identity (merrell 2002).

7

The Mexican Mind: An Interlude

Personalismo

The classical grandeur frequently displayed in Mexico oratory—at political rallies, poetry readings, conferences, banquets, weddings and other ceremonies, in the classroom, and occasionally even in street talk—bears witness to the importance of personal appearance, public demeanor, and private composure.

I am alluding to the touch of *personalismo* that pervades Mexican interpersonal relations. *Personalismo* comes to the fore when content takes a backseat to style and form. The substance or content of what is said and done gives way to rhetorical aplomb. Smooth talking takes precedence over tightly structured arguments. The charismatic attraction of the person in the spotlight becomes all-important; what is actually said and done often becomes less important. This practice contrasts with the relatively demure, properly worded, and appropriately articulated delivery valued by citizens of U.S. and northern European cultures.

The Mexican individual's worth is at times gauged by words more than deeds, by speech more than action. There is hardly any "strong, silent" John Wayne type capable of being elevated to mythical status. The linguistic economy of Abraham Lincoln, the homey quipping of Ronald Reagan, or the "give-em-hell" pragmatism of Harry Truman would not command the same respect in Mexican culture. In Mexico, intellectuals, writers, and intense, eloquent, dignified, and energetic men and women take center stage. The stoic Amerindian from Oaxaca who became president of Mexico in the last century, Benito Juárez, is an exception. No recent U.S. president commanded as much respect among Mexicans as did John F. Kennedy. In addition to his Catholicism, he had education, intelligence, aristocracy, youthful image, lovely jet-set wife, charismatic demeanor, and exceptional oratorical capacity. He had what Mexicans like: *personalismo*. If one has it one has it, and if not, not. It comes naturally, and for this reason it's difficult to cultivate.

In Mexico, *personalismo* is for the most part a projection of one's public image, a public self. Private and family life can be another matter. In Anglo-America's individualistic, money-grubbing culture, the same apparent distinction is not as sharp between private and public life—though, as argued briefly above, the distinction in Mexico is not as clearly definable as some scholars would have it. The "let it all hang out" autobiographies of celebrities where no holds are barred and there is little to no respect for members of the immediate family are virtually unknown in Mexico, where one's family is considered a private affair, and nobody else's business. Engaging in *personalismo*, in contrast, is chiefly a matter of one's public persona. In public life the person makes the position, not the other way round. The person *embodies* what she is given the empowerment to represent, and the same can be said for Mexico's institutions. The presidency *is* the president, the Church *is* the physical structure and the Virgins and Christs and all the saints that are contained within.

In the United States, by contrast, a new arrival in public office must strive to conform to the "job description" that goes along with her taking a seat behind an oak desk. In Mexico, when one officeholder goes, enter the next chief, and the personalized office is up for a radical change because now somebody else *is* the office: the office is reshaped into the form of another human being. On the Mexican scene it might appear to outside observers that there is an endless string of alliances, manipulations, fraudulent elections, and appointments through nepotism. However, this image of Mexico is actually the outcome of a paternalistic, status-seeking order in which each person, flaunting her *personalismo*, maneuvers to take over the spotlight and impress the audience out there over her competitors. The most captivating public figure is the person who gets her way, come what may. She does so by the dint of her personal charm and her ability to occupy the center of public attention. In this regard, political legitimacy is embodied chiefly in the person, not the abstract category "presidency."

The aloof, relatively detached, impassionate, and impersonal individual of the sort that often holds public office in the United States would hardly stand a chance in this arena of stars. In the Mexicans' eyes, the future is in the hands of outstanding individuals, not unseen and impersonal forces. History owes its becoming to dynamic individuals; they make it and they hold its destiny in their grasp. The idea of some intangible community spirit that pushes history along is discarded in favor of the energetically gyrating arms of the most charismatic and gregarious figure among the cultural giants that happen to be out there. What has become important for the Mexican is often not so much an abstract model, ideology, or program, but rather, *this* leader on *this* day, right *here* and *now*. The present is all-important, and she who makes the present what it is, creates time and space, gives expression to the community, molds history, and forges visions of the future. Conservatives and liberals, reactionaries and revolutionaries, all advance solutions to whatever problems might happen to be plaguing the country. A swing in one direction or the other might indicate altered ideological sentiments, or it might simply be a show of force. Quite often, however, it is an indication of whoever was able most effectively to captivate an expectant audience. In short, what we have in *personalismo* is the flip side of the will of the people that provides the glue holding ancient Spain's monarchical system together. This flip side consists of whoever becomes the most compelling individual around, whether she is capable of leading the people or not.

In this respect, Aztec emperor Moctezuma II of old and Francisco Madero, who became president after the fall of Porfirio Díaz in 1910, didn't have what it takes to captivate their respective audiences. Their *machismo* (see glossary), charisma, will to dominate, and *personalismo* left much to be desired. In contrast, Cuba's Castro—or Castro's Cuba (however one wishes to cut the cake)—is the living repository of *personalismo*. Castro in the beginning was the epitome of confidence, having the capacity to move history as history bore testimony to his powers and his prowess. Cuba was a nation of people in search of a hero, and some of those remaining on the island believe they found him—though their number has recently been dwindling. For these people, leadership is of the most basic sort. It is coterminous with the leader, the man himself. Theodore Draper (1965, 9) hit the nail on the head over three decades ago. Castro is more keenly in tune with the charismatic leader principle than Marxism, communism, or any other ideology or doctrine or movement: Castro *is* his own ideology, doctrine, movement. He *is* his office; he *is* the Cuban revolution; Castro *is* Cuba and Cuba *is* Castro.

In this sense, those who enjoy more than a moderate dose of *personalismo* are not necessarily "rugged individualists" of the North American sort. The individuals with *personalismo* are at the same time many and one. They are one, and they embody the entire community. They are not one in the sense that members of the community would say "I want to be like Mark McGwire or Sammy Sosa" or "I want to be like Madonna or Jennifer Lopez," in reference to their favorite individual endowed with *personalismo*. Rather, members of the community pay due respect to their image of the successful individual not simply because they want to identify with her or him, but also because they realize that she or he is there and they are here due to some turn of events that elevated her or him to special public status. Perhaps someday some other person among them will have a chance. If Lady Luck happens to smile favorably on someone within the community, she will not simply become "like" someone else, some icon, for example, Sammy or Jennifer. She will continue to be herself on her own terms. She will continue to be one, private, and he will become many, a public icon coterminous with the whole of the community.

Mexican *personalismo* isn't a matter of "autonomous individual me" against the community in the dualistic North American sense. It is more akin to what I call *contradictory complementary* "me" *and* "we" (see glossary). "Me" is contradictorily complementary with other "me's" among the community, the "we," in the sense that each individual is at one and the same time an individual and continuous with other individuals in the community. The individual is an individual and she is one with the community of individuals. There is no absolute distinction between "me" and "we." There is incessant mediation between individuals such that there are no rigidly distinguishable individuals at all. "Me" *is* "we" and "we" *is* "me." There is no pernicious contradiction, no simple either/or choice, but rather, the individual "me" is tantamount to the whole, "we," the community. "We" contradictorily complement each other in making up the community.

Consequently, a cultural icon like Sammy or Jennifer happens to be where she or he is for now, but, given the perpetually changing nature of the "mes" and the "we," some other "me" may become an icon, "we," in the future. If this occurs, that "me" will have become another "me," and the "we" will have changed as a consequence. Thus between one "me" and another "me," there is no clear and distinct and fixed *identity* in the space between the *either* and the *or*. From within that space, something else, something new, emerged. A private "me" became a public "me," the one became the many and the many the one. Thus in Mexico it is not necessarily "me" as potentially the best against all the rest, as is often the case in the highly competitive U.S. environment. In Mexico, all "mes" tend contradictorily to complement one another to make up the community. The inadequacy of classical logical principles in regard to broad cultural issues once again becomes painfully apparent. Allow me to clarify this point as much as possible before moving on.

People in the United States tend to take things either in one way or the other. This practice often reduces the world to a vast set of either-or choices. The concept of race is a good case in point. In the United States, an individual is usually classified as African American in spite of the fact that his features and skin color might reveal more Anglo American than African American traits. Yet he is considered black, no doubt about it as far as most citizens of the United States are concerned. Political leanings are also often conceived as either-or affairs. Two politicians may be classified as Democrat and Republican, even though any fine distinction between them would be difficult to trace. Yet when an abstract label is slapped on them, they are placed into two different political worlds.

Mexicans do not place such stock in abstract categories. Much more than their North American counterparts, they tend to take an individual for what she is, right *here*, right *now*. They often do so as a consequence of that individual's capacity to project *personalismo*. She might be corrupt, vindictive, and endowed with little administrative capacity. Yet if she has personal charm, she makes people feel good about themselves, promises the sky to whatever audience she happens to be addressing, and creates grand visions of the future. Appearance and reality, or the ideal and the concrete, with respect to this individual, might create the idea of a *contradiction* of tendencies wrapped into the same person. However, there are no clearly definable contradictory characteristics in the order of, "She is *either* 'black' *or* 'white,' she is *either* a 'Democrat' *or* a 'Republican,'" as we would expect to find in the United States. Rather, the relationship is *complementary*. In this respect, citizens of the United States finally came to admit a fellow racially and ethnically hybrid citizen, Tiger Woods, as *both* black *and* white, and also of a few other sources of racial and ethnic heritage; and at the same time he is *neither* black *nor* white, properly speaking. In other words, the North American public finally sees the golf star for what he is, of *hybrid complementary* nature. Mexicans have been privy to this sort of complementarity for centuries. The novelty of these fuzzy areas is a novelty for us, not for them.

The difference between contradiction and contradictory complementarity is in a nutshell this. In the United States, contradiction tends to be: East is East and West is West and the twain shall never meet, and the Mississippi River clearly and distinctly divides the one from the other. Contradictory complementarity would render East and West as a couple of abstractions that may be used for convenience. But "reality" is much too elusive and wily than to allow for such reductions. East is what it is, and whatever it may be it cannot be without a nod to West. Moreover, East cannot be what it is unless it contains at least a tinge of West along the borderline separating the one from the other, and indeed, some of West pervades East. And the same must be said of East within West. In this manner, you can't have the one without the other, and in fact the one is *in* the other, and vice versa. Thus in Mexico an Indio (Amerindian) might be considered a mestizo after changing his conduct and lifestyle. By a flip of the coin, a mestizo might become an Indio by taking up the latter's traditional form of life. Or, a politician might be now a quasi-socialist, now in sympathy with the downtrodden peasants and a liberal, now a rightist and fighting for fewer trade barriers, and he can put on a number of hats besides.

Contradictory complementarity interrelations allow one to take on *both* one characteristic *and* another, *and* then another, *and* another . . . according to the circumstances. After one has donned many hats in one's interdependent interrelations with one's family, friends, and associates, it cannot be said that one is *either* this person *or* that person. Such categorization would be too easy. Rather, it can only be said that one is *neither* this person, *nor* that person, *nor* that person . . . but in the next moment one might quite likely become someone else, someone complex and enigmatic, someone whose nature is well-nigh indescribable. A famous Brazilian bossa nova composer, Antonio Carlos Jobim, once quipped: "Brazil isn't for beginners." Brazilian music and Brazilian culture simply cannot be jammed into convenient pigeon holes. Much the same can be said of Mexico. Thus the wily ways of Latin American cultures.

Is all this not a study in contradictions? Of course it is! That's why Mexico is Mexico! From the North American's vantage, Mexico is no more than a bundle of contradictions. From the Mexican's perspective, however, we have what I call contradictory complementarity. It is of the very nature of *personalismo*. For Mexico and Mexicans, "our leader" is "*our* leader," whoever she happens to have been in the act of becoming what she is becoming. The difference between the North American view and the Mexican view is the difference between fixed categories, on the one hand, and a world always becoming something other than what it was becoming, on the other hand. Contradictory complementarity is not simply an either-or affair. Rather, it is a qualification of something as of *both* one nature *and* another nature, but at the same time as *neither* of one nature *nor* of the other nature, for it is always becoming something else.

The preceding paragraphs are a lot to swallow in one gulp. Moreover, it might appear that my contradictory complementarity is just another abstraction, and that the distinction I am trying to make between Mexico and the United States is another dualism. Thus I must be thinking like a North American according to my own set of abstractions. Am I not? In that case, who am I to think I can stand above and beyond both the North Americans and the Mexicans and pontificate about their likenesses and differences?

The point is well taken. The fact of the matter is, however, that I am condemned to language if I want to write this book. Language condemns me to use abstract categories, since there is no way I can nonverbally act out what I *feel about* Mexico, my *experiences of* Mexico and the Mexicans, my *reading about* Mexico, and my *thoughts on* the subject of Mexico and the Mexicans. In other words, I can't act all this out as if in a radically HC spatial setting and PC temporal setting. If I could dance what I feel, I would. But I can't, for I am condemned to the liberties and the limitations, the beauty and the bane, of language.

That much said, allow me to move on to another predominant Mexican characteristic while the concept of contradictory complementarity is in the process of digestion.

Machismo

The personalistic leader's qualities—at least as far as men are concerned—are by their very nature linked to an overpowering sense of machismo.[1] The very concept of machismo seems quite self-contradictory. During the conquest and colonization of Mexico, women were often considered physically and mentally inferior to the macho male, on the one hand, and placed on a pedestal as the repository of everything pure, good, and saintly—and hence superior to the macho—on the other hand. Male-female relations were packed into the stereotyped mold of the dominant-aggressive male and the submissive female, a passive, self-sacrificing, obedient wife and mother. Yet Salvador Reyes Nevares (1970, 15), writing of contemporary machismo in Mexico, argues that it is basically due to the flight of the male from underlying feelings of weakness vis-à-vis the *mariana* image and, as compensation, a show of strength in confrontation with the Malinche image. This apparently inextricable element of machismo is not necessarily inherent to Catholicism. Machismo actually runs contrary to the traditional emphasis on a contrite, crucified, broken, and impotent Christ, a "macho turned inside out" (Nelson 1971, 75). Machismo continues to evince this sacred-secular dualism, nonetheless.

As already noted, during the colonial period, the mestizos were neither Amerindians nor *peninsulares*. They were relegated to cultural limbo and rarely enjoyed any royal road to power, respect, or *hidalguismo*. The criollos did not enjoy quite the same privileges as the *peninsulares* either. Consequently, mestizos and criollos had hardly any recourse but to take on a somewhat subservient role. However, their compensation for loss of political power and social standing evolved into the *macho-mariana* syndrome with respect to the *peninsulares*. The colonial haves became specialists in the dominant aggressive-male stereotyped macho. In contrast, the have-nots became the submissive-feminine stereotyped masses of Amerindians,

African-Americans, mestizos, mulattos, and often even many criollos. This duality eventually evolved into the patron-client or *paternalistic* interrelations that exist in modern Mexico. It isn't so much that the new lords of independent Mexico sought power in order to retire to the good life on their estates, to become overpowering dictators, or to get rich. Rather, vaingloriously or ineptly, they actively pursued supreme sovereignty for themselves and their entire community. In so doing, they took on the values that were measured in terms of "manliness, personal valor, a capacity for imposing oneself on others" (Paz 1961, 71).

We have it from Mexican philosopher Samuel Ramos (1962) that the conquest of Mexico had as one of its principal themes the rape and exploitation of Amerindian women. The offspring of this violent union developed an "inferiority complex" as a result of the "original sin." The mother became somewhat devalued and subdued as a person, and the Spaniard, rather than a hidalgo or a person of merit, became dominant to the extreme. The mestizo son had little alternative other than to assume the role of his Spanish father. He was *both* American *and* European and at the same time he was neither Amerindian nor European— once again we note the contradictory complementarity inherent in Mexican culture. Yet he chose not to associate with the downtrodden and suffered perpetual frustration in his efforts to become "European."

In this regard, Octavio Paz observes that it is "impossible not to notice the resemblance between the figure of the macho and that of the Spanish conquistador. It is the model—more mythical than real—that determines the images the Mexican people form of their men in power: feudal lords, hacienda owners, politicians, generals, captains of industry." This set the stage for three centuries of colonialism. After the paternal arch stone of monarchism was violently rejected between 1810 and 1824, machismo emerged in reinvigorated form and continued to reign until recent years. It has given vent to the institutions of *caciquismo* and *caudillismo*, and it has aided and abetted Mexico's patriarchal and paternalistic society. The term "machismo" later became an epithet used in conjunction with certain male behavioral patterns. This meaning of the word is the focus of Paz's controversial essay, "The Sons of La Malinche" (1961, 65–88).

Machismo refers to the cult of aggressive masculinity. That is its expression, its manifestation, and its thrust. Sex is power, authority, domination, repression, aggression, violence. In one of the most grating definitions, it is the masculine ideal in Mexican culture and society. Regardless of social standing, the macho is revered for his sexual prowess, his action orientation (both physical and verbal), and his raw aggressiveness. Stridently masculine, he is outwardly and allegedly sure of himself, apparently conscious of his presumed inner worth, and prone to gamble everything on the self-confidence that he will in the end have things his own way. He may express his supposed inner confidence by overt action if he is a caudillo or revolutionary, or he may do so verbally if he is a leading intellectual, lawyer, or politician. (Macho tendencies are common throughout the Spanish-speaking countries of the tropical areas, though they are less pronounced in Brazil, where there are wide regional distinctions. In Argentina, Chile, and Uruguay, the situation seems to be more akin to southern European cultures than to the rest of Spanish America, given the high index of Spaniards and Italians in the area [Andreski 1966, 47].)

According to tradition—a tradition that is waning—among Mexican males there is a nondomestic inclination present in machismo. This inclination is neatly encapsulated in the attitude that the woman's place is the home and the church and the man's place is the street—carousing with *compadres* or business associates, mistresses, and so on. The celebrated and maligned Don Juan image of the male and his "pregnant in the summer and barefoot in the winter" mentality regarding the woman of the household is, of course, a stereotype that does violence to actual male-female interrelations. Nevertheless, there is a drop of truth to the image. Although the stereotype holds among many urban males, especially of the lower middle and lower classes, male-female relationship among peasants is more likely one of a certain contradictory complementarity rather than dominance-subservience. This characteristic is partly one of necessity, since, given scarce incomes and subsistence agricultural practices, both husband and wife must occasionally share responsibilities and engage in work outside the home.

Nevertheless, traditionally, the wife has often been excluded from public life, and the husbands dedicate considerable time to ritual drinking—which the wives usually resent—and wife beating. This syndrome, I'm sorry to report, is still quite common.[2] Moreover, it is usually assumed that the wife must remain in a state of dependency, since the male member of the household is in charge of the financial affairs. When Mexican males migrate to the United States without their families (as they increasingly have since the economic crisis of the early 1980s), conflict stemming from machismo is minimized. Since the husband sends money back home, his wife remains dependent on him. This is convenient for the husband. By ensuring his wife's dependency on his purse strings, he remains dominant and can at the same time effectively abdicate any active role he might otherwise have had to shoulder in the household. Thus the relationship supports the "woman in the home, man in the street" aspect of machismo (Rothstein 1983).

As a result of macho mores calling for shirking household chores and general domestic affairs, the home can become a matriarchal domain, especially in the father's prolonged absence. Still, the assumption among males and females alike is that of male dominance. This causes a conflict among the offspring. What is a child to do? Honor the father and obey the mother, or vice versa?—a schizophrenic sort of oscillation of the "I obey but I do not comply" dictum. But if the father's macho behavior is undeserving of such honor, where does that leave the child? And if the father's role is to dominate the mother, then to what extent is the mother's word the last word? The mother often openly shows her disdain for the father's machismo. At the same time, she complies with his wishes and commands; later, when the father is not around, matriarchy resumes its hold on the home. The father shows his disrespect for the matriarchal tendency in his home, and he attempts to force an exaggerated authoritarian form of patriarchy if and when he is around. To aggravate this conflict, women often admire a member of the opposite sex who has manly good looks with a tendency toward machismo, which encourages the sons to fashion themselves to fit the mold. Yet, in the home, they sense contempt on the part of their mother toward the macho characteristics of their father. The vicious circle is unfortunately self-perpetuating.

However, such apparent dualisms are incapable of telling the whole story. Between Malinche and Mariana, between the macho as superior and as inferior, there is no clear and distinct line of demarcation. Rather, there is, once again, contradictory complementarity. The macho is, in a manner of speaking and according to cultural stereotypes, *both* superior *and* inferior to his counterpart. In this sense, contradictory terms can cohabit that same cultural sphere, no matter how tension-ridden and violent the union may be. That same macho is in actual practice *neither* the one person *nor* the other one, *neither* superior *nor* inferior. He is perpetually in the process of self-expression, of identity switching, which actually entails becoming something Other than what he was becoming. As Octavio Paz puts it, the male of the species—and for that matter the female as well—is always on the cultural stage acting out some role or other. Hence she or he must at every moment reinvent herself or himself (compare to the discussion in Chapter 6 of "me" and "we," one and many). Perhaps now we can get a sense of the male-female relationship within Mexican culture: The *macho* is not so *macho* that he does not concede a *macha* role to his female counterpart, and she evinces her *machista* tendencies in subtle ways so as to avoid diminution of the *macho*'s self-image.

Indeed, it is a complex contradictory complementary interrelationship. The terms "man" and "woman" are in certain respects contradictory. Yet they are also complementary. There is the one within the other and the other within the one. As both "man" and "woman" flow along the cultural stream, they become what they will have been becoming according to what the situation might happen to bring. Of course, much the same can be said of male-female relationships in the United States, or anywhere else in the world for that matter. Still, traditional male-female roles, like all other roles in the United States, tend to be either-or affairs to a greater extent than in Mexico. In the United States, it's more a matter of "I'm one up, so you're one down," or "I win, you lose," all indelibly oppositional in nature. The machismo complex, in contrast, is more subtle than one would expect at the outset. It finds no genuine counterpart in the United States. Hence its enigma, its mystery. Hence the difficulty of "getting that certain feel" for it.

Now for a turn to the third and final qualifying term with respect to Mexican cultural tendencies.

Caudillismo

As with machismo, I cannot adequately account for the term *caudillismo*. Nevertheless, I must render a sense of *caudillismo* relevant to the story being unfolded here in order to provide a "feel" for Mexican culture.

Caudillismo, an institution that continues to highlight the "I," has its roots in *caciquismo*, a local rather than national phenomenon. In current usage the term "cacique," at times carrying pejorative connotations, ordinarily designates someone who exercises local dominance. When a cacique's sphere of influence expands to engulf the entire national scene, he takes on the countenance of a caudillo. What are the prerequisites for this caudillo? In order to lift himself by his own bootstraps and climb up the social ladder of success, he must be charismatic, a classical orator who is able to present a captivating image of himself, and be prepared to risk all in a violent palace revolt or a revolution. He must engage in *populism* (see glossary). He must at the drop of a hat be willing to shun the criollo elite and appeal to the working class. He then might put on a three-piece suit and cater to the entrepreneurial class. Later, he promises the sky at middle-class rallies. The next day might find him eating tortillas and beans with a group of peasants under a tree near their cornfields and commiserating over their problems. These practices often call for strong-arm tactics that have led to rebellion after rebellion by wannabe caudillos in competition for the coveted presidential seat.

Until recent times caudillos have been ubiquitous on the Latin American scene. Venezuela, for example, suffered from one of the most self-perpetuating stream of caudillos in the history of the continent. First there was José Antonio Páez (1830–1846), who was replaced by two brothers, José Gregorio y José Tadeo Monagas (1846–1861); then Paéz (1861–1863) decided he was ready for another try at it. After an interim, Antonio Guzmán Blanco (1870–1887) pushed his way into the presidential palace, followed by Joaquín Crespo (1887–1898), Cipriano Castro (1899–1908), and Juan Vicente Gómez (1908–1935). After the Marcos Pérez Jiménez dictatorship (1952–1958), and until the country became oil-rich, rarely had it remained free of the grip of *caudillismo*. The history of most other Latin American nations has followed comparable, though less spectacular, paths forged by the "will to power" of those who are most capable of getting their way.

Carlos Fuentes in his novel, *The Death of Artemio Cruz* (1964), masterfully constructs the picture of a caudillo mind helping forge postrevolutionary Mexico out of the ashes of destruction. Artemio Cruz's chief goals in life included wealth, power, domination, authority, and the respect he felt he had earned but never received from the prerevolutionary criollo aristocracy. He shaped his destiny virtually from nothing. The son of a mulatto mother and a landed criollo father in the tropical plains of Veracruz, he crossed the mountainous region to the high plateau, fought in the revolution, took advantage of men and women at every opportunity, became a member of the newly enriched class, and played out his role to the end of his life of corruption, subterfuge, and betrayal. This is will to power, Mexican style. It is the notorious road to *caudillismo* paved with the blood and sorrow of those who were sacrificed for the benefit of ends that remain more in the mind and in human relations than in sprawling mansions, lavish lifestyles, and money in foreign banks. Like Artemio Cruz, the caudillo manages to impose his will on all those around him. At the same time, the very word "caudillo" is magical. It's a magnet that by its very nature appeals to the sentiments.

Juan Domingo Perón, Argentine dictator from 1945 to 1955, once remarked that the people don't think, they *feel*. They *feel* the magnetic attraction for their caudillo leader. The caudillo is the people and the people are embodied in the caudillo; in a certain sense, the caudillo is the fatherland and the fatherland is the caudillo. In this respect, Perón's wife, Eva Duarte Perón, "Evita," was one of Latin America's supreme caudillo/as. Evita knew that caudillo/a power is the avenue toward fulfillment of what is conceived as a more noble goal: to be the person everybody else would like to be. Conscious pursuit of power, however, takes a backseat to a desire for the esteem. Coming along with this esteem is the desire of everybody to emulate the caudillo/a who has risen to the upper echelons of society and culture. All folks admire this confident, dynamic, charismatic individual. S/he garners esteem, and by the force of her/his will s/he usually exercises control over those who esteem her/him.

Control and *esteem* are the watchwords. Logically and rationally, it would seem, one who is being controlled should resent the source of that control. If one holds another individual in high esteem, it shouldn't be the result of that individual's control over the person granting him the esteem. But that is not exactly the case regarding the caudillo image. The caudillo is able to control precisely because he is esteemed, can grant favors and expects them in return, can dole out punishment as well as rewards, can cast into exile and place in comfortable offices, can give exuberant praise and knows how to receive it, and so on. He who controls does control and can remain in control because he receives esteem, and he who esteems the esteemed does so with the hopes that the opportunity may present itself, someday, sometime, for him to ascend to a position of control. This condition might be unbearably oppressive were it conceived within the Anglo-American relatively more capitalist, consumerist socio-cultural setting, where almost everybody is in a do-or-die competitive conflict.

The Mexican condition is quite otherwise, and it must be considered on its own turf. Relations are more complementary and less oppositional than in those in the United States. Those who are in power are esteemed for who they are and for the hows, the whys, and the wherefores of their ascending to the position of their power. Were the esteemers to be given the chance, they would replace those in power with neither regrets nor re-morse. It is not that they are necessarily bloodthirsty. Rather, the comple-mentarity of weblike, nonlinear interrelations has taken a turn, and now the outs have found a way in and the ins are out and once again looking in. That's okay. Perhaps they will get another break some day, and an op-portunity will once again show its face.

Controlling others and at the same time reaping their esteem: the "tragedy" and the "comedy" and the "irony" and the "romance" of *caudil-lismo*. It is potentially a virtuous rather than a vicious circle. Often, and unfortunately, it can also be a bizarre mixture of comic virtuosity and vi-cious tragedy. Yet there is irony and romance to it. In the final analysis, what, precisely, is a caudillo anyway? Definition of the term is much like definition of the word chicano(a), according to feminist activist Cherrié Moraga (1983, 90–144). The daughter of a chicana mother and an Anglo father, Moraga writes that she was not in tune with the meaning of the word until she *felt* it after a long series of painful experiences. Chicano(a), like caudillo, macho, and *personalismo*, is a word of the sort that if you have to ask its meaning you wouldn't understand it anyway. So don't ask, just *feel*. Difficult, and virtually impossible, it would seem. So how can one properly qualify *caudillismo* and caudillos? In large part one can't, not really. That is, one can't in textual language while looking inside from the outside and at the same time trying to get a *feel* for a concept in a vicari-ous mode from the inside without being able to get both feet in from the outside. One must somehow try to get a *feel* for that cultural space in no one's land that is everywhere and nowhere. Let me at least offer a few helpful suggestions on the caudillo image.

Spanish writer and historian Victor Alba sees the caudillo as a natural evolution of the colonial *encomendero* and the nineteenth-century hacienda owner. The caudillo, "like the patrón, must be a just man (or at least appear to be so)." If a caudillo is by nature severe and inflexible, he is also amiable and paternal when the need for such qualities arises. He must be "a *macho*, a he-man, if he wants to enter politics," yet he is capable of moments of compassion (Alba 1969, 349). Mexican President Porfirio Díaz, dictator from 1876 to 1910, personified the caudillo-macho boss who was a blend of *personalismo*, machismo, and populism. As such, he never ceased to add a personal touch to his office, which ingratiated him with those who supported him. On the other side of the coin, as was noted above, Francisco Madero, who became president after Díaz, proved timid, vacillating, and ineffective. Consequently, he simply didn't satisfy the expectations of the public. For his thwarted efforts, he was soon overthrown by Victoriano Huerta. The personification of a revolutionary caudillo in Mexico awaited the entry of Pancho Villa on the scene. As we shall note, Villa possessed, to a considerably greater degree than Madero, all the attributes that characterize machismo and *caudillismo*.

As Juan Perón put it, there must be an individual yet collective *feel* for the caudillo. He is *felt*, not merely cognized, *sensed*, not merely intellectualized, and interpreted *concretely* without the need for willfully executed *abstract* categories. There is an intimate quality about the caudillo that should get one in the guts. The caudillo is what he is without the need of anyone's saying what he is. Whatever meat and potatoes of abstract categories there may be with respect to a caudillo, they are all masked by the sizzling spice of the *personalismo* he exudes at every moment. He is *neither* simply what he is *nor* is he not what he is. He is always *something else* because he has been capable of filling that which potentially defines the caudillo as what he *might be* or *would be* or *should be* as long as he is able to exercise his god-given talent for captivating the people. Once again we recall the term "contradictory complementarity."

I cannot overemphasize the importance of *concrete* human interrelations within a caudillo/a setting. This is far removed from the relatively *abstract* linkage of authority found in the United States. The U.S. president is an individual with his own personality and character traits, his own behavioral patterns and idiosyncrasies. But this individual is to a large extent coterminous with the nature of whoever may occupy the presidency at whichever time. The concepts of president and presidency in the United States are abstract terms. They correspond to an institution. Whoever happens to occupy the position of president acts out a role within a particular slot in the abstract set of categories that make up the politics of the United States. The president is there now and is of utmost importance when carrying out his duties acceptably, and he is gone tomorrow.

In Mexico, in contrast, the caudillo, *El Presidente*, is who he is: he is *Presidente*, the living incarnation of the *presidency*. He *is* the *presidency* and the *presidency* concretely *is* who he *is*. There is no clearly defined abstract category; rather, the term takes on its meaning in accord with the caudillo, here and now. During the culminating moments of the caudillo's career as caudillo, I must reiterate, he is tantamount to the fatherland itself. He does not simply fill a slot that could have been filled by one of a given number of other individuals. He is prior to that slot and hence *is* that slot; he is, so to speak, filling the legitimacy vacuum as described above. When he is no longer caudillo, no longer embodiment of the nation, when someone else has displaced him, there is another caudillo. Now the old caudillo, a fallen god, exists only in memory. In this regard *caudillismo* is an extension of the responsibility that the colonial paternalistic-patriarchal lord ideally shouldered.

Throughout history caudillos have come in many countenances and many guises throughout Latin America. Juan Manuel de Rosas, who dominated the Argentine republic from 1835 to 1852, was athletic and charismatic, and he could ride with the best gauchos around. Dr. José Rodríguez Francia (1811–1840) of Paraguay was a cultured aristocrat, while his contemporary, Antonio López de Santa Anna (1828–1844) of Mexico was a rich criollo, and Diego Portales (1830–1837) of Chile was a wealthy entrepreneur. The Guatemalan Rafael Carrera (1838–1865) was an illiterate Amerindian, as was Benito Juárez (1857–1872) of Mexico, but the latter was an educated liberal politician who found it necessary to exercise caudillo-like power. The Bolivian José Mariano Melgarejo

(1864–1871) was an illiterate mestizo alcoholic, while Andrés Santa Cruz (1829–1839) of Bolivia and Rufino Barros (1872–1895) of Guatemala were exceedingly cruel and barbarous military men, and Gabriel García Moreno (1869–1875) of Ecuador was a professor and religious fanatic. Then there was Evita, offering a complementary matriarchal image that elevated her to the status of one of the greatest caudillos of them all.

Some caudillos were honest and forthright; others were hardly more than thieves. Some believed in and attempted to institute justice, others arbitrarily meted out barbaric and vindictive punishment. Some were of humble demeanor, others suffered from delusions of grandeur. There simply is no stereotypical caudillo. Yet all have a few loose and limber characteristics in common. For this reason, and due to the implicit, tacit, only vaguely definable *concreteness* natural to the term "caudillo" in contrast to the abstract relations qualifying U.S. politics, the conclusion of this section is comparable to that following the previous section: *either-ors* become fuzzy, borders fade, and the *both-ands* and *neither-nors* emerge. This characteristic bears testimony to the flux and flow of Mexican culture. This contradictory complementary interdependency interrelationship within Mexican culture cannot be overemphasized. It emerges from very profound and very subtle differences between Anglo-American culture and the cultures to the south. Germane to these differences, one must add, are differences of MC time and PC time and LC cultural space and HC cultural space.

I trust that this chapter, capping the previous chapters of historical content, has made you able to intuit the road toward "getting it." You should be able to "get a certain *feel*" for what it is that makes Mexicans Mexicans and how their *feel* for themselves and their culture is radically Other than Anglo-Americans' *feel* for themselves and their culture in the United States.

Further Reading

Anda 1996, Brusco 1995, Campa 1993, Cypess 1991, Dealy 1992, Díaz-Guerrero 1975, Díaz-Guerrero and Szalay 1991, Finer 1988, Fuentes 1971b, Goldwert 1980, Gutmann 1996, Hamill 1992, Johns 1995, Krause

1998, Lasky 1994, Lieuwen 1965, Lynch 1992, Macías 1982, Meyer 1972, Mirandé and Enríquez 1979, Nelson 1971, Peña 1998, Rodríguez 1998, Rodríguez O. 1997, Rubenstein 1998, Ruíz 1998, Schurz 1964, Shorris 1992, Stavans 1995, Stevens 1973, Szanto 1997, Vallens 1978.

Notes

1. In this section I make exclusive use of the masculine pronoun, for obvious reasons, although women have their own very characteristic form of machismo.

2. Yet the term "macho" has been used to express one of the most overrated stereotypes regarding Mexicans and Latin Americans. Moreover, the male role has recently been changing, especially in the cities, as Matthew C. Gutmann (1996) convincingly argues.

8

Making Today's Mexico: The Nineteenth Century and the Mexican Revolution

Lingering Problems

Mexico's emancipation was hardly more than a *political* liberation. The Catholic monarchy was replaced by the idea of a sovereign state. But below the surface, little had changed. I write "idea of a sovereign state" because in spite of the newly emancipated nation's having adopted a republican doctrine, the ideal did not become reality. The problem was that emancipation was not accompanied by a genuine restructuring of the *economy* and *society*.

After independence, heated debates transpired between conservatives and liberals. The criollo conservatives supported Church, *hacendados*, army, and what few foreign interests existed in the country. The liberals, criollos with a scattering of mestizos, had from the beginning cast a suspicious eye on the clergy (though they were not anti-Catholic), the large landholders, the army, and in general the upper-crust criollos. The conservatives were more centralist than federalist; it was the other way around with the liberals. In 1824 with the ousting of Agustín de Iturbide, the conservatives fell from grace, and the liberals, after drawing up the constitution of 1824 modeled largely on that of the United States, perpetuated the idealism/realism tension discussed in Chapter 4. In spite of the good intentions behind the constitutional document, it did not take into account the unequal distribution of land or the need to educate the masses of

Amerindians and citizens of mixed ethnic heritage. Moreover, the tendency was toward centralization of power in Mexico City, as had always been the case in colonial times, rather than the creation of a federal republic. The result was three periods of *caudillismo:* (1) General Santa Anna (1821–1855), who, as already noted, was either conservative or liberal, whichever seemed to fit the occasion; (2) Benito Juárez (1855–1876), an Amerindian president and liberal supporter; and (3) Porfirio Díaz (1876–1910), who came in as a liberal but later took on all the trappings of conservatism.

Santa Anna embroiled his country in the Mexican-American War, which saw the loss of over half of Mexico's territory. North Americans moving west began taking up residence in the remote province of Texas. In face of the inevitable, Santa Anna extended them an invitation, with the idea that an injection of new blood into the area would be beneficial. In 1835 the North Americans rebelled against Mexico's tax demands and stormed the Mexican garrison. Santa Anna, outraged, gathered a motley army of six thousand and marched toward Texas to punish the rebels. He found a few of them at an old mission, El Alamo, and massacred the lot of them. Two months later Sam Houston led an army against Santa Anna and, crying "Remember the Alamo," defeated the Mexican army and took Santa Anna prisoner. In exchange for his freedom, the Mexican chameleon-president gave Texas its independence. Santa Anna returned to Mexico in disgrace as a *malinchista* (see glossary), a traitor who sold out to the foreigners. In spite of this setback, the wily Santa Anna would once again rise from the ashes.

The United States admitted Texas to the Union in 1845, with a covetous eye toward the territory in the West, including the states of New Mexico, Arizona, California, and parts of Colorado, Utah, and Nevada. War soon broke out. It was no contest. The U.S. population was 17 million to Mexico's 7 million. The North American army numbered over 100,000, including 60,000 volunteers; the Mexican military might consisted of 20,000 soldiers, and of them too many officers—Latin American armies have always been top heavy. The United States had seventy warships, Mexico had six. The year 1847 saw North American troops sweeping down from the north while General Winfield Scott landed troops in Veracruz and proceeded toward Mexico City. During that same year the

U.S. flag was raised above the Mexican National Palace. On February 2, 1848, the Treaty of Guadalupe-Hidalgo was signed. In exchange for $15 million the Mexican government turned over 890,000 square miles. Mexico was in shambles when the hated gringos departed.[1] So much for Santa Anna's legacy.

Conservatives and liberals had no alternative but to continue their squabble over what was left of the country. And squabble they did. The liberals and the Zapotec Amerindian Benito Juárez soon had the upper hand. They called for elections, drew up a constitution, and dreamed about putting their Reform Laws of 1857 into effect, thus broadening individual freedoms and breaking the Church's hold over almost half of the nation's agricultural resources. Ignacio Comonfort was elected president and the conservatives revolted, threw Comonfort out of office, and jailed Juárez, only to free him later. But the liberals were not to be denied. Juárez returned to the capital city in 1860 and the Reform Laws were put into effect. The conservatives now appealed to debtor nations to intervene, since Mexico had defaulted on its payments. England and the United States declined the offer. Only France came to the rescue in 1862, sending troops and Maximilian as emperor, accompanied by his wife, Archduchess Carlota. The Mexicans never accepted them and finally repelled the French troops, captured Maximiliano in 1867, and put him before the firing squad. Juárez, after defeating Porfirio Díaz, returned to the helm.

Juárez, a liberal, was instrumental in breaking the Church's back. Land was confiscated and put up for auction. Most of it was sold for a pittance to rich criollos and mestizos. The provinces were given a relatively liberal dose of autonomy, and many of them fell sway to local caciques. Meanwhile, illiterate Amerindians and peasants, most of the mestizos, and African Americans and mulattos, who together made up almost 90 percent of the population, saw their patronage pass from the Church and conservative criollos to conservative criollos and liberal criollos, peppered with a few mestizos here and there. The difference was that they had lost whatever protection the Church offered against abuses and they gained a new class of capitalist patrons. Juárez the Amerindian played politics favoring the fair-skinned crowd and left his own people to suffer the consequences. Things went from bad to worse. Nevertheless, Juárez has gone down in history as a national hero, a president of the people who defied the conservative clergy, threw the French out, and brought freedom to the Mexican populace.

Porfirio Díaz was now chafing at the bit. He raised an army, entered the capital city, called for elections, and sat in the presidential chair in 1876. Having espoused the principle of "effective suffrage, no reelection," he gave up power to his vice president in 1880 and then resumed it in 1884 and held the reins until 1910, conveniently forgetting about "no re-election" on the pretext that the country was not yet ready for full-fledged democracy. At the very least, Díaz brought stability to Mexico for the first time in its national history. He also centralized power. He developed the country's infrastructure, built up the economy by inviting foreign invest-ment and extracting little from them in the way of taxes, kept the rich happy, controlled the countryside with his rural police (a three-thousand-man force called *rurales*), and made peace with the Church. As a liberal, he became more conservative than most conservatives. He did this by adeptly practicing the ways of the caudillo: putting on the charm, making the people think he was giving them what they wanted, and doing every-thing possible to keep himself in power.

To his credit, Díaz brought what on the surface looked like progress. While the dictatorship (with tongue in cheek dubbed *díazpotism*) was so-lidified, mining boomed, the first steel mill in Latin America was con-structed, new industries appeared, and foreign trade expanded manyfold. The railroad grew from 187 to over 12,000 miles, foreign investments poured into the country, and foreign bankers finally became confident that Mexico was not a high risk for loans. Foreigners investing in Mexico and taking up residence there flourished. Díaz surrounded himself with economic advisers and administrators, the *científicos* (scientists) (see glos-sary) who sought to apply scientific methods to their society in order to bring it up to par with the rapidly developing nations of the West. This meant more liberal concessions to foreigners. As a popular saying had it, Mexico became the "mother of foreigners and the stepmother of Mexi-cans." Every four years Díaz methodically had himself reelected so that rich Mexicans and foreign businesses could continue to thrive.

Mexico City prospered, but little wealth trickled down to the workers, who rarely ate more than tortillas and beans and consumed a cheap fer-mented drink made from distilled cactus juice called *pulque*. In the countryside, some three thousand families owned sprawling tracts and lived in magnificent haciendas, while millions of Amerindian and mestizo peasants saw their lifestyle become even more hopeless. More and more of their communal lands were taken from them, and those who did not bow down to the new hacienda system and take on a lifestyle much like medieval serfs fled further into the mountains, deserts, and jungles. A glaring disparity continued to exist between the glitter of Mexico City (which rivaled the best of Western cities) and the countryside. A long road remained for Mexico before she could become truly modernized. Díaz's immortal words encapsulate the dilemma: "Poor Mexico, so close to the United States and so far from God."

The People Begin Finding Their Voice: Political Revolution

In 1910, Díaz told a North American news correspondent that it was finally time to step down and allow free elections to take their course. A wave of enthusiasm followed. Francisco I. Madero emerged and captivated the imagination of the Mexican middle classes in the capital and provincial cities. This was apparently more than Díaz had bargained for, and he decided to throw his hat in the ring also. Elections were held, and Díaz claimed all but a few hundred votes. Electoral fraud was apparent. Madero, now facing a reprisal, decided to flee to Texas, where he issued a call to revolution for November 20, 1910. Initially the revolution was a disaster and Madero once again took up hiding in the United States. But unrest prevailed, and soon the country was in arms. Díaz boarded a train for Veracruz and left for France. Elections were held in 1911, and Madero won handily.

Madero came from a rich hacienda family in the state of Coahuila. Educated in Europe and familiar with the U.S. political system, he was a reformist, not a true revolutionary. His government was chiefly experimental, piecemeal, and pragmatic. Bear in mind that this was the beginning of the first revolution of the twentieth century, and there were few models to follow. Most importantly, however, Mexico now had a new leader. Madero, hailed with considerable enthusiasm, was seen as a breath of fresh air after the final years of *díazpotism*. This small man, who had a high-pitched voice and nervous mannerisms, was anything but a caudillo figure. Nevertheless, he was considered to have liberated the country from years of tyrannical rule. Madero allowed free speech and proposed to restore the constitution of 1857 and return lands to the peasants. But he had no economic program to speak of. To make matters worse, he kept Díaz's old army with few changes, turned his eyes away from increasing violence and corruption, and failed to enact promised reforms. His popularity soon plummeted. Evidently Madero did not possess the wherewithal for taking charge. He simply didn't live up to the expectations of a powerful revolutionary figure.

To make a long and complex story short, when Madero became president, many of the military leaders remained loyal to the Díaz backers who longed for a return to the good old days when the rich people had things their way and the poor people accepted the fact. One general, Victoriano Huerta, was straining at the leash to get at Madero any way he could. He entered into secret collaboration with U.S. Ambassador Henry Lane Wilson (no relation Woodrow Wilson who was president at the time) in a plot to depose the weak-kneed Mexican president. Henry Lane, going against the orders of his president, was at least indirectly instrumental in Huerta's removing Madero, throwing him in prison, and then having him mysteriously murdered while being transferred from one house of detention to another. Outraged at the assassination of their "apostle of democracy," peasants and city people alike rebelled against Huerta the "usurper."

Now enter the peasant revolutionaries, chief among whom were Emiliano Zapata of the state of Morelos and Francisco ("Pancho") Villa (whose real name was Doroteo Arango) of Durango to the north. Morelos, just south of Mexico City, was the first area colonized by the Spaniards after the rape of Tenochtitlán. Cortés had built a palace in Cuernavaca, capital of the state, where today tourists gaze at impressive murals by Diego Rivera. Aristocratic colonial families took up residence in the area, attracted to the ideal climate. During the time of Juárez and the Reform Laws, Church land and much of the Amerindian communal land, called *ejidos*, was auctioned to rich criollos (see glossary). By the end of the nineteenth century, Morelos had become the richest sugar cane–growing region of Mexico. The land was fertile and wealth was concentrated among some seventeen criollo families who shared thirty-seven haciendas and twenty-four sugar mills. The Amerindian communal lands were by this time virtually nonexistent. Resentment over the loss of communal fields ran deep. Emiliano Zapata, a mestizo peasant, shouldered the responsibility of defending the peasants' grievance against the criollo landowners. Zapata was always respected as a leader of courage, honest, and integrity. He never ceased his relentless struggle against those who had deprived his people of their land. He is often thought of as the only "pure revolutionary" of the Mexican civil war.

To the north, Pancho Villa reportedly had his beginning as a bandit after he killed a *rural* (rural mounted police) who molested Villa's sister with rape on his mind. Realizing he was now condemned to lead the life of a fugitive, Villa wisely went into hiding. He had for years opposed the Díaz regime, and now he found what he considered a just cause against the local politicians and caciques. After the revolution broke out, his skills as a guerrilla fighter and organizer boosted him up the ranks as a wily revolutionary leader. By 1913 he commanded a large army, the Division of the North, whose soldiers became known as the *dorados* (brown ones), so named for their khaki uniforms purchased across the border in the United States. Villa imposed makeshift reform programs in the territories he controlled, giving land to the peasants and building schools. His justice was in large part at the barrel of a gun, however. Villa was generous with his friends and brutal toward his enemies. Consequently he became a folk hero to the peasants and an opportunistic, cutthroat bandit to middle-class and upper-class Mexicans and foreigners residing in northern Mexico and the southwestern United States.

The peasants in the countryside and the working class in the cities now turned to the newly *mythified image* of Madero. He was now personified as the revolutionary "caudillo slayer" from the north, rather than Madero the mild-mannered reformist. Consequently, it was Huerta's turn to suffer the villain image. He was vilified, scorned, and branded a brutal sadist and a drunkard more often than not stoned on marihuana. *Corridos*— popular songs of the oral tradition—were sung in praise of Pancho Villa. But they were full of bile, contempt, and satire regarding Huerta. Actually, Villa was not quite the Robin Hood, nor was Huerta quite the scoundrel and bloodthirsty assassin that the popular image portrayed.

Historian Michael Meyer in *Huerta: A Political Portrait* (1972) put these and other myths to rest. The truth, however, is often far from popular images. If, according to the people, Villa was the invincible eagle, Huerta was a vulture who must fall. And fall he did, in 1914, less than a year after he took office.

With the demise of Huerta, the revolution was basically in the hands of four leaders: Villa and Zapata, Alvaro Obregón and Venustiano Carranza. The first two represented peasant interests, whereas the latter were more favorably disposed to the interests of the middle class. The first two were revolutionaries in the somewhat genuine sense, the latter two were re-formists who did not take to confiscation of foreign property, wholesale redistribution of land, and radical workers and peasants' rights. After a few skirmishes in 1914, shortly after the ousting of Huerta, a reunion was called to hammer out differences. To the chagrin of those who supported the middle class, at this gathering, called the Convention of Aguas-calientes, peasant factions clearly dominated. Nevertheless, heated debates were self-perpetuating, and no agreement seemed to be forthcoming. At one point Villa proposed to Carranza that they draw their pistols and publicly commit suicide so the congregation might come to order—a supreme expression of machismo, typical of the best of caudillo. In an act of frustration the majority finally chose the less politically ardent Eulalio Gutiérrez as interim president. Carranza and Obregón went off in a huff, and Villa and Zapata didn't trust this newcomer. The civil war carried on virtually unabated, with Obregón, Carranza—who arrogantly called him-self First Chief of the Revolution—and others of middle-class interests going into battle against the peasant groups, chief among the leaders of which were still Villa and Zapata.

Before long, Zapatista and Villista troops knocked on the door and briefly entered Mexico City. More at home on the land, however, they soon disbanded this strange setting and entered the more familiar coun-tryside. Shortly thereafter, Villa was for the first time defeated in an open battle (deviating from his familiar guerrilla tactics) with Obregón in 1915, and by 1916 Obregón and Carranza clearly had the upper hand. Carranza eventually took the reins, was elected, and oversaw the constitu-tion of 1917, the most progressive in the world at the time. It stipulated return of subsoil rights to the state (Article 27), free and compulsory primary education (Article 3), and labor rights to organize, strike, and bargain collectively (Article 123). Peasant and labor factions and radical and revolutionary elements were still powerful, and this constitution was written chiefly for their appeasement. Carranza the moderate reformist, however, had no intention of putting the radical articles into effect. Consequently, he soon fell from grace like other fallen eagles, especially in 1919 when, under his orders, Zapata was enticed into a hacienda for peace talks and was killed in an ambush. In that year Carranza sensed the end was near. He loaded a train with money and as many personal belongings as he could take and headed to Veracruz, where a ship was waiting. On the way, he was intercepted, hunted down in the jungle, and shot. His cohort, Alvaro Obregón, then became president from 1920 to 1924.

Thus ended the second phase of the Mexican Revolution. Now was the time to regroup. Obregón developed ambitious programs designed to revive a sense of national pride. Capital was injected into education, the arts, and public works. Workers' rights and land reform were also revived in an effort to put a smile on as many citizens as possible. Young teachers journeyed from the cities to the countryside to teach peasants, children and adults alike. Mexican mural art saw its dramatic beginning. Development of Mexico's infrastructure boomed. Workers organized and began pressing for better conditions and a bigger piece of the pie. It was also a time to buy off disgruntled generals (with what were called "silver bullets") and beat the rest into submission or kill them. (Pancho Villa was assassinated in 1923.) The political system had to be stabilized as well. This task was left to Plutarco Elías Calles, president from 1924 to 1928. Calles was instrumental in organizing the National Revolutionary Party (PNR, 1929), which, with alterations and amendments and a couple of name changes, remained in control until 2000, when National Action Party (PAN) candidate, Vicente Fox Quesada, garnered the most votes.

The Hour of the People: Social Revolution

Winds of change again swept through Mexico in the 1930s. The Great Depression caused hardships. Exports declined, industry suffered, capital fled the country, and unemployment went through the ceiling. Many citizens were questioning the purpose and achievement of the much ballyhooed Mexican Revolution.

Then came Lázaro Cárdenas, president from 1934 to 1940 (the term had been extended to six years). A mestizo with Tarascan Amerindian heritage, Cárdenas had revealed his concern for the plight of the common people while governor of Michoacán. He was humble and austere in his personal life. He did not smoke or drink, and, after his election, he moved out of the Presidential Palace at Chapultepec and into a modest home. He was always ready to lend an ear to the complaints of the poor. Jokes abounded that he had no time for ministers, ambassadors, and dignitaries, but spent hours chatting with peasants from the countryside. In spite of his refusal to take up the customary social graces, he was no pushover for foreigners and rich and powerful Mexicans. While in office, he proved he was a daring visionary leader capable of reviving some of the dreams of the revolution. Until his time, many promises were forthcoming but few were delivered. Most importantly, no president had confronted the problem of the landless peasants. Cárdenas distributed some 49 million acres of land to the poor and built them up into communal land holdings *(ejidos)*. He organized labor and peasant groups and nationalized foreign-owned mines, factories, manufacturing concerns, railroads, and oil fields. In fact, if Cárdenas had accomplished nothing else, he would be lionized by the Mexican public for his nationalization of oil. The Mexican state-owned oil industry, PEMEX (Petróleos de México), is today inseparable from the concept of the Mexican nation. Recent presidents have privatized foreign mines, utilities, factories, banks, right and left, but nobody dared touch PEMEX. It is the very embodiment of Mexican nationalism.

Nationalization came about in 1938. The oil companies literally owned the oil fields in the state of Veracruz. These companies were virtually tax exempt, they did what they pleased with the workers, and they had their own laws and private armies to back them up and protect their investments. After a confrontation between Cárdenas and the oil giants over worker grievances, the Mexican president issued an ultimatum. It was not met. Then, with a bold stroke of the pen, he nationalized the oil.

Ex-president Calles, from his exile in Los Angeles, branded him a "communist." The charge was widely repeated, especially since Cárdenas had recently granted asylum to Leon Trotsky and enthusiastically helped the Republican cause during the Spanish Civil War. But Cárdenas was no Marxist. Rather, his concern was with the people themselves and a return of Mexico's resources to the nation with the sole purpose of bringing the promises of the revolution to fruition.

Cárdenas has gone down in history primarily for his agrarian reform program and his nationalization of oil. He was also instrumental in centralizing governmental power beyond the dreams even of Porfirio Díaz, in preparing the way for the subsequent industrial takeoff and in turning the ruling party—which he rechristened the Party of the Mexican Revolution (PRM)—into a powerful instrument of the presidency. Cárdenas, in short, realized the *social revolution* to complement the earlier *political revolution* that culminated with the initial organization of the ruling party (PNR). Now the stage was set for the *economic revolution.* Perhaps unfortunately, the creators of that aspect of the revolution have been vilified: in the popular mind they sold the nation out to foreigners.

Enter the Young Tigers: The Economic Revolution

Prior to the elections of 1946, outgoing president Manuel Ávila Camacho (1940–1946) orchestrated a further solidification of the official ruling party, and its name was changed once again. Its newly baptized label was the Institutionalized Revolutionary Party (PRI). The PRI nominated as official candidate for the presidency Interior Secretary Miguel Alemán, who was destined to become the president most vehemently maligned for catering to foreigners. Many historians and political scientists, in contrast, identify him as the architect of modern Mexico. His change of policy continues to shape the country today: accelerated influx of foreign capital, massive industrialization, emergence of a middle class, chaotic urbanization, neglect of the country's social problems, and dependence on the world market.

Once in office, Alemán moved the government sharply to the right. Firmly believing that economic development must precede social reform,

he supported growth over justice, agriculture for export over small peasant plots, high-profit businesses and factories over workers' needs, efficiency over social programs. Mexico filled its coffers during World War II
when it exported massive quantities of raw materials, agricultural products, and workers to the United States. Now it had the makings for rapid
growth. And an extraordinary economic boom there was. The government invested heavily in construction of roads, dams, and irrigation
canals. Through fiscal incentives, foreign investors found Mexico enticing. Large commercial farmers received protection against pressure by
landless peasants. This was a program designed for concentration of
wealth. It also gave birth to a new wave of corruption. Public works enriched elected officials and high office bureaucrats. Alemán himself
bought large tracts of land around Acapulco before the government developed it for tourism. The assumption now had it that government is big
business and big business is government. The two simply could not be
separated.

At the close of Alemán's presidency, on the surface Mexico appeared
stable and peaceful. Currents of dissatisfaction ran deep, however. Conservative, right-wing, and Catholic groups still distrusted the government.
During the Cárdenas years, these groups had formed the Unión Nacional
Sinarquista (National Sinarquist Union) whose focus was God, Church,
and family. They emphasized *hispanismo*, considering Spain the genuine
source of their inherited traditions, and opposed what they saw as Anglo-
American cold, cruel, impersonal materialism. Leftists ardently opposed
Mexico's pro-U.S. policies that had now become commonplace. They followed various interpretations of liberal, Marxist-socialist, and communist
doctrines. Longing for the heyday of statism and quasi-socialism of the
Cárdenas years, they were seething over Alemán's 180-degree political
turn. All was not well in the country that experienced the first genuine
revolution of this century. The years that followed would prove to be a
telling tale.

That tale will come later. For now, let us return to further consideration of what makes Mexicans Mexicans in order better to understand the
evolution of Mexico's politics, economics, and social and cultural trends.

Further Reading

Bauer 1974, Becker 1996, Brading 1980, Brenner and Leighton 1984, Britton 1995, Burns 1980, Cline 1963, Cockcroft 1968, 1991, Cruz 1998, Cumberland 1968, Folgarait 1987, 1998, Frank 1998, Grisword 1990, Herrera-Sobek 1990, Holland 1997, Katz 1998, Levy and Szekely 1983, Livermore 1969, O'Malley 1986, Rodríguez 1969, Ross 1955, Salas 1990, Sanderson 1984, Simpson 1967, Stein 1994, Turner 1968, Wilkie and Michaels 1984, Wolfe 1963, Womak 1970. Fiction and documentary: Azuela 1983, Campobello 1988, Fuentes 1964, 1997a, 1997b, Garro 1967, Guzmán 1965, Reed 1969, Revueltas 1990, Rulfo 1971, 1994, Traven 1963, 1969, Usigli 1971, Yáñez 1971.

Notes

1. According to one story, "gringo" originated in a song brought by U.S. troops: "Green Grow the Lilacs, Oh." "Green Grow" became the Spanish "gringo."

9

Problems That Wouldn't Go Away

Because They Are Distinctly Mexican

Regarding Mexico's mind-numbing diversity, one might have the inclination to ask: What is the likeness between a bank teller in Tijuana and a peasant in Yucatán? An unemployed man who cleans windshields at an intersection in downtown Mexico City for a handout and a hotel clerk in Cancún? A government bureaucrat at Ciudad Juárez and an Amerindian woman weaving a serape at the tourist market in Guadalajara? A multimillionaire retailer in Mexico City and a bus driver on a rural highway? One response to these questions in years past might have been: They all share their distinctive "Mexicanness." Then comes the question: How can one word incorporate such diversity?

Qualifying the *essence* (fixed nature) of ethnic groups is now looked on as a highly questionable enterprise. Indeed, it is virtually impossible when taking a nation as diverse as Mexico into consideration. The difficulties are too numerous to enumerate and discuss here. Nevertheless, two problems should be given at least brief attention. First, differences between Mexicans far outnumber their likenesses. Yet there is a certain sameness within the myriad differences. Thus, one might wish to conclude, we can talk about samenesses after all. Not so, however, because of the second difficulty that Mexicans share with all people: there is not, nor can there be, a fixed essence that characterizes the Mexican people and sets them apart from any other collection of humans. Whatever a given Mexican may be at a particular time and space, she is always in the process of becoming someone other than who she is, and who she *is* in the process of becoming someone other than who she *was* in the *process of becoming*.

Yet an impressive array of intellectuals, from philosophers to psychologists to poets, have attempted to account for Mexicanness. Allow me to tell the story of a few such attempts. I have already mentioned Samuel Ramos, who in *Profile of Man and Culture in Mexico* (1962) writes that the Mexicans are caught up in "feelings of inferiority," although Ramos concedes that this general interpretation does not necessarily apply to each individual Mexican. The origin of this sentiment goes back to the days of the conquest, when the Amerindian way of life was destroyed. What remained was a vacuum, where there once existed some of the most magnificent civilizations the world had known to that time. Now, a vacuum. Only people who have suffered devastating traumatic experiences can sense the consequences of such a vacuum: Jews, African Americans, Latinos in the United States. The terrible trauma suffered by the Amerindians of Mexico involved an institutionalized effort by Church and Crown to impress on them by the cross or the sword the idea that their cultures were wrong-headed and that the conquerors had brought the right culture for them.

After generations of subjugation through violence and indoctrination, the Amerindians could not help but take on a profound sense of their inferiority. This inferiority did not become manifest, however, until after Mexico gained her independence. At this point the Mexicans had no alternative but to embark on a search for their own identity. As Leopoldo Zea (1963) writes, with independence, Mexico—like other Spanish American republics—rejected everything Spanish as "decadent." In the Mexicans' eyes, Spain had failed to play a significant role in the scientific revolution and lagged behind in industrial development. Her thinkers were lodged in pre-Enlightenment thought, and as if that were not enough, her monarchical form of government was hopelessly archaic.

Where, then, could Mexico turn? In intellectual and poet Alfonso Reyes's (1952) ironic quip, Mexico had invited herself to Western civilization's banquet after the table had been set and everybody was seated. The clash of cultures during the conquest and colonialism had resulted in a small upper crust of criollos, a massive Amerindian base, and a growing contingent of mestizos. Ethnically, there was diversity, but on the surface—or so it appeared—there was a monolithic Catholic-monarchical state. Now ethnic diversity remained, along with another vacuum, a social-political-economic vacuum or a legitimacy vacuum, as discussed in Chapter 6. Once again, according to Ramos, a sense of "inferiority" began to pervade. What was the answer? Imitate! Imitate the best the West had to offer. Where was the best found? Chiefly in France, seat of Enlightenment thought and a cultural Mecca.

So France it was. During the Porfirio Díaz era (1876–1910), the Paseo de la Reforma in Mexico City was designed in Parisian fashion. The Palace of Fine Arts, construction of which was initiated during the time of Porfirio Díaz, had a distinctly French flavor. Houses in Lomas de Chapultepec sported Mansard roofs, steeply pitched to shed snow in a locale that had never known hardly enough snow to lighten the surface of the city for an hour or so. In cultured circles, French novels were read and discussed. They were read in French if possible, and if not in Spanish translation. Yes. France was the model, and Mexico was the imitator. As is often the case, the imitator imitates to the extreme, excessively highlighting that which is imitated. And so it was in "cultured Mexico," the Mexico of "decent people." Spain was no longer the land of nobles and bullfighters and Hispanic cultural circles, for respectable Mexicans had France on their mind. Mexicans ate, drank, talked, and dreamed things Parisian. This obsession with another culture brought the Mexicans' "sense of inferiority" to the surface.

At least, so we read in Ramos. The Mexican "sense of inferiority" of which Ramos writes, however questionable as a catch-all term for qualifying Mexicanness, is nonetheless revealing. Popular sayings such as *Como México no hay dos* ("Mexico has no equal") testify to a defensive sort of nationalism. Assertion becomes defiance in an attempt to conceal doubt and, more specifically, an admiration for the United States and other cultures coupled with resentment: a love-hate relationship. Ramos recalls sentiment toward North Americans voiced in high regard for their knowledge, wealth, and material advancement, but with the corollary, "however, we Mexicans are macho." Defiance and doubt, envy and admiration, esteem and dislike.

This apparent dualism of tendencies does not quite do justice to the Mexicans, however. At the risk of endlessly repeating myself, Mexicans are Mexicans and they would never be otherwise. Mexicans also hold *malinchistas* in contempt. As the popular account goes, Moctezuma "betrayed" his people and gave in to the conquerors. Santa Anna ransomed Mexican territory to the United States in return for his life. Porfirio Díaz sold Mexico down the river. More recently, we have presidents Miguel Alemán (1946–1952) and Carlos Salinas de Gortari (1988–1994), who sided up to the United States. All are to a degree considered *malinchistas* who catered to the "foreigners." At the same time, and rather ironically, middle-class upwardly mobile citizens of the country welcome "Made in America," considering goods *Hecho in México* ("Made in Mexico") of inferior quality.

If Ramos wrote about Mexicanness up to and including the first years after the Mexican Revolution, Octavio Paz in *Labyrinth of Solitude* (1961) addresses himself more specifically to Mexico's posture vis-à-vis the United States.[1] Significantly, he begins his penetrating and penetratingly painful series of essays with his reflections on the Pachuco culture of Los Angeles during the late 1940s. This chapter serves as a point of departure for his meditation on Mexico's culture, that is, chiefly the male culture of proletariat Mexico. According to Paz, the imitator becomes a dissembler, an actor, and culture becomes his theater. But there is a difference between a dissembler and the actor of a play in a theater within culture. An actor surrenders himself to a role and then sloughs it off, like a snake its skin, when the curtain falls. The dissembler never surrenders himself to some other self; the dissembled self is his only self. He is condemned to play the role throughout life. The mask takes command of him and becomes his very personality.

But what is that personality, that self? Something transient. We read in Paz (1961, 42) that "to simulate is to invent, or rather to counterfeit, and thus to evade our condition. Dissimulation requires greater subtlety: the person who dissimulates is not counterfeiting but attempting to become invisible, to pass unnoticed without renouncing his individuality. The Mexican excels at the dissimulation of his passions and himself. He is afraid of others' looks and therefore he withdraws, contracts, becomes a shadow, a phantasm, an echo." Instead of "walking," he "glides," instead of "stating," he "hints," instead of "replying," he "mumbles," instead of "complaining," he "smiles." In sum, he must endure *(aguantar)*. He must be able to put up with whatever fate has in store for him.

Perhaps, Paz speculates, dissembling emerged during colonial times. The Amerindians and mestizos could not say things outright, loud and clear, with a strong and confident voice. They said what they had to say in a whisper, with head bowed somewhat, or perhaps between clenched teeth. They had to disguise their anger and their fear, their joy and their sorrow, their mistrust and their suspicion, so as to take on the forlorn, distant, passive, stoic countenance that has stereotyped them throughout the centuries. They learned to avoid saying what they said directly, but by way of vague suggestions, subtle nuances, and through indirect means. In other words, they spoke in terms of *indirectas* ("insinuations," a way of saying something subtly in a round-about or indirect fashion), by vaguely implying that what they said was really not what was being said but in reality something else, something perhaps provocative, critical, or maybe even flattering.

Dissimulation in its extreme form becomes mimicry, imitation. The *subaltern*, whether Amerindian or mestizo, blends into whatever context there is (see glossary). During this process, he becomes indistinguishable from all other items of perception and conception. He becomes one with the environment, silently, immutably. He becomes appearance, blending in with everything else, so that he appears to be something other than what he *is*, and at the same time other than what he *is not*. He *is* what he *is not* and he *is not* what he *is*. He becomes mimicry itself. He progresses—or digresses, if you wish—from "somebody into nobody, into nothingness. And this nothingness takes on its own individuality, with a recognizable face and figure, and suddenly becomes Nobody" (Paz 1961, 45). There is the saying about the president who asks his aide what time it is. The response? "Whatever time you wish, *Señor Presidente*." Or consider the quip about the new maid in a middle-class household who, when asked through the front door if anyone was home, responded, "There's nobody home, *señor*, only me."

These are instances, extreme and exaggerated to be sure, of little self-affirmation and much self-denial or cancellation. "Naughtization" is perhaps the proper word. But it is too presumptuous and pedantic. We should just call it dissimulation, self-denial. The subaltern Mexican denies herself, and at the same time goes through a morsel of self-affirmation. This is to imply that the self is not a fixed commodity. Rather, it is always becoming something other than what it was becoming. It is flow, flow along with the flow of life and the life of culture, flow that flows to nowhere and nowhen in particular and to everywhere and everywhen in the most general sense.

Every moment presents a slightly new picture. At each juncture one must adapt to slightly varied circumstances. Consequently, the Mexican must perpetually engage in an act of creating herself. She must at every turn modify herself. She modifies herself with such frequency that, in the words of Octavio Paz (1961, 43), she almost ceases to exist.

Thus Jorge Carrión misses the mark somewhat, I would expect, when he writes:

> The Spaniard is force, authority, order, law, author of pain and suffering. The Indian, in contrast, is passivity, submission, delicate contemplation. . . . The idea of Mother Spain has no meaning for the Mexican; as far as he is concerned, Spain is the repository of violence, masculine mobility and activity, and authority: Spain is the Father. Father Spain and Mother Aborigine are the symbols that mix into the psychological complex that makes up the Mestizo, the Mexican. (Carrión 1952, 53)

According to Carrión, the masculine/feminine and the Spanish/ Amerindian pair of dualities conjoin racially and ethnically to make up today's Mexican. The problem with Carrión, as with most other observers of the Mexican scene, is that the one side is considered the aggressor and the other side the victim, the one side is totally superordinate and the other side is subordinate, the one side inflicts pain and suffering and the other side passively takes whatever is dished out.

Dualisms, all! Rigid dualisms, incapable of patterning the flow of culture.

The Problem with Dualistic Thinking

Such dualisms are liberally sprinkled throughout the numerous treatises on Mexicanness from the 1950s to the present. It is as if Mexican culture were simply a matter of polarization between male and female, rich and poor, cities and countryside, Western and Amerindian, and so on.

This dualistic thinking regarding Mexico must go the way of the dinosaurs. Cultures, modern and traditional alike, are *interdependent*, *interrelated*, *interactive*, and highly unpredictable (see glossary). In fact, *interdependency*, *interrelationship*, and *interaction* exist in all aspects of Mexican culture. Amerindian and mestizo women from traditional cultures care for the children of the privileged class; they come into contact with gardeners from the countryside who cannot help but influence these young minds. Children of all levels of the middle class, in spite of their video games, McDonald's fast food, U.S. movies and TV programs, professional football on Sundays, and so on, cannot escape the fact, however much they might wish to do so, that they are surrounded by traditional Mexican culture. Assuming their lifestyle is "modern" and hence their mind-set and behavioral patterns are also modern is like supposing a child born of North American parents working for Wal-Mart in a foreign country will become a teenager virtually identical to the typical teenager living in Muncie, Indiana. Environment and context cannot help exercising their force.

All aspects of Mexican culture are *interrelated* in such a manner that nothing is capable of acting independently of anything else. Everything is *equally interactive*, even though on the surface there are apparently rich/poor, city/countryside, modern/traditional dualisms. Deep down, however, the have-nots are *equally interactive* with the haves. Given these *deepermost levels*, where conscious and conscientious, and willful and intentional behavior wanes, there is no telling what *interaction* will emerge from the complex cultural matrix. Thus *unpredictability* exercises its force. This unpredictability is the result of the dependency of every part of culture on every other part of it. Cultures are processes, never products. They are not cause-and-effect sequences; they are events. They are not things moving along like trains on a track; they are perpetually self-organizing into unseen and unseeable wholes in a multiplicity of diverging and converging directions rather than predictable wholes and their parts in terms of statistical averages.

Yet dualisms apparently continue to rule the roost in many considerations of Mexican and other cultures. Cultures are for some reason or other often seen as hardly more than oppositions between the powerful and the helpless. The idea generally has it that the powerful form a bloc. They are unified, quite stable, concordant, and allied toward common economic, social, political, legal, moral, and aesthetic goals. The weak, in contrast, are diverse, dispersed, disorganized. The haves are into structure, control, domination, manipulation; the have-nots are reduced to a diversity of interests, with no central organizing force.

Such dualisms straitjacket our mind, pushing us into pathways of least resistance and forcing us into seeing and conceiving cultural worlds in terms of blacks and whites. They blind us to the diversity of cultural practices; they shunt off alternative views that might give us a glimpse of the rich cultural subtleties before us. These subtleties play out their role on the wider stage where differences between PC–MC time and HC–LC space are at a maximum, especially in the contact zones. This stage is also of the nature of hybrid cultures of the sort marvelously exemplified in Mexico. Allow me to offer some clarifying examples.

A Picture Puzzle of N-Dimensions

Today's Mexico is a complex, virtually chaotic mix of colonialism and modernity, imitation and distortion, conflict and conformity, antagonism and acquiescence. Whoever rises to the top of the gush of Mexico's cultural becoming might appear to be a cut above everybody else. But not necessarily. He who happens to be of the haves at the top depends on those have-nots below, and they in turn depend on him. This entails an intricate interrelationship that renders everybody *interdependent* and *interactive* with everybody else in such a manner that there are no isolated, autonomous souls standing beyond the whole of the group. The entire cultural concoction is a flow of exchanges and replacements. If on the surface it might appear that rich/poor dualism rules, below the surface, the unexpected can occur at every bend in the stream. The idea of culture as a set of static, intransigent pairs of oppositions is a pipe dream.

In the beginning, the forging of Mexico might have seemed to be the product of clear and distinct delineation. Very quickly, the cultural milieu became pluralistic, and it is radically so in our time. Take the case of an imaginary Amerindian from the central plateau of Mexico today, almost five centuries after the conquest. If asked who "discovered" America, without hesitation she says, "Why, your ancestors, of course." She is either consciously or tacitly giving a nod to the "superiority" of European over pre-Hispanic civilizations. This is cultural awareness as it should be according to the properly endowed haves of the conquest and colonization and the aftermath of independence. If, on the other hand, our Amerindian retorts, "Well, *patrón*, as I see it, according to your account, Columbus 'discovered' your so-called America. But actually, we had no need of anybody to invent us and tell us who and where we were," she questions the supremacy of the "discoverers" and subverts the very idea of "discovery" (in the sense of to reveal, to be the first to know).[2] As far as she is concerned, there was no discovery, for nothing was concealed so that it might be revealed. There was no unknown entity in waiting expectation of its being placed in the light of knowledge.

Response to a comparable question regarding the problem of identity might be exceedingly more complex for a mestiza woman from the same area of the country. Part of her heritage is Native American, and another part perhaps peninsular, which is streaked with Arabic cultural presuppositions and propensities. The matter of her cultural heritage, her identity, and her proper posture vis-à-vis the pressures of today's society is a mixed and confusing bag of tricks. One might tell her that she really should choose, choose who she is, choose her attitude with respect to herself, her background, her political inclinations, her behavior and relations with others in society, and her role in the economic life surrounding her. Indeed, she should choose. But whichever choices she makes, she will remain separated and at the same time integrated; she will embrace and she will resist; she will interrelate and become part of an interlocking concoction of conflicts and contradictions. Along these lines María Lugones writes:

If something or some is neither/nor, but kind of both, not quite either.

If something is in the middle of either/or, if it is ambiguous, given the available classification of things, it is mestiza, if it threatens by its very ambiguity the orderliness of the system, of schematized reality.

If given its ambiguity in the univocal ordering it is anomalous, deviant, can it be tamed through separation? Should it separate so as to avoid taming?

Should it resist separation? Should it resist through separation? Separate as in the separation of the white from the yolk? (Lugones 1994, 459)

Yes, *choice*. We are all condemned to the imperative of choosing, choosing what our world is and who we are in interaction with it, whether we like it or not. We might think that a good choice is between an *either* and an *or*. That would be the easy answer. But culture is not a simple matter. There are always alternatives emerging to make themselves known along the cultural flow. These alternatives present themselves as other possibilities. Possibilities consist of many things rather than merely two things from which an *either-or* choice can be made. Moreover, when a choice is forthcoming, things never simply stay put. What has been chosen comes into *interdependent, interrelated interaction* with everything else to become something other than what it was.

Choice is not a matter simply of *either* one thing *or* another thing but of many possibilities, only a few of which can be perceived and conceived at a given time and place. Between an *either* and an *or* there are many other possible options at many possible times and places. And there is no telling when and where one of them will pop up. When taking multiple possibilities into consideration, we must entertain the notion that culture is process, marvelous process. This notion plays havoc with the idea of a fixed identity. Within cultural flow, our mestiza, like all of us, *is*, and at the same time she *is not,* who she *was,* for she is always becoming someone else, as she chooses, or chooses not to choose, along the stream of culture.

All this might appear to be nothing but riddles. But I see no other means of writing what I must try to write. Besides, whoever told us there must be *either* knowledge *or* darkness? A matter of dominating *or* of subservience? Of raping nature *or* living a sordid animal existence? Of razor-sharp binary choices between relatively simple *eithers* and *ors?* Any and all answers to all questions eventually meet their Others, and eventually there may be a happy meeting ground, or some alternative or other may pop up between the *neither* and the *nor*.

Yes, choice. Like learning another culture, it's no simple matter. Allow me to offer an example of how choices bring about change in the cultural flow of things.

Back to the Underdogs

The have-nots in Mexico, and elsewhere, actually enjoy a degree of what I call "cultural guerrilla power." Cultural guerrilla interaction at the contact zone invariably pushes new terms into the gaps between erstwhile opposites. Allow me a tangential shift in order to suggest an important practice on the part of the have-nots for the purpose of getting their way with the haves.

Sociologist John Fiske (1989, 1–21) offers the jeans craze in support of his lingering dualistic thinking. Regular jeans evoke the image of country, work, tradition, community, and relative classlessness and changelessness.

Designer jeans, in contrast, are upscale, bringing forth the idea of urban life, social distinction, leisure, and contemporary "yuppie" values. But then along come the cultural guerrillas who, in a show of contempt for society and its values, chose to mutilate any and all jeans, fading them, tearing holes in them, putting patches and daubs of paint over them, cutting them off, wearing them more loosely than normal. In the next scene we have the late capitalist system manufacturing jeans that way and selling them at inflated prices as stylish, the way to dress like the "in crowd." The moral to the story is that the monied powermongers succumbed to cultural guerrilla pressures. Dominance from above was not as intransigent as it appeared at the outset. Culture changed due to the rebellious upstarts from below. Nevertheless, the assumption still often has it in "cultural studies" programs that there is a "dominant culture" and a "subservient" or "popular culture," and the former exercises *hegemony* over the latter (see glossary). It all threatens to become quite dualistic, even though that is not what most of the cultural theorists originally had in mind.

This threat of dualism can be buffered by Michel de Certeau's (1984) contention that the would-be dominant group of capitalist societies is perpetually subjected to contestations and negotiations by the guileful ruses, subversive trickery, and cultural guerrilla tactics of the so-called subaltern groups. Allow me to begin with an example close to home. In de Certeau's conception, the dominant classes are powerful, but they are also laden with bureaucratic baggage; they are overweight and sluggish. In contrast, the underprivileged are lean and mean, nimble and flexible, creative and mobile. The powerful construct the fortresses of capitalist might: shopping malls, schools, parks, stadiums, and public monuments. The weak make their own space in and leave their mark on those memorials to the virtues of capitalism: graffiti, shoplifted goods, and defaced shrubs, signs, windows, and painted surfaces. In order to do so, however, the weak must be constantly on their toes; they must remain vigilant and seize the proper moments to engage in their subversive acts whenever and wherever they can. There are numerous ways of altering standard procedures and methods that characterize the subtle, stubborn resistance of the have-nots. Since they lack their own space, they have to get along in a network of already established forces and representations. They have to make do with what they have. In their cultural guerrilla strategies, they take certain pleasure in getting around the rules of a constraining space.

Making do with what one has: strategies for survival when one is of the have-nots. This entails constant improvisation, from trivial levels up to the top. As an exercise in cultural guerrilla triviality, shoplift an item worth $10 and buy a pack of gum, and you've doubly manifested your contempt for those who wield power. Take a couple of tools from the auto repair shop where you work, and soon you'll have a well-equipped workshop of your own. You may never belong to the power elite, but you'll give them enough pricks in their buttocks when their back is turned to help make life miserable for them.

Of course these are petty, insignificant, "I obey but I do not comply" tactics in comparison to today's serious problems that affect millions of people—and from the proper haves' view, they are quite illicit and immoral. However, if your friends and coworkers adopt these and similar strategies to throw monkey wrenches in the works at all levels, then collectively you have-nots may eventually have your way of getting even with and occasionally even taking sweet revenge on the haves. You are doing things your way, in spite of what the rich and the powerful think you're doing. You are *neither* producers of cultural artifacts *nor* full-blown consumers according to the ideal social image. You are somewhere in between. That is precisely the art.

The dominant culture must have everything given in blacks or whites. But the have-nots are superior to such oversimplified binary imperatives. In a rather tacit sense they know everything is either *neither* the one thing *nor* the other, or it is *both* the one thing *and* the other, take your pick. They *neither* exclusively buy *nor* do they exclusively not buy, when they shoplift and purchase some gum. They engage in another activity entirely. They *do* buy, but they *don't* buy everything they take; they buy a portion of it, however small. And they *do not buy*, for much or most of what they take remains unpurchased. From another, complementary perspective, they *both* buy *and* they don't buy. Put the two possible incongruous activities together and we have the have-nots' subtle moves that complement the dominant culture's *either-or* imperatives.

My examples are simple, everyday happenings. Yet I would hope they offer an image of the subtle interrelationships between haves and have-nots. The haves can live with *either-or* imperatives quite well. They can do so because they have the power and the purchasing capacity. The have-nots are not so fortunate. They must do the best with what they have. What they have is cultural guerrilla subversion. They behave as if they knew their place in the social hierarchy, and then, with a wink of the eye, they do a quick sleight of hand and the haves have been had while they think they are in control. The have-nots, I repeat, create loose and limber ways of rebellion within the gaps between the *eithers* and the *ors* with their wily moves. They have no other way, for they are the have-nots.

In other words, according to standard, two-value logic, we should simply have the powerful and the weak, those in control and those who have no say, the *dominant* and the *subalterns*. It is an *either-or* proposition. According to cultural guerrilla logic, in contrast, it is possible to don a different mask for each occasion. One can be virtually all things to all those who are in control. One can be intermittently *both* one thing *and* the other: buying a little and stealing a little, showing civic responsibility by throwing trash in the proper receptacle and later that night strewing the contents of that same receptacle along the sidewalk, catering to the boss in the morning and stealing from the company in the afternoon. Concomitantly, one is like an antihero. One is like the inverse of Forrest Gump, the all-American character in that prize-winning movie: one is *neither* the one thing *nor* the other on a permanent basis, for there is always the possibility of engaging in some act that falls *neither* within the *neither nor* the *nor*. One is always someone else entirely and then someone else, always emerging from within the interstices. So between the *either* and the *or* one always seems capable of finding something to fill in a portion of the excluded middle, thus bringing it into the equation.

All this is to say that the ordinary concepts of popular culture, folk culture, and guerrilla culture are not a monolithic mass of faceless dough. They are always in transition, with no readily apparent purpose or direction. In their composite they make up guerrilla culture, which is anything but reducible to a set of descriptive features. Guerrilla culture is in a manner of speaking identityless; it lacks identifying features; it eludes every effort conceptually to pin it down. Yet there *is* identity; it is, I would suggest, forever transient. It is, in a word, like all forms of identity, *process*. It defies fixed labels and definitions. Once it has been labeled, it contradicts that very label; once it has been defined in terms of what it is in contrast to what it is not, it has already altered itself to the extent that it is neither the *is* nor the *is not* but now something else.

With respect to the have-nots of Mexico, we see the dictum cited in various spots above, "I obey but I do not comply," from within a broader perspective. The two terms "obey" and "comply" enjoy a contradictory complementary relationship. It is never a question of *both* obeying *and* complying, as we might ordinarily expect. Neither is it a matter of *either* obeying *or* complying. There is *neither* obedience *nor* compliance, at least in the ordinary sense of the terms. Rather, there is noncompliance in a creative way that on the surface might appear to be so much compliance. At the same time there is obedience, yet underneath the surface there is nonobedience. Such *neither-nors* are often the norm in a radically heterogeneous cultural milieu.

After this digression on everyday cultural hybrid life in Mexico, let us turn to some particularly Mexican characteristics in order to set the stage for further consideration of the country's twentieth-century social, historical, and political milieu.

Further Readings

Bruhn 1996, Camp 1989, Drucker 1991, Gutierrez 1991, Handelman 1996, Herrera 1983, Hoyt-Goldsmith 1994, Jamis 1988, Mazón 1983, Oppenheimer 1998, Raat 1992, Staudt 1998, Suchlicki 1996, Tangeman 1995. Fiction and essay: Campos 1993, Castellanos 1992, 1998, Esquivel 1994, 1997, Paz 1991, Poniatowska 1992.

Notes

1. Paz, I must add, has received seething criticism regarding what is considered his "male-centered" view of Mexican culture of the early 1950s. The fact remains, however, that he was living and writing during a half-century in the past, and his views were common among most Mexican intellectuals.

2. I once heard a self-educated Amerindian from the state of Oaxaca respond to a comparable question in this fashion.

10

Particular Mexican Ways

Form, Formula, Formality

Octavio Paz (1961, 31–32) writes that the Mexicans' proclivity for hermeticism, for sealing themselves up as a defense against those who wish to penetrate their inner secrets, "manifests itself not only as impassivity and distrust, irony and suspicion, but also as love for Form. Form surrounds and sets bounds to our privacy, limiting its excesses, curbing its explosions, isolating and preserving it."

A fondness for ceremony, formulas, and formalities: that is the norm in Mexico. This tendency is derived from both the Mexicans' Hispano-Arabic heritage and their Amerindian heritage. In conforming to the form, the individual is not totally caught up in free-flowing spontaneity, creativity, and invention of novelty at each and every juncture. That would be too chaotic for comfort. There must be at least a modicum of security, some sense of the harmony within the cultural universe. When an individual decides to engage in an act of invention, there is a pattern to follow: it is the form. Customary courtesies, formalism in attire, declamatory style in addressing oneself before an audience: all are matters of orderly and harmonious patterns.

Mexican formalities are not usually rigorous and orderly. They do not follow the same set of procedures for all seasons and all occasions. They evince some constancy, yet there is always a degree of deviation from the norm, depending on the conditions that happen to present themselves.

This characteristic is in part the result of the Moorish love for geometrical harmony and order coupled with the Catholic Counter-Reformation, which spilled into the Baroque world's obsession with ambiguity, vagueness, and uncertainty. It is symmetry wedded to asymmetry, balance to unbalance, order to disorder. It is a fusion of the rational and the irrational, whose form of expression becomes paradoxical. The Counter-Reformation proclaimed the superiority of divine mysteries of faith, of incomprehensibles over rational clarity, of the tragic sense of life and the restlessness of struggle over the ideal of the self-confident individual who is always in control. Mexicans continue to live within the Baroque mind to a remarkable degree.

Let us consider some of Mexico's formalities with respect to their everyday comings and goings. This may help us "get a feel" for what makes Mexico Mexico and Mexicans Mexicans.[1]

Some Particular Forms

A particular Mexican custom that is subtly and profoundly entrenched in human interrelationships, keeps friendships alive and vital, and provides sustenance for emotional needs, is the *abrazo*, the "embrace," a warm hug between men and women, men and other men, women and women, and adults and adolescents.

When two men embrace, heads tilt to the left and on the right side of the other person, and torsos become clasped, tightly or somewhat loosely depending on the intimacy of the relationship between the two. When man and woman embrace, perhaps there might be a peck on the cheek, and perhaps not. The *abrazo* might appear to be a rather trivial custom of relative unimportance. But we shouldn't sell the custom short. It serves to break down psychological barriers and allows warmth to flow into the lines of verbal and nonverbal communication between humans. It is an institution, a ritual. It is fit for all occasions, from rigid, rule-governed ceremonies to the workplace to the afternoon meal to encounters in the street or market to free-for-all tequila-doused fiestas. With neither embarrassment nor shame, two men can meet at the airport and give each other a vigorous *abrazo*, then walk toward the baggage claim, laughing boisterously, with periodic backslapping. Two women surprised by a chance encounter at the shopping mall, after an *abrazo* and a brief exchange, stroll arm in arm toward the coffee shop. For a non-Mexican to enter into the confidence and ultimately enter into personal and intimate relations with a Mexican, the *abrazo* must become second nature. It is one of the Mexicans' most profound means of expressing their feelings for one another.

The *abrazo* is only one of many formalities found in Mexican culture, where everyday courtesies abound. Human interdependent, interrelated interactions converge into and diverge from them. Courtesies are the grease that keeps the wheels rolling along the Mexican cultural terrain, however smooth or however rocky. They are the sliding standard creating and undoing family and courtship and marital ties, religious conventions, business affairs, casual and intimate friendships, male bonding and female unities. At the same time, courtesies assert distinctions between men and women, adults and children, rich and poor, powerful and weak, leaders and followers, celebrities and common folks, bosses and workers, priests and parishioners, and between social classes, ethnicities, and races. In brief, courtesies keep cultural processes alive; at the same time they maintain cultural distinctions within a hierarchical society. This is the case of politicians, business associates, those of the upper crust, *niñas bien* ("stylish women"), *juniors* (irresponsible playboy sons of the rich and famous), and *pelados* (resentful lower-middle-class and lower-class urban males).

Formalities were customary even in pre-Hispanic cultures. Moctezuma addressed himself to Cortés with the courtesy when entering Tenochitlán: "Welcome to *your* city, my lord." The practice remains in effect. The typical Mexican, when receiving a prospective friend or associate in her home, may say, "Welcome to *your* humble abode." The home might be a million-dollar mansion, yet, in conformity with the proper formalities, it is a "humble abode." The saying is "my house is *your* house." That's literally the message. But it is a mere formality. Yet the saying is figurative but is to be taken as if it were literally true. It is not the case that it must be *either* true *or* untrue; it is *both* true *and* untrue; it is *neither* true *nor* untrue; it is a figure of speech and it is as if it were to be taken at face value. The guest is treated like a king or queen, even though the home may be poverty stricken.

Such formalities derive in part, as already noted, from Hispano-Arabic customs. The Spanish conqueror came to the Americas in search of riches. But wealth was only a means to the all-important end: to become someone important whom others meet with a slightly bowed head and a lowered voice, someone who paternalistically doles out patronage and favors. From that time on, formality of speech, comportment, dress, and appearance became paramount. A person worthy of proper respect must show his better side, whether that means being warm or demanding, generous or reprimanding, tolerant or coldly aloof. Appearances are important above everything else: they create the desired image that elicits proper acknowledgment of the individual. They set up a window through which to view the world that exists for the individual, and they form a shield protecting the individual's innermost self.

All this is courtesy. The word "courtesy" calls for formal standards of refinement, style in speech and behavior, manners that include an ostentatious show of hospitality, gentle demeanor, effusive friendship, and warm, personal interest in others. That is the generous side of the Mexican. The other side demands due respect from those of lower social rank. This other side can evince cold, rude, callous behavior toward those who are outside one's sphere of family, friends, business associates, and political circle. That side of the Mexican shows a face exuding pride and envy, respect and contempt, support and rejection, sympathy and disdain. For those on the Mexican individual's positive side, there are no bounds to her generosity, but for those who find themselves on her negative side, there may be no limits to her spite, cruelty, and vengeance.

Long afternoon lunches with friends, relatives, and associates, as well as the custom of socializing on Friday evenings after a week of work, testifies to the need to nurture human ties. The cult of human interrelationships provides spiritual food when loneliness would otherwise inhere. Quality time with special people fills a void. It brings out the best in women and men. It renews their sociability and their motivation in the workplace, where human interrelations rather than production-oriented goals are of prime importance. That, once more, is the positive side. On the negative side, Mexicans consider those people outside their intimate circle of friends, relatives, and associates to be just that: *on the outside*. These people merit little consideration at work or play. The non-Mexican whose knowledge is limited to stereotypes of Mexicans harbors a complex, confusing mix of the Mexicans' two complementary sides, and consequently they remain a mystery. A mystery, for they are looked upon as possessing contradictory and irreconcilable personality traits. A more adequate conception of the Mexican mind and manners would consider them not in terms of *contradictions* but of *complementarities*.

In Mexican interrelationships there can never be one thing without its complement. As complementarities, all aspects of the Mexican mind and manners are in a liquid embrace as they flow along with the changing currents of culture. This becomes evident, especially when we consider the ideal of interdependent, interrelated interactivity, insofar as the terms bear on the concept of complementarity. Western thought during the twentieth century has turned increasingly toward the notion of complementarity. It is not mere coincidence that quantum physicist Niels Bohr proposed a complementarity principle regarding the world of quanta. During the first two decades of the twentieth century, it seemed that the subatomic world was *neither* exclusively either thing-like *nor* energy-like; it was *neither* exactly particle *nor* wave. The problem is that the quantum world couldn't tolerate a phenomenon that was *both* wave-like *and* particle-like in the same instant. A perplexed physicist once coined the term "wavicle" for this bizarre subatomic unthing-thing. The term is quite apropos. A "wavicle" is *both* particle *and* wave, and at the same time it is *neither* particle *nor* wave. In the wave, there is the makings of a particle, and in the particle, there is a trace of a wave. Very roughly, this is Niels Bohr's complementarity rendition. Metaphorically, I would suggest, it is of the nature of *cultural complementarity*. Exactly what does this concept have to do with the problem at hand?

The Mexican people are not exclusively *either* cold *or* warm, caring *or* uncaring, tolerant *or* demanding. They manifest *both* the characteristics of the apparent oppositions of behavior, *or* they manifest *neither* of them but some mixture in between. Granted, one must maintain appearances above all else. But appearances alone do not the Mexican people make. Appearances are virtually worthless as far as the Mexican is concerned, were it not for her inner worth. Outward appearances and inner qualities, values and importance . . . or particle and wave: like love and marriage and horse and carriage, you can't have one without the other. This is because the one is interdependently interrelated and interactive with the other.

In times past, Mexicans tended to accept or reject a newcomer in terms of whether or not she was *buena gente* ("good people"). In addition to outward appearances, this focus rests on the person's inner worth, her capacity to acknowledge and practice the customary formalities, to say and do the right thing at the right time and the right place. Another popular expression now rarely heard in Mexico is *buena reata*. The meaning is comparable to *buena gente*. Literally it means "good rope." This is revealing. *Reata* in times past referred to a "rope" for tying, especially for joining mules or donkeys in single file for transportation of goods. The *reata* implies ties that allow for freedom of movement yet bind one to the whole of which one is a part. One has freedom, yet one is constrained; one belongs to a close-knit community, yet one has a degree of autonomy for self-expression and individual creativity. One's self and one's community are *complementarily intertwined*.

A *buena reata* or *buena gente* is the Mexican who knows when and how to work, as well as how to spend leisure time with family and friends and associates. It is a two-hour lunch at a downtown restaurant with a few margaritas and a congenial atmosphere spent chatting about trips to the United States and Europe, the latest soccer scores, politics, and family. Then it's off to the office to get some business done. *Buena gente* is a couple of automobile mechanics having lunch at the local restaurant in a popular neighborhood. While eating tacos and whistling at and offering sexual innuendoes to the young ladies passing by on the sidewalk, they are enjoying each other's company. There is hardly a thought of anybody or anything outside their little circle of family and friends. *Buena gente* is the administrator who is always ready to express sympathy, respond to a family emergency or misfortune, or lend a hand whenever possible, with respect to those who work under him. *Buena gente* is also the priest who is on a personal basis with his parishioners and admonishes them in a positive way and with a smile, while occasionally even giving them a comforting *abrazo*.

For the outsider or newcomer, the most effective approach at the outset is a show of humility, moderation in all things, respect for authority. The outsider may gradually enter into a less formal and more friendly association with the members of the group, observing them closely and taking up their expressions and gestures, learning, learning, learning, but never attempting to teach them how things are done elsewhere or how they should be done. First, a newcomer should keep his mind open and his mouth shut. Then he may very carefully and tentatively enter into the group's confidence by exercising the appropriate courtesies. There is hardly anything more ingratiating to Mexicans than the outsider who properly uses their slang, gestures as they gesture, tells a joke that happens to be "in," even though they've heard it dozens of times.

In sum, a person's inner worth is as important (and at times more important) than a person's background credentials, work ethic, skills, and talents. It is more a matter of turning on the charm than of efficiently and appropriately getting things done, more a matter of how she says what she says than of what she says, of how she does what she does than what she does. It is the individuality and the personal and emotional and intellectual uniqueness of the person that is most admired. In the United States, the law-abiding, talented, productive, effective, successful person usually commands the greatest respect. In Mexico, loyalty, generosity, sympathy, thoughtfulness, and personal charm, as well as social status, authority, prestige, and power, are often valued more highly. A person is not judged so much on the basis of material accomplishments as on the quality of her character. This is frequently more important than her technical skills and dedication to hard work. Ambition, industry, and furious activity are admired, but not as much as interpersonal relationships.

Blame or Shame?

Do you obey the law because you do not wish to be *blamed* for not doing so or because you don't want to suffer the *shame* of violating it? If you break the law and catch the blame for it, do you fear the guilt this will bring? People in the United States seemingly wish to avoid blame at any cost, so there is a deterrent regarding violating the law. A blame-free life is the ideal. Catholic Mexico, in contrast, is less caught up in guilt than are Protestant cultures. Blame is often not seen as the problem. Shame, on the other hand, is to be avoided at all cost. One obeys the law because one does not wish to suffer the shame of not doing so: one *obeys*, according to all outward appearances. But one might not necessarily *comply*.

Once again the dictum "I obey but I do not comply" says it effectively. "I pay my due respects by obeying the spirit of the law, even though the circumstances are not conducive toward my complying with the letter of that same law." This implies a split between *private* and *public domains*, between saintly composure in the home and streetwise, roguish conduct outside. It is the image of human interrelationships among friends, family, and associates in conflict with the image of hard knocks out there in the world, where each person must depend on his own resources. This might lead to the assumption that the notorious maxim of the colonial period, "I obey, but the sordid affairs of everyday life call for more practical measures," is basically an *either-or* affair. "I obey" brings along the baggage of the ideal image. "I do not comply" puts one in the cutthroat social environment. Things are not so simple, however. There is no genuine dualism in a sociocultural milieu of multiplicity, pluralism, hybridity, nonlinear and asymmetrical hierarchization. Between *private life* and *public life*, the home and the street, there is the *both-and* and the *neither-nor* offering a concoction of alternative responses, many of which are forthcoming in daily practices whenever and wherever.

In this manner, relations inherent in the interdependent, interrelated human interactions engulf customary polarities (colonizer/colonized, lord/serf, private/public, home/street) with alternatives. These alternatives lurk behind the scene, at any moment willing and ready to make their appearance and disrupt the action. *Both* the one side *and* the other side of the complementarity are essential. However, *neither* the one *nor* the other can be absolutely prioritized. In the first place, each side of the complementary pair needs the other one—they are *codependent*. In the second place, an alternative (in fact many alternatives) can at any given point make its presence felt, either explicitly or implicitly. The twin authoritarian pillars of Spanish colonial society, king and church, bred a hierarchical system in which *vergüenza* or "shame" takes precedence over *culpa* or "guilt." There's no harm in occasionally taking a subtle detour around the law, if appearances are maintained and if one can avoid getting caught. In Protestant cultures, individual conscience counts more; in Catholic cultures, appearances might take priority over conscience in regard to wrongdoing. As long as appearances are maintained, there is no loss of face. Someone who is caught red-handed must face the consequences, which involve loss of face and shame. That is a more serious issue than the revelation of one's guilt.

Blame

In recent years it has become customary to avoid blame whenever possible in the United States. Nobody is really to blame for anything, it seems. It's always somebody else's fault, or it's an act of God. The "Who me?" attitude is endemic. This, perhaps, is a sign of the times. There was Richard Nixon of Watergate whose statement of "confession" was, "Mistakes were made." There were Ronald Reagan and George Bush whose response was often "I don't recall" with respect to Irangate. Then there was Bill Clinton's "I did nothing improper." Following these and a host of other shining examples, people of all walks of life in North America make every effort to expurgate themselves from all culpability. Whenever the individual can place himself in a positive light, it's "me" exaggerated to the nth degree. When something is not as it should be, it's "Who, me? No way Joseee."

This attitude is nothing new in Mexico. It has prevailed since the colonial period. The "Who me?" syndrome is implicit in basic linguistic practices throughout the Hispanic community. I allude to the reflexive use of verbs entailing action or reaction on the part of inanimate objects and their interrelationships with human agents. If, say, I push my coffee cup off the table with my elbow, I might conveniently say in Spanish, "Se me cayó." Literally translated, this would be roughly, "It fell on me (to me)." Of course I was the agent of the action and the cup was the recipient. Yet my customary verbal expression makes the inverse out to be the case. It is as if the cup fell of its own accord and entirely against my will or effort to the contrary. It is as if I were absolving myself of all blame or guilt over the accident. Of course, it was an accident. I did not knock the cup over intentionally or through some malicious act. Yet in order to remain free of all guilt, it is as if I were to say that the cup acted on its own and was autonomous of my will and good intentions.

Comparable syntactic constructions abound. *Se me rompió mi camisa* ("My shirt tore itself on me [to me]"), *Se me mojó mi libro* ("My book got itself wet on me [to me]"—because I left it out in the rain), *Se me olvidó la cita* ("The appointment forgot itself on me [to me]"), and many other expressions, are of the same sort. Reflexivity gives the appearance of an inanimate object or a human capacity that nonetheless acts on its own and independently of the human agent. Naturally the Spanish speaker does not actually think of herself and her actions in the bizarre way suggested by the computer-like interpretations of the expressions in English. Yet she uses her language in this way, and it creates tendencies toward a particular attitude on the part of the individual and her interrelations with the world.

What, actually, do these linguistic nuances tell us? Perhaps not much. Not much, if we simply comment on these verbal practices. So, let's go a step further. Consider the possessive in English with respect to body parts. We tend to say "My head aches," "My arm was broken," "I had my appendix removed," and "My mind isn't functioning today." In Spanish, and above all the Spanish of Mexico, one would usually say *Me duele la cabeza* ("The head hurts to me"), *Se me rompió el brazo* ("The arm broke itself to me"), *Me quitaron el apéndice* ("They took out the appendix"), and *La mente no me funciona hoy* ("The mind isn't functioning for me today"). In each case it is as if the human agent were somewhere, at some focal center about which her body and mind and spirit, and indeed the entire universe, revolves. It is as if the agent were her own center of the universe, a universe whose center is everywhere—that is, wherever a human agent exists, there the center exists—and whose circumference is nowhere.

Don't get me wrong. I am by no means suggesting that all Mexicans rationalize their mistakes in the manner that seems to have become common for all people in the United States in recent decades. Apparently many people in the United States have become less prone to take responsibility for their actions. Many of us try to avoid accepting our share of the blame for any errors we might have committed or paying the consequences—many politicians in the United States are prime examples in this respect. Neither do I wish to imply that the recent wave of self-centeredness that seems to be sweeping this country is the stock-in-trade behavior of Mexicans. What I am saying is that the Spanish language has, at its roots, the implication that the speaking subject is an individual of intrinsic worth. This is not the hard-nosed individual of the North American sort who literally bulls his way through every problem. It is the individual whose inner worth enables him to win friends and influence enemies and hence often get his way.

The Mexican individual who is admired possesses an inner quality that shines forth in spite of the sordid conditions in which he might live. He has an inner worth that is revealed in the dignity he evinces. What is this dignity? It emerges from his modesty, his merging into the background while expressing adulation and eulogizing others, his gracious willingness to step aside to allow another person a place in the spotlight. It also emerges from his unwillingness to highlight his own self, to resort to braggadocio in order to attract attention, to fall into the practice of self-aggrandizement and self-praise. He becomes apologetic for what he expresses as his shortcomings. He expresses his insecurity over whether he can successfully carry out a task or not, whether he is capable of meeting his responsibilities, whether he will be able to perform adequately. This is not to say that a genuine sense of modesty exists. The individual might think he can move mountains; yet he maintains an admirable mode of composure. He never ceases understating his own talents, knowing quite well that he will be able to execute the task given him.

The basic difference between the Mexican and the North American is this: the Mexican stresses inner worth; it is the nature of his individuality, who he is, how effectively he enters into human relationships and keeps them properly oiled. The North American more frequently stresses outer worth, what he can do, what he has in terms of material possessions, his professional and technical background and training. Mexican individualism is more attuned to *who* one is, *how* one handles oneself, and *what* one knows and *how* one expresses oneself. North American individualism is more focused on *what* one can do, *what* one says about one's capacities, and *what* one is worth materially. The Mexican individual defines himself in terms of his opinions, which are his and nobody else's; hence he is eager on all occasions to express himself, for self-expression is expression of the individual. The North American individual might be opinionated, but he tends to keep matters more to himself. If he wishes to divulge his opinion, he often acknowledges that it rests on the basis of "I once read," "According to leading authorities," "My doctor says," and so on. In this manner, expression of his individualism is more a matter of his ability to cite authorities than of having developed his own ideas.

In the United States, those who command respect are talented, productive, successful, industrious, and dynamic. There is also some attention to loyalty, thoughtfulness, generosity, and a contemplative, introspective attitude. These are precisely the qualities that are highlighted in the Mexican mind, while raw talent, a hell-for-leather attitude toward human relationships, comportment at the workplace, and sheer productivity are to an extent played down. North Americans generally respect those who are well-known—our cultural icons and celebrities in recent years—for their recognized capacities. These capacities might include a politician who voted for a progressive education bill or a tax cut, a medical researcher who discovered a cure for a disease, a corporate executive who reenergized her company, or a teacher who won a national award. These qualities demand respect for the person on the basis of what she has done in the past. Mexicans tend to respect people for their professional position, social status, and above all their concern for proper personal relationships. These are qualities that require emotional investment: respect for the person is for the person's inner worth that is presumably the same, yesterday, today, and tomorrow.

The North American would like to set an example by demonstrating that she is a workaholic. The Mexican may see this as quite foolish, for the proper example is a matter of personal interrelations. The North American works hard and plays hard and does both to win. The Mexican works and plays among family, friends, and associates, chiefly for the purpose of deepening the bonds between them. The Mexican, like the North American, admires those who get ahead, even though she realizes she does not have the same competitive drive. However, she is more prone toward stressing her own inner worth, and she awaits the opportunity to show herself capable of reaching new heights of status, prestige, and power in the future. In general, North Americans judge people on the basis of their accomplishments and *what* they can do. Mexicans judge people on the basis of the kind of individual they are: whether they have character, whether they show consideration and thoughtfulness toward others, and *how* they perform. North Americans usually stress material needs, Mexicans more often stress emotional needs. North Americans see Mexicans as too emotional, the Mexicans see North Americans as too robotic. North Americans want zest in life, and it comes through buying power; Mexicans also want buying power, but it is considered a means toward quality of life.

After all is said and done, one must be aware that Mexico remains chiefly a paternalistic society weighted in favor of the upper class. Equality is hardly more than an ideal. Inequality is the norm based on gender, ethnic background, wealth, and social standing. For three centuries Mexico existed under a hierarchically structured, centralized colonial system. Within this system, the equally hierarchically patterned Catholic Church exercised paramount influence over lives and customs until the 1920s, when church-state separation finally became part of the Mexican revolutionary society. This in itself renders Mexico and the United States two quite separate yet *interdependently* and *interrelatedly* united worlds.

It might appear that in the last few paragraphs I erected a set of dualisms regarding the distinctions between North Americans and Mexicans. The problem is with language: it invariably brings along a satchel of apparent *either-or* dichotomies. However, assume that the differences and distinctions between the two cultures are not simply *contradictory,* but *contradictorily complementary,* such that in the best of all worlds, what the one lacks the other can contribute and vice versa. Then perhaps we can get into the proper mental flow. If so, we might consider the following Mexican trait and how it complements U.S. cultural tendencies.

"Excuse Me Just a Little Bit"

Mexicans love diminutives, going back to the pre-Hispanic fascination with statuettes and other minuscule items that abound among the artifacts found at archeological sites. It is in part the product of the Spanish language, which so liberally gives itself to diminutization, to *empequeñecimiento* (a monstrous noun meaning "the act of making small").

Diminutizing ideas, things, and happenings tends to deemphasize them. It puts them at the level of apparently relative unimportance. This habit of diminutizing complements the Mexican individual's tendency toward modesty, whether it is artificial and somewhat hypocritical or genuine. Of course, modesty is occasionally false modesty; hence, the act of diminishing is precisely to take attention away from the thing diminutized and toward the speaking subject. At the same time it is an act of diminishing the importance of that very speaking subject such that she appears of lesser importance than the subject she would like to present herself to be. She by no means considers herself of unimportance, but of an importance that is highlighted by a form of irony. The irony comes through emphasizing what *is not* the case in order to shift attention toward what *is* the case. In other words, she is to be taken as *neither* a matter of importance *nor* of unimportance, but rather in terms of her inner worth, which goes beyond ordinary *either-or* categories. The Mexican resists ordinary labels that tend to underrate individual worth.

Diminishment

Diminishment complements the act of *dissimulation* (discussed above). For over four hundred years the Amerindians, mestizos, mulattos, and occasionally even the criollos knew their place, and if they overstepped their bounds there was often retribution of some sort. Thus, as already noted, it became necessary to dissimulate. Anger and emotion, violence and tenderness, love and hatred are disguised. As a consequence, the individual tends to fade into the background, thus diminutizing herself. Although there is resignation and humility in her voice, she retains a certain challenge vis-à-vis her onlooker's eyes and mind. When she begs her pardon, quite often the response given her is, *No hay de que*. The phrase is difficult to translate, perhaps "There's no need," "It's nothing," "Think nothing of it," or "Pretend it never happened." Thus her onlooker diminutizes himself also, ironically, such that attention is diverted away from him and at the same time drawn toward him.

In the marketplace one overhears *papitas* ("little potatoes"), *carnitas* ("little bits of meat"), *frijolitos* ("small beans"), *blanquillos* ("little eggs"). At work there are *papelitos* ("little sheets of paper"), *chambita* ("this little job"), *cochecito* ("little car"), *despachito* ("little office"), *colita* ("little waiting line"). At home one uses the words *salita* ("little living room"), *camita* ("little bed"), *platito* ("little plate"), *salesita* ("little salt"), and so on. Diminution has many uses and as many interpretations. A woman forty-five years of age can be addressed as *señorita* if she is unmarried, and at times even if she is married. This is a compliment. In contrast, if one wishes to demean a man of forty-five one can call him *señorito*. One can refer to one's *zapatitos* ("little shoes") that are old yet immaculately shined with affection and pride. In contrast, one might speak of one's *pantaloncito* ("little pants") or *vestidito* ("little dress") in less than endearing terms if it is old or out of fashion. Diminutives can mean the opposite of that which they would ordinarily imply in other respects. If I invite you for a *cervecita* ("a little beer") and a *taquito* ("a little taco"), we might be in for a few hours of beer belches and taco chomps. Yet it all started with a couple of diminutives.

There are various forms of diminutives: *ito(a)*, *illo(a)*, *iño(a)*. Mexicans use all these diminutives in forming intimate personal relationships and in describing themselves and their everyday affairs. As the popular cha-cha-cha song of the 1950s goes: *Tengo una muñequita, de boquita chiquita* ("I have a little doll of a girl, with a tiny little mouth"). An important aspect of the institution of diminutives is, once again, an emphasis on style and form rather than substance. This stems from the habit of making suggestions, vague illusions, and indirect allusions, instead of saying things outright. There is beauty in keeping what one wishes to say somewhat vague and uncertain, and in downplaying its attracting any attention. This diminishes disharmony between persons, viewpoints, and attitudes and brings about more harmonious personal interrelations and actions. It helps create a more intimate environment in which one's inner worth takes priority over extrinsic values.

The tendency, however, brings about a diminishment of the dissembling individual to the extent that she can at times appear to fade out of existence. As the popular saying goes when one is asking permission: *Con permisito* ("Excuse me just a little bit," or "If you will allow me just a little bit"). The irony, of course, is that permission is permission. It is not a material commodity that comes in large or small quantities but an intangible quality. Yet it is treated as if it were a substantive thing. This tends to desubstantialize the speaking subject, to convert her into form rather than essence, style rather than content. Yet there always remains a personal touch that keeps interrelationships alive.

North Americans might tend to view Mexicans' disposition for diminutizing things in a negative light. How can they take themselves positively and seriously if they reduce everything to a minimum? North Americans must think big, and the bigger the better. Mexicans tend to look at the world through a magnifying glass with the concave side toward them; North Americans tend to look at it through the same magnifying glass, but with the convex side toward themselves. A major (though not *the* major) difference is that a Mexican businessperson would rather think small and make a large profit per item sold, while the North American businessperson thinks big and makes big profits on a massive number of small profit margin items moved over to the customer. It's not a matter of one method necessarily being either better or worse than the other. They are just different. That's all.

Making Deals

Speaking of business, let's consider life in the workplace for a moment. There it's the same story. North American and Mexican characteristics are not diametrically opposed, but there exists a certain tendency toward differences in their attitudes and behavior that can at times reach extreme manifestations.

Mexicans, Octavio Paz (1961, 9–64) writes, delight in fantasy and dreams. North Americans, in contrast, usually wish to plant their feet on rock-hard reality. Mexicans are relatively suspicious of others; North Americans tend to be trusting. Mexican nature tends toward pessimism, in spite of the fantasy and dreams; North Americans are by and large optimistic. Mexicans are cynical, skeptical, sarcastic, given to cruel, biting jokes; North Americans prefer lighthearted jests, friendly teasing, slapstick comedy, and relatively innocent banter. Mexicans revel in novelty, foreign things; North Americans are more animals of habit, wanting the same as always and tending to shun foreign ways. Above all, North Americans tend to highlight strength, willpower, and raw physical power, doing and accomplishing; Mexicans often stress the individual as a person of contemplation, thought, and understanding, who is at ease with people of all types and from all walks of life. In short, North Americans are more prone to admire hard work, organization, and efficiency; Mexicans admire the individual who also shows personal interest in individuals and is sympathetic regarding their problems.

On the North American side, there is impersonal structure, productivity, and proficiency; on the Mexican side, there is group effort grounded in personal relationships. The North American entrepreneurial hero usually gets things done through astute managerial techniques; the Mexican hero stands out as much as his North American counterpart, but through generating a desire on the part of the group to work together. The chief difference is between abstract human interrelations and patrimonial, paternalistic interrelations. On the one hand, in the United States one works everything out on paper and expects the corporation to run as planned, and if it does so, then there has been success. On the other hand, in Mexico one has little faith in paper theories, methods, techniques and strategies; rather, one relies on inner resources, personal charm, and the ability to work things out on the spot. We want things done according to a plan; they improvise.

Success in Mexico is often gauged by dreams and visions and talk about doing things in the future. Still, to a great extent, the Mexicans live for today, for the dream itself, instead of rolling up their sleeves and working for its realization in the future. Consequently, grand projects often don't take on the same urgency in Mexico. For example, a project may begin with one administrator. Then a new administrator enters and abandons the project because it was not his baby. Perhaps money in the coffers dwindled and the project could not be completed. Public works begun are a tribute to the person who was instrumental in overseeing their initiation, but unfinished they are the deceased testimony of dreams unfulfilled. In the United States, in contrast, projects are more frequently brought to completion, and once completed, they are maintained, in spite of the fact that the project's prime mover is no longer the authority figure.

In short, when things aren't going as planned, North Americans strive to make them right. Mexicans tend to take whatever comes *(aguantar)*. They often assume that trying to change things might make matters worse. So they improvise with what they have.

The Way Things Might Appear in Mexico

I repeat: Mexican society is traditionally hierarchical, patrimonial, paternalistic, authoritarian. Status and social and professional standing are the byproducts of obtaining and exercising power and authority, which is never shared but remains within the sphere of influence of the president, administrator, director, boss, teacher, priest, or the father of the family.

This is not to imply that the Mexicans, with respect to whatever activity, do not work together with their leader. The leader got where he is by the strength of his will, determination, physical appearance, personal charm, ability to hold people's attention, his way with the opposite sex, his impressive sentimental and emotional displays, and, finally, to an extent his background training and professional aplomb. He is able to get the most out of the personnel under him by the force of his charisma, not by cajolery, demands, threats, punishment, or, when all else fails, by salary increases.

Aguantar now comes into view with greater force. If one's leader has all the personal qualities, one follows, in spite of undesirable working conditions and low pay. One follows because one feels admiration, dedication, loyalty to one's superior. So one puts up with one's place in the organization or community, often in mute, passive silence. Traditionally, questioning authority is looked on as a serious offense. Direct confrontations are relatively rare due to the authoritarian nature of the culture and the sensitivity of Mexicans toward anything that appears as a loss of dignity. *Aguantar:* the bane and the beauty of Mexican ways. *Aguantar* can become the reason for advantages taken, and abuses and violation of the law, but also the reason for the smooth functioning of social and cultural processes that to the outsider appear much like a chaotic mess and the wanton exploitation of humans by humans. The community, in its own way, works together quite effectively, within HC environments, PC time, and in nonlinear fashion.

Yes, *aguantar*, because one's leader is who she is and because of family and national traditions. Not necessarily because of what the leader, family members, or nation have accomplished in the past, but because of the compelling image they command. This is comparable to the romantic notion of the individual who is capable of standing out and taking charge, no matter what the situation. It is also comparable to family and patriotic pride in the face of setbacks. Mexican leaders are excellent at formulating ideas and articulating them, but they occasionally fall short in the implementation and execution department. When the vision is not realized, blame is often placed elsewhere. This can create tension, ill will, and difficulties at all levels. Yet the show usually goes on. By a comparable token, members of the family occasionally commit shameful acts, but they are pushed under the rug whenever possible, and the family maintains appearances. The nation might fail to measure up to the world's expectations, yet patriotism does not suffer a whit.

The dream is what's important. Dream the dream, and when it fails to come to fruition, create another dream. Mexicans dream, but always with their eyes wide open. Deep down they know their dreams are dreams, and when one dream fails there is always an unlimited number of dreams available to take its place. Indeed, life is a dream. North Americans and most Westerners, in contrast, take their dreams much more seriously, but without awareness that they are dreams: the dreams are for them reality just as it is.

How do Mexicans dream the dream? Through awareness that what *is*, could always have been something *other than* what it *is*, by taking themselves dead seriously, but not their social, political, economic, and cultural world. They dream by virtue of their awareness of themselves and their world, taking much of it with a grain of salt, through humor, cynicism, irony, skepticism, darkly cryptic remarks, and laughter. They would like to avoid bad news about their dreams (projects, the workplace, family, circle of friends and associates). They would rather just dream the dream. Consequently they often place more emphasis on courtesy and social graces than on what is actually accomplished. Interrelations between friends and associates often take precedence over technical know-how, experience, and organizing ability. The workplace, school, political arena, and church thus have a familial, homelike atmosphere. As a result, adulation, flattery, and loyalty toward she who has risen to the top are often comparable to the attitude toward mother or father: the chief characteristic of maternalism or paternalism. The upside is that this adds a certain intimacy to human interrelations. The downside is that this attitude toward superiors can pander to sensitive egos. The attitude takes on the guise of support for those in positions of authority, whereas those who occupy the lower rungs on the social ladder could perhaps better their condition with a little criticism and perhaps even some civil action.

Adulation, flattery, and pandering to upper-class Mexicans by lower-class Mexicans is gradually changing. A striking indication of this change occurred during the first two years of President Ernesto Zedillo's (1994–2000) administration. Zedillo criticized individual politicians, jurists, and bureaucrats, along with all three branches of the government, for their empty formalities. On numerous occasions he downplayed his own importance and asked that his audience resist the temptation to indulge him. Was this false modesty or was it a sincere attempt to downgrade customary formalities and patronizing practices? It's difficult to tell. Certainly generations will pass before deeply entrenched customs change substantially, and before straightforward honesty displaces flattery as the norm.

With the diversion in this chapter through the flows of everyday Mexican life, I trust Mexico's mix of interdependent cultural tendencies and propensities have become a bit more intelligible. Indeed, Mexican cultural flows play on *contradictory complementarity* in the most complex manner imaginable. With this in mind, we give further consideration to some Mexican cultural dispositions within the social, historical, and political arenas.

Further Reading

Anzaldúa 1987, Castañeda 1995, Dealy 1992, Foster 1989, Hinds and Tatum 1985, Ingham 1986, Ramírez Berg 1992, Riding 1989, Rowe and Schelling 1991, Stavans 1990, Vélez-Ibáñez 1996. Fiction and essay: Fuentes 1971a, Lawrence 1951, Lowry 1965, Romero 1967, Zea 1969, 1992.

Notes

1. For the following I owe a debt to De Mente 1996, Shorris 1992, and Stavans 1995.

11

Making Today's Mexico: Or, How and Why Are There Two Mexicos?

A New Look at Machismo and Malinchismo

Novelist José Agustín (1990) writes that President Miguel Alemán (1946–1952) is one of the chief culprits responsible for the country's rampant *charrismo*, *guarurismo*, and endemic corruption. *Charrismo* is from *charro* and refers to a "cowboy" type, usually considered a coarse, ill-bred, tawdry, and uncultured person romanticized in dress and style in the mariachi bands that have become popular in many parts of the United States. *Guarurismo* is from *guarura*, a bodyguard, an armed individual accompanying wealthy and/or powerful officials, who themselves often become perpetrators of violence.

Alemán, alias "Ali Baba and his forty thieves," was responsible for the new wave of capitalism. It included foreign investments in Mexico as never before, attractive enticements to Mexican citizens with promises of enrichment if they kept their money in the country, a snub for the working class, and the rise of crooked bureaucratic practices. At the same time, Alemán actively promoted the arts. He commissioned the trio of great muralists, Diego Rivera, José Clemente Orozco, and David Alfaro Siqueiros, to create works in numerous public places. Those were the days of comedians Tin Tán (Germán Valdéz) and the internationally renowned Cantínflas (Mario Moreno). Those days saw the golden age of Mexican cinema, starring the likes of María Félix, Dolores Del Río, and

Pedro Infante, and films by the Spanish director Luis Buñuel. In music, Cuban Pérez Prado moved his big band sounds to Mexico, where he influenced popular music for a couple of decades.

Nevertheless, most conservative Mexican traditions continued virtually unchanged. For instance, Diego Rivera created a mural at the extravagant Hotel del Prado in the center of Mexico City that he entitled *Sunday Afternoon Dream in Alameda Park* in honor of a park situated across the street from the hotel. The socialist painter included the phrase "God doesn't exist" by nineteenth-century Mexican atheist Ignacio Ramírez. The staunch Catholic public, seeing this as a desecration of Mexican nationalism, reacted so vehemently that Rivera was forced to remove it from his work. (Actually desecration of traditions had hardly changed when, some four decades later, Loco Valdéz, a comedian with a wildly popular TV show, referred to the venerated Amerindian President Don Benito Juárez as "Bomberito" ["Little Fireman"]. His show was immediately canceled.)

Charrismo and *guarurismo*, along with a term that became popular in the 1970s and 1980s, *grilla*, have to do with Mexico's particular form of *machismo*. (*Grilla* refers to Mexico's political environment replete with rumor, hearsay, scandal, slander, backstabbing, and corruption.) *Charrismo*, *guarurismo*, and *grilla* aid and abet the notorious and notoriously cruel, malicious, barbarous expressions of *machismo* with respect to masculine/feminine, dominant/subservient, active/passive, and other binary oppositions. Women are especially singled out as the focus of this mind-set, which is more prevalent in Mexico than in most other Western societies. Traditionally, and quite unfortunately, women are to be possessed violently and even sadistically if the occasion demands or, alternatively, with flattery, flirtation, charm, intimate gestures. The reaction of the Spanish father-conqueror and the Amerindian mother-conquered tells the beginning, however mythical and however contrived, of this practice in the minds of many Mexicans today.[1]

According to the mythical image, the Spanish male satisfied his sexual urges on the conquered and supposedly inferior Other. This Other was occasionally devalued, sometimes even dehumanized. The mestizo, product of this often violent union, lived with the stigma of abandonment by the father, who was somewhere else pursuing other conquests. Even when the Spaniard stuck around, perhaps entering into marriage with the object of his sexual desires, there might remain a certain Catholic shame over what had been done. This shame revealed itself in resentment over the existence of the male mestizo offspring, who derived from his mother what he often considered his undesirable characteristics. The mestizo at least sensed some form of supremacy over his Amerindian mother, which compensated somewhat his lesser status at the side of his father. This sense of heightened social status in comparison to his mother played a role in creating the particular Mexican attitude toward women. Consequently the mestizo male was characterized, or wished to characterize himself, in terms of brute strength, masculinity, the imposition of his will, and his capacity to conquer all odds, especially regarding his relations with the opposite sex. Mexican machismo combined the Spanish-Arabic sense of honor with the Amerindians' humiliation over the conquest. At least this is how Samuel Ramos (1962) characterizes the Mexican myth.

Women, as a counterpart to the macho mentality, manifested a certain tendency to become martyrs. Those suffering souls have been embodied in the myth of the *llorona,* who drowned her children in a river to spare them the hardships of life and is now condemned to wander about, especially at night, mourning her loss. Of course the macho mentality is more myth than reality as well. It is the fantasy and the dream of many mestizos to exercise dominion. And if the object of that dominion can only be women, then he will have to settle for that. At least he is dominant; at least he lives up to the myth, in however impoverished a fashion. If the mother has been brutalized by the father, then at least she has her children, with special privilege granted to the male child. As befitting her martyr status, she denies herself and indulges her children. She becomes the "saintly mother" for her mestizo offspring, who express uncommitted love and veneration for her. But what is her condition, really? Suffering, exhausted, indecisive, uncertain, often verbally beaten into submission; and if that is not enough, she sometimes acquires piercing feelings of guilt. The myth of the "macho" father and the "suffering" mother is replete with aberrations that belie that very myth. The mythical mother gives her all to her husband and especially her children. Yet she may be caught up in vanity, pride, narcissism, sometimes ignoring her husband's desires and her children's needs. All this, I must emphasize, is myth. But when the myth lingers in the mind, reality is always somewhere trailing along behind.

The myth is a double-edged sword. Why do Mexicans venerate the mother-martyr? Where did this idea of the mother as sacrificial victim come from? Suffering appears as an indispensable accompaniment to love and marriage. At the same time, in terms of the practical affairs of domestic life, women in many ways rule the roost. They organize the household, dole out punishment in the absence of the father, and make virtually all decisions regarding domestic affairs. They take care of their duties with efficient dispatch and take pride in doing so. At home they are virtually the boss. Where, then, is the abnegation? The uncertainty and indecision? The vacillation? The frailty? Why do they not exercise the same determination with respect to other affairs? Why doesn't their pride in their competence at home and in female circles carry over into the larger society? Mexican women's admirable capacity to shoulder their limited responsibilities so effectively is their response to their victimization in the larger society. That, perhaps, is their greatest inner strength and a mark of their mythified weakness.

Strength and weakness, wife and mistress, lover and victim, mother and martyr, saint and sinner. Who is she, this archetypal Mexican woman? As noted above, there are at least two archetypes: María and Malintzín or Malinche. María is the mother of Christ, embodied in the Virgin of Guadalupe image in Mexico, where the deeply rooted Guadalupana (Marianist) cult reigns. Malinche was Cortés's mistress and betrayed her people. Margo Glantz (1995) writes how Malinche became translator, messenger, and mistress to Cortés, who with her sired Martín Cortés, the mythical primordial mestizo. Thus Malinche became mediator and intermediary through language and then passed from maid to mistress to messenger. Messenger because in the chronicles Malinche is recorded as a *faraute*, a "messenger," who, in the theater of the day in Spain, was a character, elaborately and often clownishly garbed, who appeared and gave the audience a few clues regarding what they were soon to see. Another term that appears in the chronicles in conjunction with the *faraute* is *bullicio* ("noise," "racket," "uproarious activity"). *Bullicio* is noise that has no meaning, nonsensical, as was apparently the case of this strange new language that met the conquerors.

Moreover, according to the myth, Malinche also performed the function of an *entremetida* ("intruder," "meddler," "intervenor"). As such, she is a mediator but hardly a moderator. She is a go-between, a penetrator of two languages and two cultures and two colliding classes of humans from those cultures. As *faraute* bringing *bullicio* yet reducing the *bullicio* through her *entremetida* acts, Malinche is an intermediary merging audience and actors. Conquerors and conquered were both actors and spectators in that great drama. Both sides invented an imaginary world they themselves played out to the hilt. For the conquerors, what happened was destined to have happened as an extension of the region-inspired "reconquest" of Spain from the Moors. For the conquered, what happened was also fated: the prophesied return of the shamed god, Quetzalcoatl, to reap vengeance on all.

Surprisingly enough (or perhaps it was to be expected), Cortés was dubbed by the Amerindians "señor Malinche." He was the incorporation, the embodiment, of "Marina la voz," or even "María la voz." Malinche brought sense from nonsense; Cortés used this sense to reap destruction and establish a new order. Malinche announced the tragedy that was soon to transpire on that stage now called the Valley of Mexico; Cortés became the villain and Moctezuma the victim. Equally surprisingly, some chroniclers refer to Cortés as "Cortés Malinche." Cortés is the individual. Malinche becomes the surname, the generality, the community, in which communion takes place through intervention, intermediation. Malinche is the mediator. She is the mother of Mexicans who betrayed her people and got laid by Cortés. Everything is wrapped into one grand mythical image.

The Virgin of Guadalupe is one of Mexico's principal images and merits contemplation. Defined as the Mother of Mexico, as an expression of national consciousness, and as the ultimate archetype of the feminine incorporation of the Mexican heart and soul, Guadalupe is the shadow and the mirror of all Mexicans. The Amerindian goddess Tonantzín and the Virgin of Guadalupe as Tonantzín's Catholic counterpart merge and mesh along the contact zone between peninsular and Amerindian cultures. They become, at that contact zone, orthographically *Guadantzín* (Guadalupe + Tonantzín = Guadantzín). Guadantzín is a cultural hybrid par excellence. Malintzín-Malinche, the other mask presented by the archetypal mother-goddess, the violated one, merges with Guadalupe to create the image of mother and mistress, messenger and mediator, intermediary and intervenor. The fusion and confusion of these images produces one of Mexico's most supreme examples of hybridity manifesting *both* one characteristic *and* the other in an image that is *neither* the one *nor* the other. *Guadalupanism*, the practice of this hybridity, becomes in David A. Brading's (1973) words "neoaztequism," an anticonquest, anti-Gachupín, and to an extent even an anti-Catholic (i.e., Catholicism in the orthodox European sense) image and force.[2]

This brief return to the past allows us to sense with greater force how Mexican cultures can live with HC meanings within PC time to a considerably greater extent than mainstream U.S. culture. Mexican traditions are alive. They are embodied in every Mexican; they manifest themselves through every utterance, every gesture, every act. Let us now turn to another theme running through Mexico's history and influencing its present.

Two Mexicos?

Octavio Paz in *The Other Mexico* (1970) alludes to one Mexico, that of modernity, consumerism, and bright lights. Then there's the Other Mexico. This is the Mexico of the Guadalupe-Tonantzín and Guadalupe-Malinche tradition. It remains occult until making its terrible presence *felt*—such as in the October 2, 1968, massacre of hundreds of reform-minded protesters at a plaza in Mexico City called Tlatelolco.

For a long time, something about Paz's qualification of Mexican society rubbed me the wrong way. It was just another dualistic split and I was trying my best to avoid them. Then came Guillermo Bonfil Batalla's *México Profundo* (1996). Bonfil Batalla's interpretation, apparently of dualistic nature, also places things in a different light. The author presents Mexico on two planes: (1) *Imaginary Mexico* reveals the collapse of the "developmental model" the West has imposed on most of the "developing" areas of the world, with disastrous consequences, and (2) *México Profundo* contains the traditional human resources Mexico has always possessed and should use to construct the nation's authentic future.

But I am getting ahead of myself. Let me backtrack a little and explain what I mean by the "developmental model." The idea had it in the 1950s and 1960s that Latin America could develop in the same way the United States developed. The keyword was *modernize*. Modernization, U.S. style, would bring vigorous industrialization, education for all, democratization with clean elections, and a politically aware, nationalistically minded middle class that would emerge with the sole purpose of fomenting development. In order to modernize after World War II, many Latin American nations adopted the *import substitution industrialization* (ISI) model. The idea was that the Great Depression had limited exports, and the area had to begin producing its own goods. This was done by protecting big business and industry from foreign competition through high tariffs, prohibiting importation of many luxury goods, and slapping quotas on imports of other goods. Imports used to further economic development were given top priority. Mexico, in particular, began entering the ISI dance after the populist reforms of the Cárdenas period.

ISI was the capitalist way. During the 1960s a socialist alternative, *dependency theory* (DT), entered the scene. It went something like this. After World War II the world's capitalist economy expanded by leaps and bounds. A division of labor emerged in this global system, roughly between the industrialized countries (the *center*) and the less developed countries (the *periphery*). The central, developed areas demanded agricultural products and minerals. The peripheral areas needed capital to bring about their modernization. Exporting raw goods brought revenue. With this money, a capital intensive industrial base was established, following the U.S. and European modernization model. Wages were kept low in the factories, the mines, and the countryside in order to generate money for industrial development. Materials for that development in the form of manufactured goods became more and more expensive in comparison to raw goods. Concomitantly, an increasing volume of agricultural products and minerals were required to buy the same amount of manufactured goods. Wages deteriorated even more, and Mexico fell further behind. The peripheral zones, according to DT, were nurturing the central zones while becoming themselves increasingly undernourished.

This center-periphery model DT proposed was gobbledygook as far as ISI was concerned. According to the capitalist ISI model of development proceeding along the lines of the United States and Europe, an aggressive middle class would arise in Latin America whose interests would focus neither exactly on the center nor on the periphery. Middle-class citizens would be obsessed with improvement of their nation as a whole. They would bring about development by the force of their dynamism. However, the ISI hypothesis was problematic, due fundamentally to four factors. First, there was no relatively coherent middle-class consciousness in Latin America. So-called middle-class professionals did not see their status as an end in itself, but a stepping-stone to the more respectable upper class. In other words, the hidalgo mind-set persisted. Second, education for all, improvement of wages and working conditions and higher wages, and social programs were not on the middle-class agenda. Middle-class and upper-class politicians passed legislation with an eye toward protecting their own interests rather than helping the disadvantaged classes. This hindered the development of democracy and the creation of a conscious and conscientiously educated citizenry. Third, industrialization in the United States and Europe was in the beginning *labor intensive*. It required masses of workers. Middle-class and upper-class Mexican entrepreneurs wanted nothing to do with labor intensive development. They would be satisfied with no less than the most advanced technology, which set the grounds for *capital intensive* development. This type of development was too expensive for frail national economies and provided relatively few jobs. Fourth, businessmen and factory owners, wary of unstable political conditions, wanted big profits now. That way they could get rich quickly and get out if political and social conditions deteriorated. Capital intensive development calls for a relatively small force of skilled laborers and few unskilled laborers. Most of the area's labor was unskilled. Unemployment remained high as a consequence. Because few Mexicans had plenty of money that they were willing to invest in their country, investors from the United States and Europe were invited into Mexico, especially during the 1950s and 1960s. The result of all this? Relatively few jobs, low wages for unskilled labor, and expensive imported goods. DT saw all this as the consequence of misguided ISI policies.

The dream of ISI modernization had followed the "trickle-down theory." The reasoning was this. If the upper classes could find the key to prosperity, they would expand their holdings and create more jobs. Due to keen competition in the marketplace, wages would increase, educational and social programs would expand due to aggressive action on the part of the working classes, and a more equitable system would emerge: democracy in the U.S. mold. But this did not happen. The answer, as far as DT was concerned, was to socialize. Bring the economy under state control in order to create a foundation for equitable development. During the 1970s, under Presidents Luís Echeverría (1970–1976) and José López Portillo (1976–1982), statism became rampant, and populism became the modus operandi. Echeverría threw off his business suit, donned a *guayabera* ("*guayabera* politics" they called it, after the open-necked, loose-fitting shirt common in the Caribbean area) and tried his turn at rubbing elbows with workers and peasants. These populist tactics caused foreign investors to become uneasy with the threat of nationalization. Domestic investors began eyeing banks in Texas and elsewhere as a safe haven for their money. Peasants invaded private lands, and worker unrest became more evident. To top it all off, students began protesting and guerrilla movements began emerging in the countryside.

Then came the oil. State-owned Petróleos de México (PEMEX) discovered vast new oil fields in Tabasco and northern Chiapas, as well as off the coasts of Tabasco and Campeche. Between 1972 and 1977, oil production increased dramatically, as Mexico's proven oil reserves rose to 72 billion barrels, fifth place in the world. The world price of oil jumped in 1979, quickly doubling PEMEX earnings. A mood of euphoria overtook the country. Mexico could finally leave underdevelopment behind and join in the consuming frenzy with the best of the affluent West. As President López Portillo put it, Mexico in the past had to manage poverty, but now was the time to manage wealth. Mexico would soon become a member of the league of opulent nations. At least that was the dream.

Businesses thrived, and the Mexican government began expanding its economic and social programs at a dramatic rate, much of it with borrowed money under the assumption that oil would pay the debt. Although massive corruption cost the country billions of dollars, black gold held its charms. Pump it out and sell it, and fortune for all would be just around the corner. Between 1978 and 1981 economic growth rose to 8.5 percent annually. However, by 1978, export of manufactured goods had begun to lag, food exports were dropping, and importation of food staples was on the increase. To make matters worse, the oil boom had created an overvalued peso. This meant that exported goods went at higher prices, which hurt competition. The bottom soon fell through. In 1981 the world recession brought about a glut of oil on the international level, and prices dropped. The Mexican government continued to borrow money to make ends meet. In 1982 the country's debt had risen to $82 billion, approximately 60 percent of the gross domestic product. Economic growth was slowing drastically, plants were shut down, and unemployment was on the rise. President López Portillo was backed into a corner.

The Mexican president once proclaimed that he would defend the peso "like a dog." The barking dog had now lost his bite. López Portillo suspended foreign exchange of money for the first time in Mexican history. He then nationalized the banks and froze all foreign accounts, blaming the economic crisis on the rich who had exported their capital out of the country with the remark that "we cannot stand around with our arms crossed while they tear out our guts." To López Portillo's way of thinking, this served as justification for a 75 percent devaluation of the peso. When the "bad dog," President López Portillo, left office, he built an impressive mansion on a hill northwest of Mexico City. The Mexicans later referred to it as *El cerro del perro* ("the dog's hill"). López Portillo has gone by the name of "López Porpillo" ("López because he's a crook"), as in the saying *Encarcélenlo porpillo* ("Put him in jail for being crooked").

Where are the myths of Mexico in all this? ISI, following the idea that Mexico's inner resources have the makings of equitable development, failed in part because the conquerors were the haves and the conquered were the have-nots. DT, following the idea that structural changes should be imposed from above, failed in part because the haves were still the conquerors and the have-nots were the conquered. Conquerors and conquered, Guadantzín, and macho images: myths, with reality trailing along somewhere in the shadows. The myths of the past are still alive.

That is one interpretation. Now for Bonfil Batalla's view of the ISI-DT debacle from the Imaginary Mexico/México Profundo perspective.

What Happened to the Other Mexico?

Both ISI and DT, private enterprise with good intentions and statism with equally good intentions, were to an extent tried and tested in partial, piecemeal, and haphazard ways: ISI chiefly during the 1950s and 1960s, and DT during the 1970s. Both failed miserably. Why? Because, writes Bonfil Batalla, Mexico is not one and homogeneous. It never was and it never will be. It is actually two. It is México Profundo and Imaginary Mexico, Mexico according to its traditions and Mexico according to the image created of it by the upper crust aspiring to become a copy of the United States.

Two Mexicos

The idea is not exactly original, though Bonfil Batalla gives it a unique twist. However, I would suggest that there are actually more than two Mexicos. Mexico is certainly not one and *homogeneous;* neither is it merely two. It is plural: multicultural domains are the name of the game making up a radically *heterogeneous* milieu. In anthropologist Renato Rosaldo's words, Mexico and Latin America are "caught between traditions that have not yet gone and a modernity that has not yet arrived. From its hybrid position between tradition and modernity, the challenge for Latin America is to construct democratic culture and knowledge without succumbing either to the temptations of elite art and literature or to the coercive forces of mass media and marketing" (Rosaldo 1995, xi).

Rosaldo refers to Néstor García Canclini's (1993, 1995) hybridity thesis. García Canclini writes that modern and high culture is "hegemonic," while traditional and popular cultures are usually "subaltern." The nation-state has incorporated popular cultures into national culture for the purpose of legitimatizing it and its people at the same time that it made a concerted effort to eliminate it. However, the people resisted, revealing in the process that Mexican cultures do not follow strict "hegemonic" lines, nor are they nor have they ever been homogeneous; rather, they are heterogeneous through and through. But I'm getting ahead of myself again. Let's slow down and take a further look at the two Mexicos.

Criollo nationalism after independence foregrounded Guadalupana and Quetzalcoatl and the idea of an exclusive Amerindian flavor of Mexico that radically set it apart from Spain. But the actual presence of Amerindians was almost completely ignored. The ideological conception of the mestizos after the revolution drilled its taproot of nationalism into the country's Amerindian past. According to the revolutionary rhetoric, Mexico enjoyed a glorious past violently disrupted by the conquest.

However, the mestizos triumphed against all odds, bringing about the reforms of 1857 and the Mexican Revolution of 1910–1920. The latter movement was the culmination of mestizo expression, whose pre-Hispanic origins could not be denied any longer. Murals by Rivera, Siqueiros, and Orozco soon adorned government palaces and public places, glorifying precolonial Mexico. Amerindian symbols pervaded historical and cultural allegories in literature and the theater. Music took up Amerindian instruments and rhythms. Architecture began sporting Aztec and Mayan themes. Archaeology and folklore became the vogue. They were considered noble nationalistic enterprises and the most respectable of intellectual pastimes. Museums took their place as the repositories of ethnocentricity. The venerated Aztec emperor who replaced Moctezuma and fought against the Spaniards to the bitter end, Cuauhtémoc, staked his claim as Mexico's original national and cultural hero.

Criollo nationalism had ignored the actual presence of the Amerindians; mestizo nationalism could not. Mestizos and Amerindians became ubiquitous in revolutionary tales, painting, literature, and folk customs. Political rhetoric eulogized them, and Emiliano Zapata's image embellished nationalistic images alongside Miguel Hidalgo and the Mexican flag. Popular art and handicrafts were cherished as symbols affirming the special character of mestizo and Amerindian Mexico. Now, it seemed, México Profundo was finally enjoying its rightful place. But Bonfil Batalla writes that if the Amerindian really existed and if México Profundo is really real, and if the Amerindians "possessed positive and preservable values, then revolutionary Mexico proposed to 'redeem' them, incorporating them into national culture and, through it, 'universal' [i.e., Western] culture" (Bonfil Batalla 1995, 113–114).

The problem is that México Profundo lost out in the euphoric postrevolutionary days. Shortly after the revolution, moderation prevailed regarding the "Amerindianization" of society. The mestizo should be Amerindianized so that Amerindian culture would not be seen as barbarous, incomprehensible, or merely exotic. But mestizos should not adapt to Amerindian ways too seriously, for modernization Western style was the chief goal. Consequently, there was a concerted effort to westernize the Amerindian and at the same time Amerindianize Mexican culture.

However, with respect both to Europeanized Amerindian cultures and European cultures Amerindianized, heterogeneity stood out. Amerindian cultures in Mexico are the most diverse in all Latin America. Granted, the Amerindian Other, what Bonfil calls Imaginary Mexico, gives the appearance of unity. Yet diversity goes deep—Amerindian diversity combined with the diversity between México Profundo and Imaginary Mexico. Since there are no inner ties uniting those who dominate and rule in the country and those who are powerless, the distinction between Amerindian diversity and the diversity that exists in spite of Imaginary Mexico's attempt to homogenize society is virtually absolute. There is a striking, even shocking, degree of diversity within and between the two Mexicos. Thus there is no unified national culture, but rather a heterogeneous grouping of different and even contradictory ways of life. A northerner differs radically from a resident of the coast of Veracruz, influenced by African American Caribbean cultures. A peasant from the largely criollo state of Jalisco is a world apart from the mestizo of Yucatán, streaked with Mayan ethnicity. The Amerindian of Chiapas has very little in common with the middle-class inhabitant of Mexico City.

Mexico's ties are chiefly with Western culture, one might wish to argue. Yet what is the manifestation of that Western culture? The twangy accordion and polka rhythms of *música norteña* (music from northern Mexico) and *maquiladoras* (foreign-owned assembly plants using cheap Mexican labor) in Ciudad Juárez? Banking business in Mexico City and life in the suburbs with the Dallas Cowboys and the latest top-ranked ABC, CBS, and NBC programs on TV? The wealthy coffee grower of Veracruz who resides in Xalapa and sends his kids to college at Berkeley? The construction worker in Puebla who takes his family out to dine at McDonald's once in a while? The manager of a department store in Guadalajara who inculcates her offspring with traditional Catholic values? The street vendor of Acapulco who uses some English he learned while residing in San Francisco to hawk his wares among North American tourists? In all cases, mestizo culture predominates. But thanks to the revolution, the presence of Amerindian elements creates a heterogeneous mix that continues to differ radically in different regions, in the countryside and in the cities, and within different social classes.

The Amerindian subsistence farmer in Yucatán is not the Amerindian or mestizo peasant of the parched land in Zacatecas who makes his yearly pilgrimage to the United States and picks up a few bucks, a little English, and snippets of North American culture. The Tarahumara Amerindian of Chihuahua who is forced to raise marijuana on his minuscule plot to survive is a world apart from the farmworker on the mechanized, irrigated, and chemically laden stretches of land in Sinaloa. The exploited *maquiladora* laborer living in a shack on the U.S.-Mexican border can hardly identify with the lackadaisical specialist in a sweatshop in the Tepito district of Mexico City. The owner of a *discoteca* in the chic Zona Rosa area of the Capital City has little in common with the pistol-packing landowner of Chiapas.

Admittedly, such distinctions exist in the United States between New Yorkers and Iowa corn farmers, Chicanos in Los Angeles and Cubans in Miami, and so on. The fact of the matter is that the United States is also becoming increasingly diversified, in spite of the archconservatives' desire to make this country into their image of what it never really was and never will be. But Mexico has experienced such diversity from the very beginning.

In Spite of It All, the Myth of Homogeneous "Progress" Endures

In the early 1990s an anthology issue of the U.S. fashion magazine *Town and Country* presented a dedication to the "mighty Mexicans." It included page after page of photographs of the rich and the famous, the "beautiful people," the Imaginary Mexico that enriched itself during the oil boom of the 1970s and lucrative investments of the 1980s. We see "mighty Mexicans" in their daily surroundings, at home and in the factory, the office, and the vacation home. They sport the finest clothing and jewelry that money can buy. In each scene, there is at least some suggestion of the people's "Mexicanness."

One particular scene stands out. Beside the criolla-mestiza matron, there is an Amerindian woman in authentic native Amerindian clothing. She is a short, plump, smiling woman, obviously the maid, with bronze skin and an appreciative look on her face. This is indicative of what Bonfil Batalla calls Mexico's schizophrenia, which gives rise to one of the most heterogeneous cultural mixes imaginable (Bonfil Batalla 199, 56). I am not alluding to different cultural levels, which exist in a hierarchy. Different hierarchical levels and distinctions along the horizontal axis of a given level make up the myriad surface variations that result when two radically distinct civilizations collide at the contact zone. These two civilizations never realized any peaceful coexistence, never effectively converged, for the contact zone has always been a cultural battlefield, virtually incomprehensible in its complexity.

These two civilizations entail distinct ways of perceiving and conceiving the world, distinct values, distinct forms of life. As far as the dominant class is concerned, the respectable model for Mexican development has always been Western, from conquest to colonial times to the present. When possible, México Profundo—Amerindian culture—was largely ignored. Yet it never ceased to make its presence felt in one way or another. The presence of México Profundo was perhaps most prominent during the Zapatista revolt as a local expression of the general Mexican Revolution. Zapatismo defended its villages, its agrarian orientation, its affirmation of Amerindian life patterns developed over the centuries, its periodic punctuation of seasonal time with rites and religious ceremonies. But in the final analysis, Zapatismo was defeated. The revolution was more a defeat of Zapatismo and México Profundo than of Porfirio Díaz and the criollo oligarchy. True, the constitution of 1917 contains an agrarian article calling for equitable distribution of land, an article that was in part finally put into effect during the Cárdenas years. Nevertheless, Zapatismo was largely snuffed out. Imaginary Mexico triumphed. And yet the Other Mexico, México Profundo, remains. This creates a stuttering, hesitating, vacillating, hopping and skipping, syncopated cultural rhythm that appears out of tune with itself: Bonfil Batalla's cultural schizophrenia.

The dominant culture, Imaginary Mexico, puts on airs and attempts to take on the trappings of developed Western cultures. In the process, proponents of Imaginary Mexico try to convince themselves that they should aspire to be what Mexico *is not*. As a result, Mexico *has become, is becoming, will have become*, what it *is not*, and it *is not* what it appears *to be*, what Imaginary Mexico would like it *to be*. Bonfil Batalla observes that Mexico's "cultural schizophrenia" presents grave consequences, though this does not seem to worry Imaginary Mexico. In the first place, "schizophrenia" ends in marginalization of the majority of México Profundo. This marginalization, product of Imaginary Mexico, is nonetheless more real then imaginary. Marginalized majority Mexico is pushed aside by the minority to make way for the Mexico that *ought to exist* but *does not*. All the Others of marginalized Mexico remain excluded by decree. They thus have three choices. They can (1) live on the outskirts of national life, with minimal interrelations between their world and Imaginary Mexico, which appears alien to them, (2) live a double life, also "schizophrenic," by alternating between worlds and cultures according to whatever circumstances happen to prevail, or (3) renounce their genuine identity and try to gain acceptance into Imaginary Mexico. In spite of the choices, Imaginary Mexico almost inevitably avoids México Profundo, which is the genuine cultural expression of Mexican society. Consequently, it becomes virtually impossible "to recognize, appreciate, and stimulate the development of the extensive and varied cultural patrimony that history has placed in Mexican hands" (Bonfil Batalla 1995, 65–67).

Thus it is, Bonfil Batalla believes, that daily the Amerindian people experience "schizophrenic" Mexico. The whole heterogeneous concoction of Mexican cultures is basically split into two opposed and incompatible worlds. If you are an inhabitant of México Profundo, when you are ill, go to the local *curandero* (practitioner of folk medicine), and if that doesn't work, as a last resort try the nearest doctor of Western medicine—if you by chance have the money. Dress like a traditional Amerindian peasant during the week, then don a pair of shoes like a mestizo and take in the marketplace on the weekend. Sense the rhythms of traditional culture during periodic festivities, and on the following day in the corn field plug in a transistor radio manufactured in Taiwan and throb to a rock beat. Traditional legends and folktales must compete with Donald Duck cartoon strips, TV images pervade traditional social gatherings, tacos and tortillas must contend with hamburgers and *pan bimbo* (insipid white bread in presliced loaves), huaraches with Nikes, customary dress with Los Angeles Lakers and Hard Rock Cafe T-shirts. And so on.

"Schizophrenia." Yet México Profundo is inextricably *interdependent* on and *interrelatedly intertwined* with Imaginary Mexico. The one imposes itself on the other and the other resists. Imaginary Mexico thinks it is free of its past even though it pays homage to murals by Rivera, eulogizes the National Museum of Anthropology, and takes pride in its Aztec-laden cuisine. México Profundo falls and rises again; it remains mute but silently persists; it ceases becoming what it is becoming yet continues to become what it has always been becoming. All the while, it yields and resists, accepts and rejects; and it endures (as in *aguantar*). It endures, therefore it exists. It exists, therefore it is always becoming. In short, México Profundo survives by engaging in "cultural guerrilla" tactics, as described above.

México Profundo is in a scintillating, titillating, shimmering, oscillating hesitation and vacillation and stuttering process of syncopated undecidability. It wavers to and fro between dualistic *eithers* and the *ors* without ever settling down. This is the problem of the mestizo character that is becoming generalized for all of Mexico. However, it is not merely the case that there is no *either-or;* there is no *both-and* either; rather, there is just *neither-nor, neither* the one alternative *nor* the other suffices. Thus it is immersed in cultural pluralism. In a pluralist culture there is no single model but many models, no one and only developmental model according to Western Enlightenment visions of indefinite linear progress, but many possible models that spew off and out along nonlinear pathways. There is much probing and experimenting and trying things out just for the hell of it. Mexico has been pluralist all along. It is a mix of westernized and Amerindian cultures, with some African Mexican blended in for good measure, all embodied in a great variety of customs and conventions. As a radically heterogeneous culture, Mexico is in a position to take advantage of the best the West has to offer and choose from the rest—including México Profundo—that which lies beyond the grasp of the West. Mexico has the human resources for further developing its unique society.

We become aware more than ever how profoundly Mexico is rooted in her past. She is rooted in time, intensive PC time. We become aware more than ever regarding the two Mexicos . . . no, that's not right, many Mexicos. We also become aware how deeply communication in the many Mexicos is bound in specific contexts, where nonverbal cues are of paramount importance. In other words, the many faces of Mexico are of radical HC space with respect to their citizenry's *interdependent, interrelated, interactive* coming and going within the flow of everyday life, within intracultural and intercultural contact zones. In short, Mexico is a supreme expression of *hybrid culture*, epitomized in the reality of her myths, in her mythified reality, deeply rooted in the Guadantzín-macho images. Whether or not Mexico will be able to overcome her "schizophrenic dance" is a tale only the future can tell.

Our next step in getting a feel for Mexican culture involves a look at the numbingly complex Mexican sociopolitical system that has existed since the 1960s.

Further Reading

Barkin 1990, Bartra 1992, Castillo 1994, De Aragón 1980, Grayson 1980, Guillermoprieto 1994, Hellman 1988, Hodges and Gandy 1983, Iglesias Prieto 1997, Lafaye 1976, Peña 1997, Riding 1984, Ross 1998, Ruiz 1998, Teichman 1988, Warnock 1987, 1995, Wolf 1972. Fiction: Esquivel 1994, 1997, Taibo 1996.

Notes

1. Although, I must assert once again, fortunately, this attitude is changing, most notably in the cities.

2. I cannot overemphasize my use of the *mythical female* rather than the *real female* in this and the preceding paragraphs. Today's Mexican woman is slowly becoming as educated, as effective in whatever profession she chooses, and as capable of forging her own future as her counterpart in many other Western countries. However, the *mythical female* tends to linger in the collective mind. With time, hopefully the myth will have ceded to the realities of everyday life.

12

Along the Political Roller Coaster

Turning Point: 1968

Things seemed to be going well for Mexico. A distinct note of optimism lasted through most of the 1960s. The "Mexican miracle" was in full swing. The rather insipid President Ruiz Cortines (1952–1958) gave the *dedazo* (pointed finger, the "king's nod") to handsome, dashing young Adolfo López Mateos for the 1958–1964 term (see glossary).

López Mateos was supposed to give leftist politics a breath of fresh air. He came in with support from labor and peasant sectors. But on the eve of his election the railroad workers went on a strike that lasted for months. After lines of communication had broken down repeatedly, López Mateos finally responded by marching out the military. Over two thousand militants were jailed, including labor leader Demetrio Vallejo and Stalinist mural painter Siqueiros. The story had it that the movement had been egged on by communist elements—the Cold War now had a healthy head of steam. So much for leftist politics, it might seem. However, on the international scene, Mexico presented a different face. Fidel Castro and his revolutionaries deposed dictator Fulgencio Batista early in 1959. The United States had initially tolerated the Castro crowd as middle-class reformists who would not rock the capitalist boat. It soon became evident that Castro's Cuba was quickly moving toward socialism. The communists were establishing a beachhead in the Americas, and "domino theory" paranoia became rampant in the United States. Ex-President Lázaro Cárdenas threw his support for the Young Turks in Cuba and paid them a visit. To the consternation of U.S. observers, Mexico seemed to be making overtures toward socialist politics.

The overtures were deceptive, however. While López Mateos spouted leftist rhetoric and began the most massive land reform in the name of the peasants since Cárdenas, he was secretly cracking down on leftists who refused to tow the official party line. To complicate the issue, Mexico's policy regarding Cuba turned out to be ambiguous. Mexico stood with the United States in defense of the Monroe Doctrine against any alien power infiltrating the affairs of the American sovereign states while refusing to cooperate in the blockade of Cuba. López Mateos felt compelled to turn his liberal face toward the Mexican people, who had grown tired of the country's support for big business and foreign investors. At the same time, he had to walk on marshmallows with respect to intensified Cold War efforts on the part of the "colossus of the North" (the United States).

In 1964 it was Secretary of the Interior Gustavo Díaz Ordaz's turn to try out the presidential seat for his half dozen years. Mexico's tightrope act between supporting both Castro and U.S. anticommunist activities had been moderately successful. The country enjoyed prestige as never before. The "Mexican miracle" was lauded as a model to be emulated by developing nations the world over. At the pinnacle of her international respect, Mexico was chosen as the site of the Olympic Games for 1968, the first so-called third world country to be given such an honor. The "Mexican miracle" could now be showcased for the whole world. The year 1968 saw turmoil the world over. There were massive demonstrations and riots in China and Japan. The Tet offensive in Vietnam revealed the U.S. rhetoric by which the war would soon come to an end for what it was. The May revolution in Paris irreversibly altered the country's political, social, and intellectual direction. Martin Luther King and Robert Kennedy were assassinated. Mexico could hardly escape these winds of change. Student demonstrations in the capital city became bigger and bolder, reaching a climax with a march, 400,000 strong, toward the central plaza in August. With the Olympics a couple of months away, the government was hard-pressed to do something drastic. The opportunity came on October 2, ten days before the inauguration of the celebrated games, when 10,000 or so supporters gathered for a rally at the Plaza of Three Cultures, called Tlatelolco during pre-Hispanic times.

Suddenly the armed forces appeared and gunfire erupted. Escape was difficult, since the plaza is surrounded by an apartment complex on two sides, the towering foreign relations building on a third side, and one of the main causeways into the center of the city on the fourth side, where the soldiers were doing the gunning. After the massacre, government officials blamed professional communist-inspired snipers who opened fire on the military. Students attributed the massacre to government repression. The news media prudently played the issue down, with customary encouragement from the government. All told, a few hundred were killed and many more were wounded. There's no telling, exactly, since the plaza was scrubbed clean within hours. Later that month, when the Olympic torch proudly made its way through the streets of Mexico City, as far as the newspapers were concerned, the issue was forgotten. This was newspaper reportage, Mexican style.

Now enter President Luís Echeverría (1970–1976), followed by José López Portillo (1976–1982). Echeverría took a turn to the left, at least in his rhetoric, in order to calm the unrest. He managed to avoid scaring off foreign investors, who began pouring money into the country at an unprecedented rate. López Portillo became the self-proclaimed patriarch of the oil boom, preparing the country to "administer during a time of abundance." He was able to play the two sides of the Cold War against each other. He supported Daniel Ortega and the triumphant revolutionary Sandinistas of Nicaragua in 1979, and he later paid sympathetic lip service to the peasant struggle in Guatemala. At the same time, he enticed the United States with oil. His dream ended in 1981, when world oil prices collapsed and Mexico all but drowned in debt. He was destined to repeat the ritual that had now become endemic to the country's presidents over the past decades: enter with fame, end with shame. With massive debts, rampant corruption, a declining peso at home, and deteriorating prestige abroad, López Portillo had no chance of a last hurrah. He ended his reign literally in tears before the Mexican congress. But there was no real shame, for according to his way of thinking, blame for the tragic turn of events was not his at all.

The next president was Harvard-educated, drab, business-like Miguel de la Madrid (1982–1988). It was now austerity time in the land of Cancún tourists—as if the millions of poor people had ever known anything but austerity. It was also a time of corruption gone wild and continuing middle-class illusions of consumerism, U.S. style. The first Mexican president with a strong economic background, de la Madrid seemed as tailor-made for the job as were his custom-made suits. Short in the charisma department, he was long at tough, unemotional decisionmaking. He initially set about slashing government spending and raising the price of public services. There was a grand show about curbing corruption, and to back up the hoopla, oil chief Jorge Díaz Serrano was thrown in jail. Production and purchasing power on the part of a now diminishing middle class suffered even more, but tough financial measures won praise abroad, especially from those countries eager to continue receiving payments on the country's debt. Middle-class unrest was there, and disgruntled labor, student protests, and peasant demands made their presence felt. Yet de la Madrid stood firm. He made no promises, created no dreams, and avoided serious instability.

In 1988 Carlos Salinas de Gortari won the elections over Cuauhtémoc Cárdenas, son of the most popular president since the revolution, Lázaro Cárdenas, in what was considered by many as the greatest ballot-box fraud ever. De la Madrid had thrown a *dedazo* (see glossary) Salinas's way, most likely because of his economic know-how and his support for up-and-coming neoliberal policies. Now, as president without a genuine claim to legitimacy in the eyes of many, Salinas had to continue dealing with the economic crisis. Polls showed that 90 percent of the people believed he was in office by fraud. He must somehow gain the respect of the Mexican public, and at the same time he was hard-pressed to restore the confidence of foreign investors. A daunting task indeed. His tactics were tried-and-tested PRI tactics, which worked, at least for upper-class Mexican *sacadólares* (those who when it becomes convenient take their money out of the country and deposit it in U.S. and European banks or invest in stock and real estate) and U.S. business. Salinas used the military rather than the conference table with unions and political opponents, and he began negotiating with foreign bankers, promising to widen the door to foreign investors.

By 1989 all regulations on foreign investment had been repealed. Salinas then initiated broad neoliberal policies, beginning with reprivatization of the banks in 1999—banks that López Portillo had nationalized only a few years earlier. In 1991 the constitution of 1917 was altered to permit private citizens and even foreigners to buy up the peasant *ejidos*, communal farmlands operated by Amerindian and mestizo peasants. Tax reforms were enacted with an eye toward increasing profits and investments. Transportation, communication media, petrochemicals, and fisheries were deregulated. State-owned enterprises were privatized (in 1982 there were 1,155 state-owned businesses but by 1993 only around two hundred). Mexico's subsidized food program for the poor, the National Basic Food Program (CONASUPO), was abolished. This left small farmers in the dark and many poor people in the cities without money to buy rice, beans, milk, eggs, and other staples in the expensive supermarkets.

Most noteworthy of all, Salinas entered into talks over the North American Free Trade Agreement (NAFTA) tying together the U.S., Canadian, and Mexican economies. The only thing that was not negotiable, seemingly, was the "virginity of the Virgin of Guadalupe," as one observer noted. The poor were quickly becoming poorer and the rich, richer. In the eyes of Washington beholders, however, Salinas was flying high. And he could do no wrong as far as foreign investors and a handful of Mexican multimillionaires were concerned. These "mighty Mexican" multimillionaires were a new development for which Salinas's policies were chiefly responsible. In 1988, when he took over the presidency, not a single Mexican made the Forbes list of the world's richest people. When Salinas left office in 1994, Mexico could boast of fourteen members in the exclusive club. Only three other countries had more representatives on the list: the United States, Japan, and Germany!

Surely there must be an upside regarding the lower classes. And there was, rhetorically speaking. It came to the tune of "Solidarity." Solidarity was presumably a bond established between government and the people and between the haves and the have-nots. However, Salinas's solidarity program, designed to invest token pesos in the countryside in order to win back lost rural support for PRI, was a failure. It had little public appeal. Its prime mover, Salinas himself, lacked *personalismo*, and it was bloated with bureaucratic molasses: flow protocols and government corruption. Solidarity was showcased in the program's birthplace, in Chalco to the south of Mexico City. Chalco was once a charming Amerindian village. Now, after Solidarity, it is a miserable squatters' settlement of muddy streets and cinder-block hovels. The entire area sports multiple skeletons of unfinished public works projects and many billboards lauding PRI's dedication to the welfare of the Mexican people.

The coveted images of Imaginary Mexico never died. They occupied the eyes and minds of both the haves and the have-nots, those who knew how to get rich and consume and those who knew how to *aguantar*, while sugarplums of Solidarity danced in the politicians' heads.

Mexico Thought She Had Become One of the Big Guys

On January 1, 1994, NAFTA was finally born. On that same day, the Ejército Zapatista de Liberación Nacional (EZLN) occupied San Cristóbal de las Casas and four towns in Chiapas, demanding land, freedom, justice, democracy, and recognition of rights for indigenous peoples.[1]

Thus Mexico awoke from its dream of a utopian rite of passage from "third world" to "first world" status on New Year's Day 1994, shortly after NAFTA went into effect. EZLN had begun its campaign, and a communiqué was sent to the newly elected president of Mexico, offering the defiant interdiction: "Welcome to the nightmare." With NAFTA a reality, Mexico was supposed to start looking like Texas; instead, the EZLN rebellion made it look more like El Salvador.

Subcomandante Marcos was the focus of attention; all eyes were turned toward him and an army of international correspondents converged in his direction. Marcos was the news media's ideal "revolutionary." He had lighter skin and was taller than the Amerindians surrounding him; he pensively smoked a pipe and articulated himself effectively, with wry irony and ingratiating humor. He was eagerly interviewed, and he became an overnight celebrity, especially since he conveniently fit into high-tech media methods. Before long, T-shirts appeared with the image of Subcomandante Marcos taking their place beside Che Guevara and other "revolutionary" tourist items.

Why Chiapas? That southernmost and poorest state of the nation had received little attention since the the Mexican Revolution of 1910–1920. However, it became evident in the early 1990s that the radically unequal distribution of wealth in Chiapas mirrored that of Mexico as a whole. Nevertheless, though the fact had been hidden over the centuries, Chiapas was actually one of the country's richest states in natural resources. In 1994 it was providing almost 60 percent of the hydroelectric power for the entire country, 47 percent of the natural gas, and 21 percent of the oil. It was one of the chief producers of lumber, coffee, and beef. Nevertheless, one-third of the homes had no electricity and one-half had no running water or sewage facilities. In some of the provincial cities the Zapatistas occupied, for example, Ocosingo, 70 percent of the homes had no electricity. What is more indicative, the state of Chiapas had recently suffered corruption on a minor scale, but of such an absurd nature that it could hardly be taken without a bit of humor.

Pulitzer Prize recipient Andrés Oppenheimer (1998) tells an interesting tale regarding these corrupt political practices. He arrived at the airport of Tuxtla Gutiérrez, capital of the state, after a two-hour delay at the Mexico City airport, anticipating an interview with Marcos. From the local Chiapas airport he found that a thirty-five kilometer taxi ride through the hinterland was necessary to reach the small provincial capital. Why was there a delay in Mexico City and why was the airport not located closer to Tuxtla Gutiérrez? After some inquiry he discovered that the delay was due to the fact that the Tuxtla airport is usually shrouded in a mist and they were awaiting the signal to take off from the capital so they could arrive in Chiapas at a time when the fog had temporarily cleared. As for the inordinately long taxi ride, the airport had been constructed in 1979 at precisely this spot, in spite of recommendations to the contrary due to the unfeasibility of a landing site in that area. The land had belonged to an ex-governor of the state who had sold at a handy profit. Such are the ambitions of Imaginary Mexico.[2]

In regard to the vast gap between the haves and the have-nots, as well as rampant corruption, Chiapas is a microcosm, albeit in radical form, of the national macrocosm. As such, a more symbolic seal for the peasant outcry in the name of revolutionary leader Emiliano Zapata could hardly have been found.

"Guerrilla" Warfare to a Different Tune

Mexican business and patronage, politics and patronage, haciendas and patronage, all went about as usual in the mode that had become entrenched over the centuries. The paternalistic interrelations with all the formalities that accompanied them were serious business for the haves. The have-not Zapatistas donned masks revealing irony, sarcasm, cynicism, wit and droll humor through the words of Subcomandante Marcos. Consequently, messages forthcoming from the haves were customarily met with a knowing nod, for everybody knew what the messages were all about: control, in order to keep the traditional social, political, and economic hierarchies intact.

Throughout Mexico, for centuries the winks, sly grins, gesturing hands and eyebrows, nodding and wagging heads and know-it-all looks belied other messages. These other messages consisted of signs that usually remained below the surface. These were signs of tacit communication with nonverbal signals along implicit pathways. These were signs that at some of the most inopportune moments might be ready and willing to leap out and show their disrespect, and then quickly disappear before their subversive nature became too apparent. These were not signs of lesser but in certain respects of greater importance than the more intentional and explicit linguistic signs. They were chiefly signs of silent rebellion, of resistance when open insurrection would be self-destructive. Yes. The Mexican people, that is, the have-nots, usually knew their signs well, signs of the most subtly insubordinate nature imaginable. What is the nature of these insubordinate signs?

As noted above, it is assumed that there is a "dominant culture" and a "subservient" or "popular culture," and that the former exercises *hegemony* over the latter. This assumption is flawed in ways that are becoming increasingly evident. The dominant classes are powerful but sluggish; the underprivileged are lean and mean. They are not producers of cultural artifacts, nor are they full-blown consumers. They are somewhere in between. That is precisely the art. The dominant culture must have everything *either* in black *or* white. But the have-nots are superior to such *dualistic* demands. In a rather tacit sense they know everything is either *neither* the one thing *nor* the other, or it is *both* the one thing *and* the other. They *neither* exclusively conform to the system *nor* exclusively engage in nonconformity practices. They are in tune with *hybrid* culture, for they are acutely aware of the devious nature of all signs, and they make the best of it.

Classical logic dictates that we should simply have the powerful and the weak, those in control and those who have no say, the so-called *dominant* and the *subalterns*. According to cultural guerrilla logic, in contrast, it is possible to don a different mask for each occasion. One can be virtually all things to those who are in control. To repeat the above examples, one can show civic responsibility by throwing trash in the proper receptacle and later that night strew the contents of that same receptacle along the sidewalk; one can cater to the boss in the morning and pilfer from the company in the afternoon. One *neither* conforms *nor* does one rebel on a permanent basis, for there is always the possibility of engaging in some act that emerges from within the interstices between categories. So between the *either* and the *or*, one always seems capable of finding something to fill in a portion of the *excluded middle*.

I'll try putting this cultural guerrilla logic within Mexican everyday life. A thriving informal economy has emerged in the Tepito neighborhood and elsewhere in Mexico City. Taking a job at minimum wage of a little over $3.50 per day would hardly provide more than survival, considering the basic needs of an individual, let alone a small family, in the capital city today. A minimum wage job would be bad enough, if such jobs were available. The cold fact is that there are not even enough of these jobs to go around. What can the people do? Before NAFTA, they bought defective brand-name items (called *fayuca*) in Brownsville, Texas, and elsewhere, smuggled them across the border, and set up shop in the streets. These people didn't have permits for such illicit activity, so the police were periodically sent into the neighborhoods and the main arteries leading into the cities to put a stop to this activity that cut into legitimate retail establishments. What was the response of the have-nots? Slip the cops a *mordida* (a "bribe," or literally, a "bite"). More pressure was put on the people, but to hardly any avail. Small-time Mafia-type fraternities soon arose as the people's way of organizing themselves at the grassroots level. These mini-Mafias soon became so effective that they even had many government officials in line.

After NAFTA, the big-time merchants could get many of their goods duty-free. This presented a problem for the street-vending have-nots. How could they possibly compete when duty-free items were piled up in the department stores. The people had another answer up their sleeve. Almost overnight they set up small shops producing articles with "pirated" brand names such as Levi, Nike, Adidas, and Jordache. A small shop owner would simply buy a pair of jeans, undo all the stitches, and, using the pieces as a pattern, make a virtually identical product with cheap denim material she bought locally at bargain prices. Sometimes the products bore brands like "Levay," "Naiki," or "Soni." I've witnessed people selling on the streets from a fold-up box that could put away in a few seconds when an enforcer of the law appeared in the vicinity.

The ordinary Mexican middle-class concept of "popular culture," "folk culture," or "guerrilla culture" of EZLN or Tepito variety includes a teeming cauldron of aesthetically senseless, intellectually trivial, morally bankrupt, and virtually chaotic practices. But this is a developing country. "Popular culture," "folk culture," and "guerrilla culture" present themselves as a radically *heterogeneous*, ongoing flux of humanity and cultural artifacts. This renders them thoroughly *contradictorily complementary*, and they are always in transition, with no readily apparent purpose or direction. In their composite they make up "guerrilla culture," which is anything but reducible to any set of descriptive features. Guerrilla culture is in a manner of speaking identityless. It lacks identifying features; it eludes every effort to pin it down conceptually. Yet there *is* identity, forever transient identity. "Guerrilla culture" is, in a word, *process*. It defies all fixed labels and definitions. Once it has been labeled, it contradicts that very label; once it has been defined in terms of what it *is* in contrast to what it *is not*, it has already altered itself to the extent that it is neither the *is* nor the *is not* but now something else. With this in mind, we return to the EZLN enigma.

Mexican Masks Par Excellence

At the outset it appeared that the Chiapas rebels were unique. Unlike peasant leaders of earlier years, the "outsider," Marcos, had over the past decade taken up the Amerindian way of life. He learned their language and did things their way, while gaining their confidence and informing them of centuries of wrongdoing and how things could be made right. If EZLN was not exactly an "army of national liberation," it was at least an "army of indigenous interests in favor of local liberation." Clearly, most of the rebels did not carry weapons as modern and powerful as those that were proudly displayed on TV during the initial days of the movement. Some of them didn't even have weapons. Yet the several thousand fighters were part of a coordinated plan with a single command that articulated a consistent message. Their organization, logistics, communication, and public relations revealed years of preparation.

EZLN's appearance was an immediate problem for Mexico and especially the ruling party, PRI. There had been persistent rumors of the uprising from the daily *La Jornada* and the weekly magazine, *Proceso*, but the party machine paid them little mind, since it was almost inconceivable that several thousand peasants could launch an effective insurgency campaign. Yet the rumors turned out to confirm those critics who had been insisting since 1988 that the course followed by President Carlos Salinas de Gortari would someday lead to a major crisis. Salinas had spoken in the name of solidarity, and now it was EZLN's turn to show its own brand of solidarity. The rationale for a movement that otherwise might have appeared suicidal was actually quite laudable.

An EZLN manifesto, as expressed in the original "Declaration from the Lacandón Jungle," included:

TODAY WE SAY ENOUGH IS ENOUGH!
TO THE PEOPLE OF MEXICO:
MEXICAN BROTHERS AND SISTERS:
  We are the product of 500 years of struggle: first against slavery, then during the War of Independence against Spain, then to avoid being absorbed by North American imperialism, then to promulgate our constitution and expel the French empire from our soil; later the dictatorship of Porfirio Díaz denied us the just application of the Reform laws and the people rebelled and leaders like Villa and Zapata emerged, poor men just like us. We have been denied by our rulers the most elemental conditions of life so they can use us as cannon fodder and pillage the wealth of our country. (EZLN 1995, 311)

A later communiqué of January 11, 1994, stated: "We believe that a genuine respect for the liberties and democratic will of the people are indispensable requisites for the improvement of social and economic conditions among our country's dispossessed" (EZLN 1994).

Marco's tactic was not to take power or defeat the Mexican government but to become a mouthpiece of the people. Dignity for the Amerindians, democracy, justice: soberly reformist rather than wild-eyed, violent revolutionary goals. The mysterious masked spokesman apparently didn't have revolution on the agenda (Castañeda 1995, 79–86). On the other hand, Oppenheimer claims that from the beginning the movement was the arm of a radical Marxist movement based in Mexico City. He writes that it was not until Marcos ingratiated himself with the correspondents and intellectuals throughout the West and not until the movement gained the reputation of a unique operation that the charismatic, wisecracking leader made an about-face and denied any Marxist leanings (Oppenheimer 1998, 58–61). Whichever the case, by February 1994 the importance of EZLN had become apparent. This was not just another skirmish. It was soon lauded and slandered, but it was generally acknowledged as the world's first "postcommunist" revolution—to complement the Mexican Revolution as the first social movement of the twentieth century.

According to most reports, Marcos was "unmasked" early in 1995. He turned out to be Rafael Sebastián Guillén, a professor of graphic design at the Universidad Autónoma Metropolitana at Xochimilco. President Ernesto Zedillo (1994–2000) immediately put Operation Rainbow on the board, and a surprise attack was set to catch the wily "Marcos," thus repeating the infamous ambush of revolutionary hero Emiliano Zapata in 1919. The operation was a fiasco. EZLN, enjoying high-tech communication facilities in the middle of the Lacandón jungle, got wind of the countermovement, fled more deeply into the jungle, and the "Marcos mystique" was perpetuated. The nimble peasant leader continued popping jokes about the plodding giant, PRI, Mexican bureaucracy, while he poked fun at the world press and international opinion. He proved himself to be a master at wordplay, tragicomic inversions, and quick mental maneuvers.

All in all, the Chiapas rebellion epitomizes the image of limber "cultural guerrillas" constantly eluding the creaking bones of a lumbering power structure. While Marcos was practicing his rhetorical moves, Byzantine debates in the capital city by archaic methods beat about the bush with generalizations and without addressing the real issue. Sharp remarks from EZLN were met with stuttering, hesitation, and denials; quick communiqués were addressed by the president's advisers parroting canned responses; the monolithic Televisa network, a right arm of the government, silenced the important events while repeating the usual slogans about "solidarity." All the while, Marcos's name and the movement were avoided whenever possible, and penetrating questions went unasked.

The Zapatista rebellion is not an ideology-based revolution of the customary sort. It is reformist, yet it creates a revolutionary image in the eyes of the Mexican middle class. There were arms, but there were more guerrillas than guns. The rebels were politically and economically motivated, yet there were few aspirations outside the local environs of the Lacandón jungle. There were attempts to change domestic social policies, yet there were no overt political designs and no attempts to engage directly in politics. Once again we see that dualistic thinking breaks down. There is no simple *this* or *that*. Rather, there is *vagueness*, with all its *inconsistencies*. The EZLN is as elusive with respect to dualistic thinking as it is with respect to the official government body. Grand ideological designs imposed on the Zapatista movement simply don't cut the cake. One has to conceive of the movement from down under, not from above like some God's-eye view of things. Such a conception of EZLN was, however, beyond the scope of the folks in power.

Back to Normal: Chaos?

During Zedillo's presidency, the Mexican government failed to solve the murder of Cardinal Juan Jesús Posadas Ocampo in May 1993, of presidential candidate Luis Donaldo Colosio in March 1994, and of José Francisco Ruis Massieu, general secretary of the PRI, in September 1994.[3] Meanwhile, back in the secluded quarters where the politicians met, it was business as usual. Jorge Castañeda (1995) has suggested that assassinations result from struggles for money and power within Mexico's elite, which includes the PRI, the nation's great capitalists, the drug lords, and even to an extent the Catholic Church—although on paper there are no ties between church and state.

The struggles among the ruling elite are driven by the international economy and Mexico's entry into NAFTA, which marked leaner and meaner modes of production—*maquiladoras* or sweatshops, downsizing at all levels, severe cutbacks in social programs, wages that fall behind inflation, and higher unemployment. At the same time, the ruling party was pushed and pulled by a bloated bureaucracy, sham labor unions and peasant leagues, and, increasingly, foreign and domestic capital and powerful drug lords. The technocratic leadership was a giant step removed from the close personal ties *(personalismo)* it had maintained into the 1960s. Especially since the massacre at Tlatelolco in 1968, it had moved toward becoming a cold and impersonal bureaucratic-technocratic machine. As a consequence, Zedillo and other party and government leaders seemed out of touch with the reality of Mexican life. The distant, humorless, straitlaced Zedillo lacked charisma, oratorical capacity, and personal charm. He was unable to strike a resonant chord with the people. The official ruling family had lost its ability to coopt its opponents with enticing carrots, and it didn't have the wherewithal to apply the stick—it would most likely not dare do so even if it could, fearful of the outcry from international sources. PRI ups and downs were like Sisyphus scaling Mexico's snow-capped volcano, Popocatapetl.

As the gap grew between the haves and the have-nots, politicians and people, cities and countryside, Imaginary Mexico and México Profundo, the existence of a vacuum became increasingly evident. Wealth and power, like nature, abhor a vacuum. Something must change. So the Mexican army, it appeared, began stepping forth to fill the empty spots. Generals and colonels began to take things into their own hands in some of the rural areas. Military checkpoints existed along highways, travelers were hounded constantly, soldiers invaded rural villages where guerrilla activity was seen as a threat. Occasional torture, rape, and murder were the inevitable consequence. Mexico was unfortunately beginning to resemble other Latin American countries during the 1960s and early 1970s, when the military took over Argentina, Uruguay, Brazil, Chile, Bolivia, and Perú.[4]

The high voltage behind the changes in Mexico and elsewhere in the world is expressed in current buzzwords: multinational corporations, globalization of capital, World Wide Web, information superhighway, neoliberalism, privatization. These shifting eddies and whirlpools and major alterations of the main current and periodic flood stages and occasional destruction of check dams below are radically changing economic life, social classes and alliances, and political forces. In Mexico, as elsewhere, the turn has been toward something comparable to the classical liberal economic policies of the late nineteenth and early twentieth centuries, when big government as we now know it from the time of Franklin Delano Roosevelt to Ronald Reagan was virtually unknown. These new policies received a massive injection in Mexico with the passing of NAFTA.

Since then the story has it that the Mexican economy soon began its road to recovery. The question is, Recovery for whom? Granted, the gross national product grew by 7.2 percent during the second trimester of 1996. But the growth was basically due to increased production of made-for-export commodities in the manufacturing sector. This growth has been accompanied by Mexico's continuing austerity program. Budgets for health, social security, and education were still being cut, workers' wages were virtually frozen, and unemployment was still on the increase. It was boom for a small minority and bust for the majority that had yet to experience any kind of boom at all. To top it all off, President Zedillo's budget proposal for 1999 squeezed out less money for social programs than at any time since the Mexican Revolution.

In this chapter's discussion I have offered some statistics behind the current lamentable condition of Mexico. A further look at the nature of Mexico's leading figure, *El Señor Presidente,* might help us achieve a greater understanding of Mexico's condition.

Further Reading

Aguilar Camín and Meyer 1985, Barry 1995, Benjamin 1996, Collier and Quaratiello 1994, Gil 1992, Harvey 1998, Katzenberger 1995, La Botz 1992, 1995, Monroy 1990, Moore and Pachón 1985, Orme 1996a, 1996b, Otero 1996, Price 1973, Rodríguez O. 1997, Ross 1998, Samora 1971, Suchlicki 1996, Warnock 1995, Wise 1998. Fiction: Azuela 1985, Spota 1957, 1963, Taibo 1994.

Notes

1. In January 1994, when NAFTA became a reality, per capita income had passed the $4,000 mark, theoretically putting Mexicans in company of the East Asians and Southern Europeans. By January 1995, after devaluation of the peso,

Mexico's per capita income nose-dived to $2,600, erasing all the gains of the previous years.

2. The high plains where the airport stood were called *Llanos San Juan* (San Juan Prairie) but it had been jocularly rebaptized *Ya no se ve* ("Now it can't be seen," which, in Spanish, alliterates with *Llanos San Juan*).

3. After a prolonged and heated trial, Raul Salinas de Gortari, brother of President Carlos Salinas de Gortari, was pronounced guilty of orchestrating the assassination of Ruis Massieu and sentenced to 50 years in prison.

4. To cite a personal example, in December of 1997 I took a subway, bus, and walking tour through the parts of Mexico City that had changed most radically since NAFTA for the purpose of taking slides for use in a class I was to teach in the spring semester. I had never before met with such harassment. I was escorted out of a shopping mall, stopped by police and frisked after taking a shot of a plushy mansion, prevented from entering an area with some high rise buildings housing business offices, and followed for about 30 minutes by a couple of plain clothes agents. Twice I had to do some fast talking to prevent my camera from being confiscated, and once I was literally threatened at gun barrel by a member of the armed forces. My only explanation was that the upper crust is running scared.

13

And Now: Pre-Postmodern Mexico?

How Mexican Politics Works When It Works

Mexico's stability depends in large part on the image of an all-powerful *Señor Presidente*. He is the personification of the office of the presidency, the political system, Mexican nationalism, and in a sense the nation itself. *El Señor Presidente* is the concrete embodiment of all that. And much more besides.

As I have already suggested in passing, in the United States the office of the presidency is generally considered an abstract category. It is an abstraction in relation to the actual human being who at a given time happens to be known as the president. As an abstraction, the term "presidency" is related to concrete objects that can be named in place of it: White House, Oval Office, Pennsylvania Avenue, Washington, D.C., and all the other physical reminders of the term. The term "presidency" shares something of the nature of the concept of the university, which is interrelated with the concrete physical structures, the computer terminals, the books, the football stadium, the bell tower, the dormitories, and the grass and shrubs and trees and sidewalks and parking garages that make up the campus. They all act as reminders that this is a university. All these parts of the university, as well as students and professors and administrators, come and go. They are transient. The buildings decay, are demolished, and then are replaced. But the university as an abstract category lives on, as if it were a fixed entity.

Granted, the university also undergoes alterations. Its academic status as one university among hundreds in the United States is subject to the winds of change. The campus might be known for its aesthetic qualities. Particular schools might be rated among the top ten in the country. A scandal might be caused by a fraternity hazing when a brother dies of alcohol poisoning. A football championship might be won. And so on. Nevertheless, the category remains basically what it is in the minds of those who cherish fond memories of their experiences at the institution.

In the United States, actual living, breathing humans occupy the category of presidency. Then they move on. The category is basically what it is, while concrete human specimens enter and pass on. The abstraction and its temporary concrete exemplifications are maintained in separation. The category is conceived as a relatively fixed entity. Concrete presidents come in a variety of sizes and shapes and personalities and capacities and political leanings. Of course, the category is not really fixed. It can be tarnished. In recent history we had Richard Nixon and the Watergate scandal that brought on a more cynical view of the very idea of the presidency and of whomever might happen to fill it. Then there was Bill Clinton and Whitewatergate and the Monica Lewinsky affair. Some observers would say that the presidency has been irremediably and irreversibly tarnished. Yet it remains, and it will most likely continue to remain into the indefinite future.

In Mexico, the office of the presidency is not the same abstract, autonomous entity it is in the United States. In a very real sense in the minds of Mexicans, it *is* the president and the president *is* it. In other words, whoever occupies the presidency is the concrete embodiment of the very word presidency. The word is not really an abstraction, at least in the sense that it is an abstraction in the United States. It is concretion exemplified. Thus *Señor Presidente*'s charm, his charisma, his *personalismo*, his physical appearance, his oratorical prowess, even perhaps his ability to fulfill the image of the caudillo in the traditional sense, is of paramount importance. Thus a noncharismatic president will be incapable effectively of captivating the public and becoming a president in the genuine sense of the term. As *Señor Presidente* goes, so goes the image of the presidency. However, an irreversible event occurred in 1968 that altered the idea of *Señor Presidente* and the presidency at least as long as the official political party, PRI, remained in power. I refer to the massacre of a few hundred students at Tlatelolco on October 2. With that event, both *Señor Presidente* and the presidency suffered irretrievable damage.

Since the 1930s, Mexico's political stability depended on the myth that *Señor Presidente* is all-powerful. It was a captivating myth, even though, like all myths, it was for the most part a fiction, and Mexicans in important positions in the country knew it. As long as *Señor Presidente* could continue to enthrall his public, influence his friends with liberal doses of patronage, and impose his will on his political enemies, he would at least temporarily enjoy some form of legitimacy. Mexico City is, after all, the site of ancient Tenochtitlán, seat of pre-Hispanic theocratic authoritarianism, and the center of the equally authoritarian religious dogmatism and monarchical power during colonial times. If legitimacy in the abstract sense was lost twice, during the conquest and during independence, in a very concrete, personal, and personalized sense, it could be temporarily incorporated in the figure of whoever happened to be *Señor Presidente* at a given moment.

For Mexicans, political life exists here and now. It is relatively free of the abstract conceptualizations of the presidency and the constitution and the legislative and judicial branches of the government that prevail in the United States. The Mexican president *is* who he *is*, here and now. He is the embodiment of history, of Spanish colonial and national patrimony; therefore he provides a certain continuity to the political system. He concretizes the system. There is no need for historians to pontificate over the historical antecedents that serve to legitimate the system. All that *is* the president and the president *is* all that. The myth of *Señor Presidente* reflects the tradition to provide a unifying thread tying past to present in the hearts and minds of the Mexican citizens.

The postrevolutionary presidential tradition began with a four-year term from 1920 to 1924, when Mexican revolutionary fervor finally came under control. In 1934 it was increased to six years. It is important to note that no president can run for reelection. That is a sacrosanct principle written into the Constitution of 1917. The only president who dared throw his hat in the ring for reelection was Obregón, who claimed to have won the elections in 1928 after having served from 1920 to 1924. He was soon assassinated for his lack of respect for the young tradition. Although the president is president, he is the personification of the official political party that mythically perpetuates the image that it is itself the product of Mexican tradition. In Alan Riding's (1984, 67) words, "The presidential system has survived, not because it has subjected a passive Mexico to decades of dictatorial rule, but because it mirrors the strengths and weaknesses, virtues and defects, of the Mexicans themselves."

Since 1968 and the Tlatelolco tragedy, however, the Mexican political system has become increasingly impersonal and more businesslike. Presidents Luís Echeverría (1970–1976) and José López Portillo (1976–1982) were of interpersonal-populist bent. Their successors, Miguel de la Madrid (1982–88), Carlos Salinas de Gortari (1988–1994), and Ernesto Zedillo (1994–2000) were trained in business and economics at Ivy League universities. It is no mere coincidence that the latter three presidents blamed many of Mexico's woes on the administratively irresponsible populist tactics of Echeverría and López Portillo. This is a recent phenomenon. University-trained *técnicos* (technicians) are in conflict with the traditional lawyer *políticos* (politicians), businesslike administrators are in conflict with pragmatic hands-on populists, impersonal behind-the-scenes operators are in conflict with people-oriented executives. Presidential power has increased with the entry of the *técnicos*, and at the same time concrete links with the people offered by the *políticos* have waned. The system as a consequence has become less stable.

The system works best when the president enjoys absolute power but does not wield it absolutely. While the president is in office, what he says goes. The legislative branch has paper power but very little actual power. Even though being elected to a legislative seat brings little power, opportunities for self-enrichment through corrupt wheeling and dealing are unfortunately abundant. And pockets are filled. "We are paid to applaud," quipped one senator. The senators' and representatives' meager pay is for services rendered in the legislative branch of the government. Illicit pay for shady services is the trade-off for the lack of a political voice. (All this has been changing slightly in recent years, however, since candidates from the alternative parties, PAN and PRD, have been winning an increasing number of seats and are beginning to raise their voices.) The judicial branch, in contrast to the legislative branch, is known for its honesty in a system rife with corruption, but it does not exercise much real power either. Consequently, the president sits on top of the pyramid as negotiator, arbitrator, persuader, and mediator of interests. However, in spite of his authority, there are many things the president would not dare try to do. It is doubtful that he would, for example, privatize the oil industry or openly embrace a pro–North American policy. Such moves might lead to insurrection or economic disaster.

According to tradition, the president ultimately decides on his successor with the notorious *dedazo* ("pointed finger"). However, when the successor has been signaled, he cannot yet begin his campaign; according to the tradition, everybody knows he, as the PRI candidate, will win, and his identification as the candidate would direct much of the spotlight toward him and away from the incumbent president. So he must continue his role of *tapado* ("hooded one") (see glossary). At the propitious moment there is a *destape* ("unveiling"), and the promotion of the new *Señor Presidente* begins with a multimillion dollar phantom campaign that crisscrosses the country. It is a "phantom" campaign in that the presumed president can do no more than make vague promises. He must be careful not to criticize the outgoing president directly. After all, the current president is still *Señor Presidente*. The candidate must consequently do a tightrope act. He can show himself off, but his exhibitionism can consist of no more than a few deft moves, for he must maintain a delicate balance between his present powerlessness and what will soon be his all-powerful image. After the elections, the reigning president leaves office and loses his voice; only on rare occasions have ex-presidents actively engaged in the affairs of the country. Now there is a new *Señor Presidente*. He is invested with absolute authority, but if he is wise he will resist wielding it absolutely.[1]

All this appears as so much ritual to the North American. And in a manner of speaking it is. However, by adopting this system of elections within what was a one-party system (until the year 2000), Mexico alone among the authoritarian countries of the world has effectively resolved the problem of succession. Mexico's political system has apparently emerged from a distinctly Mexican cultural base. As such, it is unique among Latin American political systems. One may criticize Mexico's corruption, her electoral fraud, her rigidly hierarchical social, political, and economic structures, and her disparity between the haves and the have-nots. Yet, after a fashion, Mexico discovered a road to stability.

Family and Friends

The three Ps—*paternalismo*, patronage, and *personalismo*—qualify some of the greatest differences between political life in the United States and Mexico (see glossary). Mexico, thanks to the revolution, initially opened up new possibilities for oppressed and exploited people. These people could now dream dreams and work toward their realization. Due in large part to the doors that were opened, a dynamic generation of politicians, doctors, lawyers, teachers, professors, engineers, technicians, and businessmen emerged. This new generation found success on the basis of intelligence, hard work, and above all, by taking advantage of the intricate network of vital human interrelations predicated on *paternalismo*, patronage, and *personalismo*. As a consequence, it was not unusual, especially from the 1950s to 2000, to hear an account comparable to the following imaginary scenario as described by a successful member of the mestizo class. Let us call our fictional character Juan Gómez ("John Doe"), of the very class that was for the most part the underdog before the Revolution. Juan tells his story:

"I was born to a rather poor rural family in the state of Nuevo León. At twelve years of age, I went to the city to live with one of my aunts because my father died and my mother couldn't take care of her seven children. My aunt insisted I continue my education past elementary school, which at the time I thought was absurd since none of my friends were doing so. In retrospect, I cannot thank her too much. I eventually enrolled in the state University, where I became acquainted with some students from families that had recently invested their money in the right way and were quickly becoming rich. During my senior year at the University I took an active part in the campaign for state elections. One of my friend's father was elected Senator. After graduation, he offered me a job in his law firm. A few years later, I ran for State Representative as PRI candidate, and I had the good fortune of being elected to the position. I have invested my money in a cement plant, and recently the Secretary of Public Works has given me a contract for four projects that brought in a considerable sum of money. So, as you can see, life has been good to me."

And, why has life been good to him? Because of his "contacts." And now, as the crowning achievement of his efforts, he finds himself surrounded by "friends" *(compadres)* within a profoundly paternalistic web of interrelationships.

The road to success in Mexico is not solely paved with hard work, frugality, and wise business and professional decisions—as is the case of the North American myth, as exemplified in the Horatio Alger stories. In Mexico, to a considerably greater extent than in the United States, it is important to know the right people, make the proper "contacts," acquire influence through friends and relatives, gain membership in advantageous "clubs," and enter into influential circles in a respectable university (even though it must be the state university, as in the case of our imaginary Juan Gómez) and in commerce and local politics. An individual's success is not measured on the basis of much industrious activity and some good luck. Success is also the product of human interrelationships: as the expression goes, *Dime con quien andas y te diré quien eres* ("Tell me the company you keep and I will tell you who you are"). Success is less often a matter of merit than contacts. One must *tener palanca* ("have pull"), *estar enchufado* ("be plugged in," "have connections").

This is not to say that the procedure within a Mexican paternalistic system is necessarily less egalitarian than procedures in the United States, where more emphasis is usually placed on merit. The two systems are just different. There is no genuine meritocracy in Mexico that rewards the individual for what she has accomplished. But neither in the United States are strictly objective measures used for giving a nod to those who deserve jobs and advancement solely as a result of their capacities and their achievements. The fact remains, however, that in the United States there is considerably less *paternalismo*, patronage, and *personalismo* than in Mexico. Consequently, perhaps more intimate human ties could be beneficial in the United States, and perhaps a little more interest in merit could yield more effective results in business, the professions, and politics in Mexico. Just as in Mexico things are done primarily on the basis of *concrete human interrelations* instead of *abstract institutional considerations*, so also every aspect of Mexican culture is grounded more in *concrete interpersonal ties* than on *individual initiative*.

The road to success in Mexico might seem unjust and even illogical to North Americans. But from the Mexican viewpoint, it is a well-worn road that is familiar and comfortably predictable. An individual depends on friends, relatives, and associates in order to make her way to prestige and fortune. She knows what she must do to travel this customary highway, and if she excels at the game, the good life will be hers. This interpersonal road is just as reasonable for her as is the less interpersonal road for the U.S. citizen. Although the ambitious young job seeker in the United States would prefer to be considered with a greater degree of cold objectivity than her Mexican counterpart, we can hardly deny the security derived from knowing one belongs to a circle of friends, family, and associates that will always be there for support. *Neither* the one system *nor* the other is necessarily *either* better *or* worse than the other, but thinking from one side of the border or the other or at the contact zone may make it so. Both systems have their advantages and disadvantages.

The Family Here and the Others There

The Mexican and Latin American tradition of favors and *paternalismo*, patronage, and *personalismo* is by and large an extension of the family. The family as a profoundly conservative institution has survived virtually intact, in spite of pressure for modernization. In fact, it is crucial in maintaining Mexico's political stability because the structure of the political family is patterned along the lines of the structure of the Mexican family. The same can be said of the Church; it serves as a model for the family. Hierarchy is the watchword. Unlike Protestant religions, which see the individual as standing before God, the Catholic hierarchy employs many mediators. In the Church hierarchy the priest in the local parish petitions God by way of the saints and the Virgin in regard to divine mediation. In the family, the mother acts as mediator between the children and the father. In government, the president is at the apex of the pyramid, and the citizens approach him through the mediation of the *corporate sectors* and/or interest groups (see glossary).

The family is the most concrete means for understanding this hierarchy of relationships. Through the family, traditions, values, and religious beliefs are perpetuated. Much of the economy is based on family farms, factories, big businesses, restaurants, and small businesses. The extended family structure, which also includes *compadres*, *comadres*, and a host of friends, supports the young, the aged, and any visitor who happens to be under the roof at a given time. It takes care of many of the services partly supported by the state in the U.S. welfare system. The entire society mirrors the family structure. It is marked by paternalistic, authoritarian lines of responsibility. This structure has held strong in spite of the periodic convulsions Mexico has experienced. It is the glue that holds together otherwise disparate, conflicting groups and interests.

The great majority of Mexicans continue to organize their lives around the nuclear family. Traditions and customs vary from region to region and social class to social class, but family relationships tie Mexican cultures together. The family is chiefly a self-contained, self-sufficient unit, closed to outsiders. Attitudes toward politics and religion, the opposite sex and adults, and human interrelations and social customs are often taught in the home in an authoritarian way. Boys and girls are distinguished more clearly with respect to behavior and freedom and restrictions than they are in the United States. Boys are given relatively free rein and few restrictions; discipline is in many cases almost unknown. Girls, in contrast, must learn controlled, rigidly disciplined, modest behavior; they must behave like young ladies anywhere and everywhere. Children play with siblings and cousins, and they usually have fewer friends outside the immediate family circle than do children in the United States, where the nuclear family is in many cases fractured. Sunday afternoons are still a customary time for family gatherings. On birthdays, saint's days, national holidays, and other special occasions, families instinctively reunite to renew familiar interrelations, recall old times, and catch up on the latest news regarding family members.

Among the poor, two, three, and even four families may live under one roof. It is common for upper-middle-class family members to house grandparents, a widowed aunt, an ill uncle, or a pair of newlyweds who are given time to settle down and save enough money for a car and down payment on a house. The *compadre* and his spouse and their family are also part of the immediate family, and they participate in all the family gatherings that time and other commitments will permit. Everyone in the immediate family and even the extended family looks after everyone else with respect to health and medical assistance, jobs and financial security, and social affairs and general emotional well-being.[2]

The home is a world apart from the world. The term *casa* ("home," "house") is from the same root as *casarse* ("to get married"), which also means "to unite," "join." Thus *casado* or *casada* ("married") is "housed," "enclosed," a "turning within." Within the home, *casado(a)*, and with a family, there exists a minisociety within the larger society. Outside is the other world, that of the *calle* ("street"), the world of cutthroat business wheeling and dealing and political maneuvers and enemies to contend with and friends and associates from whom to solicit favors and to whom favors must be given. Brazilian anthropologist Roberto DaMatta, writing about Brazilian society, hits the nail on the head, and to a great extent what he says of Brazil can be said of Mexico. *Casa* and *calle*, home and street, the family and the Others and the larger world consist of spaces that are symbolic of moral and ethical spheres of existence. The space of the home is that of hierarchical lines of paternalistic, interpersonal, patrimonial interrelations. The street, in contrast, is everyone for himself, a relatively egalitarian, individualistic existence. The two worlds are in constant interaction: just as the home cannot be hermetically sealed from street life, so also the street is influenced by the hierarchical, paternalistic values of family and home (DaMatta 1991).

House and street spaces are also polarized by gender, class, race, and age. The street is the male's domain, just as the house is where the female has her way. In the home—as well as in social institutions modeled on the home such as the Church, bureaucracy, workplace, and schools—the immediate family and servants and the extended family and friends interact according to paternal and maternal, patrimonial and interpersonal lines following the categories of gender, class, race, and age. Mothers and daughters and servants must know their proper role. Members of the family of lower social standing must pay customary respect to those of the family with higher standing. In addition, the aged are to be respected for their experience and wisdom.

The street is a different matter. In this dog-eat-dog world, it is every individual for himself. The rich can be assaulted. The poor can engage in "cultural guerrilla" practices, and if they are so disposed, they can assault others. In this manner they may be able to put themselves on equal footing with the rich. Women can enjoy greater freedom. They can become (almost) equal at the workplace; they can come and go in the restaurants, places of entertainment, and marketplaces as they wish; they can even flirt with men. Teenagers can run wild with their newly acquired freedom. In other words, the hierarchy of the home is flattened and occasionally inverted in the street. Where flattening occurs, African Americans and mulattos and mestizos do not necessarily engage in the same formal interaction with criollos. Rather, interethnic interrelations tend to become less formal. The street is where a more open and egalitarian society surfaces. This is the arena of risk taking and danger, of adventure and excitement, of spontaneous rule making and rule breaking. It is where the individual can become something other than what she was by her own will, intelligence, cunning, physical force, and even malice. The home, in contrast, is where the hierarchy stands in much the same way from generation to generation.

Of course, in the Anglo-American United States, this distinction to an extent exists in the street in contrast to the home. However, it is considerably more pronounced in Brazil, Mexico, and Latin America. More importantly, in addition to street and home, there is a third space, which brings the first two distinctions together in a *complementary* embrace: the Other world. This is the world of intercession by means of religious-moral-ethical values. In the religious hierarchy, lines of interrelation are mediated by saints and Christ and the Virgin. Similarly, lines of interrelation between the home and the street are mediated regarding family, business, schools, bureaucracy, and politics. Mediary elements intercede and moderate and arbitrate between opposing forces and between sinners and faithful, criollos and hybrid groups, men and women, adults and children, old and young, the powerful and the weak.

However, there is another aspect to the Other of mediation. The phenomenon of mediation is not simply a matter of a mediator interceding between polar opposites. Mediation also comes through the way people see themselves in their *interdependent, interrelated interaction* with Others, that are Other than themselves as *Others*. These distinctions are not merely a matter of economics or power. These Others—Amerindians, mestizos, mulattos—might view themselves as exploited, but they see their lot as still better than *Other Others*. Thus the relatively poor might say, "We are poor but at least we don't live in the slums." Those in the slums might say, "We live in the slums but at least we have a roof over our heads." Homeless recent arrivals might say, "We live on the streets but at least here in the city we have a chance." A man might say, "We Mexicans aren't rich like people in the United States, but we know how to be real men." Or you might hear a woman saying that "In the U.S. they have more money to buy clothes, but we know how to dress properly." A mestizo might declare, "It is true that I am *prieto* ("dark skinned"), but I have European features." And so on. The stories are virtually endless. By these and other "justifications" or "rationalizations," the hierarchialized differences become finer and finer until they seem to fade out of existence. Such is apparently the way of hybrid cultures.

Actually, however, the above sentences are neither justifications nor rationalizations. Mexican cultural logic is a means for placing oneself in the gap between the two poles of an opposition, and then between the remaining gaps, and then between the new gaps that are formed, and so on. Thus it cannot be said that between one value and another value there can be no third value. In Mexican cultural logic, there is always the possibility of a third term and a different value emerging into the light of day. The social hierarchy, consequently, is reproduced endlessly. It is reproduced at every juncture, but every reproduction yields cultural practices pushed by values that are something other than what they were. Up and down the cultural hierarchy there is a musical chairs trade-off at unexpected moments that realign attitudes toward gender, class, race, ethnicity, and age.

There is security in the hierarchical structure of the institutionalized Catholic Church and the local parish, of the patron-boss and worker at the factory, shop, or market, and of local and regional and national politics. It is in a deep sense the same hierarchy found in the home. If the larger society, in spite of its familiar cultural patterns, is mistrusted due to its sheer size and its unpredictable, threatening nature, there is at least safety in the home. Speaking of family, Mexico's Revolutionary Party bred the ultimate expression of the term.

The Revolutionary Family

The old boys club that had the voice in Mexico under the official political umbrella until 2000 was often dubbed the "revolutionary family," so named by Frank Brandenburg (1964) in his seminal study before Mexico took its authoritarian turn in 1968.

Since the revolution Mexico has been ruled by an elite. In that sense it hardly differs from prerevolutionary Mexico. The difference rests in the composition of the elite. Before the revolution, with a few notable exceptions, it consisted of criollos and upper-class mestizos. After the revolution there was an entire new generation of mestizos, who through military might, political favors, or sheer opportunism by availing themselves of the land and wealth that was there for the taking after the revolution, came into their own. Once again, Carlos Fuentes's *The Death of Artemio Cruz* (1964) is an excellent case. As a young lad at the outbreak of the revolution, Cruz journeyed into the central highlands. Joining up with whichever group that at the moment appeared to have the upper hand in the civil struggle, he finally survived in big fashion. He married the daughter of a large landowner, shrewdly established political contacts, invested money in the right places, and generally imposed his will on all people at all times. He became a member of the new rich class.

This is basically the class that made up the Revolutionary Family since the time of Carranza, when middle-class reformist interests triumphed. At the outset, the revolutionary family was composed of those who ran Mexico up to and including the 1970s. They set down the policy lines of the revolution and held effective decision-making power. Brandenburg reveals the nature of the revolutionary family through the words of a Mexican senator, Manuel Moreno Sánchez, who affirmed "vigorously and courageously" on the senate floor that "an oligarchy supported by the people governs in Mexico, an oligarchy that has made possible the leading of the nation into development." Brandenburg goes on to point out that this Mexican elite is not the usual type of Latin American oligarchy. The difference is that the Mexican elite "is a revolutionary minority, while others in Latin America are of a military, clerical, large agricultural, or of a simple industrial-financial type, and [as] conservative minorities they hold back from becoming revolutionary minorities." The problem with the other oligarchic elites is that they are not serious about the problem "of transforming their people, but merely about development of properties and of their own businesses" (Brandenburg 1964, 3).

Brandenburg goes on to write that the revolutionary family can be identified by (1) the members' *dedication* to the revolution and to the dream of building a better nation, (2) *friendship (compadrismo)* between revolutionary family members, forged on the revolutionary battlefield and later in nightclubs, universities, and government buildings, (3) the members' *self-interest* or opportunism in securing and retaining power, prestige, and wealth, (4) their *fear* of being defeated politically by those who remain outside the revolutionary family and the consequent loss of everything they worked for with respect to themselves and their people, and (5) the *inertia* they have built up by forming an integral part of an apparently well-oiled political machine that operates on the basis of professed dedication to the revolution. In essence, we have the characteristics of our above *casa* (family, security within), *calle* (threatening elements outside, insecurity) and *mediating Other* (by means of the revolutionary image in place of the Church). The revolutionary family possesses all the characteristics of the immediate Mexican family. Its nature and function are by and large defined through HC space and PC time. Consequently, *interdependent, interrelated interaction* between members of the family is pervaded through and through with tacit, nonverbal, nonlinear lines of communication.

Since the time of Cárdenas the head of the revolutionary family, *Señor Presidente*, governed not so much by a three-way division of power, but rather, by means of *corporate centralism* (see glossary). Since Congress and the Supreme Court were largely paper powers, it was the more hierarchical corporate structure that held the lines of interrelationships. This *corporate structure* consisted originally of four *sectors*—peasant, labor, popular, and military—that acted much as interest groups. The lines of communication and power went through the sectors and their representatives as mediators and directly to the president, thus bypassing the more horizontally organized congress and supreme court. In this manner, the president was directly linked to the people through the sector leaders. Candidates for political offices also reflected a corporate tendency, since the decision-making process for their selection required the support of the sectors. Cárdenas changed the sectors. He dissolved the military sector into the popular sector—which now included the governmental bureaucratic body and the professional class—and he included big business as the fourth sector.

The revolutionary family up to and into the 1970s seemed to possess assets that most ruling elites in developing countries lacked. It was apparently in tune with what the masses and classes desired. The family members carried on as if they knew what the people needed, what would be good for the country, and what route to take in order to get there. They grasped the importance of social reform and economic progress. They seemed devoted to political liberalism, which included public education, public health, and social services, economic growth, higher standards of living, industrialization and commercialization, continued agrarian reform, and defense of labor rights. They also realized the importance of hemispheric and global diplomacy. They had been able to avoid excessive instability and elevate Mexico to an exemplary spot in the eyes of the world. In brief, the "Mexican miracle" was paying dividends. But the method employed during those years was import substitution industrialization (ISI), which was soon to run into a brick wall and fall from grace, especially with the economic crisis of the 1980s.

The real glitch came in the 1980s and has continued to the present. I allude once again to the transition from pragmatically oriented *políticos* to the new Ivy League university–trained *técnicos*. Especially since Echeverría, interpersonal style has waned, with a cold, often cruel, businesslike administration taking its place. Traditional charismatic political interlocutors have been left behind in the dust by the nimble maneuvers and slick tactics of the *técnicos*. As a consequence, government has become increasingly isolated from the population: it has lost the charm of its family-like structure. It is strong on economic theory and weak on human relations. The revolutionary family can no longer gaze at the sky, smell the pastures, and listen to the grass grow; it is too busy manipulating the political machine, making sure its own members are not left in the cold, and accumulating more and more money through corruption. In the past, social mobility allowed teachers, union leaders, and small landowners to enter the political ring in order to voice popular sentiments. Now an Ivy League education at Harvard or its equivalent is mandatory for the card-carrying politician. The *técnicos* had forgotten how to take off their pinstripe suits and talk to the people, have breakfast with small-town politicians, rub elbows with white-collar professionals at the office.

In Alan Riding's (1984, 371) words, by trying to make the country more superficially democratic, "more Western, more 'presentable' abroad, the system's roots in the population have weakened. It has become less truly democratic because it is less representative of real Mexicans. The more the system responds to the Americanized minority, the more blatant will be the contradictions within the country." In other words, the revolutionary family was acting less like a Latino family and more like a business consortium. Nevertheless, a compelling attraction toward Mexican ways persist, as we shall see in the next chapter.

Further Reading

Camp 1993, Castañeda 1993, Cockcroft 1990, Cottam 1994, Gil 1992, Harrison 1997, Hartlyn and Schoultz 1992, Kryzanek 1990, Lewis 1959, 1961, 1966, 1969, Orme 1993, 1996b, Pike 1992, Rotella 1998, Vázquez and Meyer 1985. Fiction and essay: Fuentes 1978, 1997b, Monsiváis 1997, Poniatowska 1992, 1995.

Notes

1. I should point out, however, that in recent years the tradition of the *dedazo* and the *tapado* has waned, and prior to the 2000 election it came to an abrupt end and something vaguely suggesting primary elections went into effect. This is chiefly due to the fact that opposing parties have been capturing seats in congress and positions in local politics at an accelerated rate and the official party is no longer winning the elections by the overwhelming majority it once enjoyed (even after discounting an estimated number of rigged ballots). The beginning of the end of the *dedazo* and *tapado* might have occurred on September 8, 1999, when four hopeful PRI candidates for the presidential election of 2000 presented a televised public debate for the first time in Mexican history.

2. It cannot go without mention that these customs have been changing with increasing acceleration over the past three decades, for better or worse. The changes are yielding a society less interpersonal and more impersonal, closer to the U.S. mold.

14

Flying High or Primed for a Fall?

Pendulum Politics

Mexican culture, like all cultures, is rhythm—the most universal of phenomena. It is the way of the entire universe, from subnuclear frequencies to atoms and molecules to life rhythms to the movements of the planets and outward to galactic rhythms.

Figure 14.1 shows the to-and-fro rhythm of Mexican politics from the most right-wing political, social, and economic programs to moderate and leftist programs. After the most violent stage of Mexico's civil war, Carranza entrenched himself within middle-class interests, although he was compelled to oversee the writing of the most liberal constitution in the world in 1917 to appease the radical political factions that continued to wield considerable power. In the face of unrest, Obregón began instituting some of the revolutionary principles embodied in various constitutional articles. Then power gravitated to the authoritarian right with Calles. Cárdenas brought the pendulum swing drastically to the left, which was followed by increasingly stabilized rhythms until well into the Díaz Ordaz presidency.

The to-and-fro flow might lend itself to idle speculation. Like rebellious offspring, ingrate disciples often take every advantage to demonstrate their independence of their masters. Thus the swings could represent political turns after mild moments of rebellion. That, however, is a rather simplistic interpretation. An economic interpretation might see the

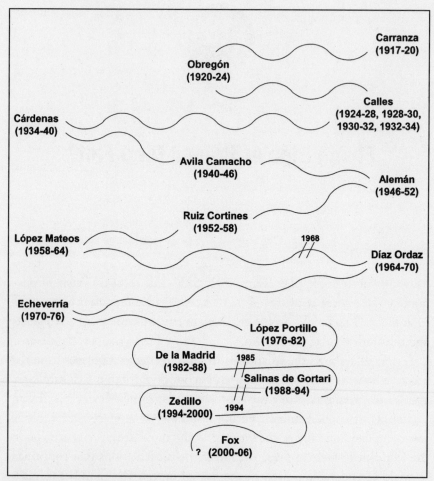

Figure 14.1   Mexico's Political Roller Coaster

flow as a series of responses to changing demands from lower-class work-ers and peasants, middle-class professionals and small businesses, and the upper class. A sociologist might view the swings as the consequence of dy-namic interaction between the social classes themselves. All these inter-pretations are to an extent correct. A more practical interpretation of Mexico's rhythms might focus on the nature of the nation's political sys-tem. From 1929 to 2000 Mexico was ruled by one party only. In a one-party system, movement must be from right to middle to left and back again in order to satisfy the demands of part of the people at least some of the time and all the people to the greatest possible extent.

It is almost as if the rightist presidents had been from one political party, the leftist presidents from another party, and the fence-straddling presidents from a third party. First, big business wants its favors and doesn't get them and begins pressuring the president by working through its special interest sector. So the president dances toward the right and does what needs to be done. After a while, the workers become disgruntled and want better pay for a day's work and more social programs. The next president brings himself in line with the changing demands. Then peasants raise their voices, wanting more attention and a piece of land they can call their own. *Señor Presidente* tries to accommodate them with a shuffle to the left. Everybody wants a bigger piece of the pie, but they must wait their turn. For quite a while, this system worked admirably well.

The pendulum effect was disrupted under Díaz Ordaz, when revolutionary Mexico experienced its first profound eruption: the massacre of 1968. Díaz Ordaz to all appearances did not begin his rule at the extreme authoritarian right. The unrest of 1968 saw him gravitate rightward, however, driven by the Revolutionary Family's fear of subversive elements. It was as if a drum began beating furiously and then was followed by a moment of hesitation, an instant of silence, the taut skins of the drums still quivering slightly, when suddenly the drums violently took off in a new direction. That's political rhythm breaking for you, Mexican style.

After the tragic event at Tlatelolco, people hardly dared open their mouths. The Olympic Games were inaugurated and closed with grand hoopla. By the end of the year it was back to business as usual in Mexico. However, the handwriting was on the wall. A time bomb existed below the surface of the calm demeanor of the Mexican people, and it could explode at any moment.

Parody Politics

Now enter Luís Echeverría and "guayabera politics." Echeverría never missed a chance to make himself over into another Lázaro Cárdenas in the eyes of the people. He encouraged land reform as no one had since

Cárdenas, opened up the universities and gave them the autonomy they had enjoyed in years past, supported students in the creation of a bitingly critical "theater of the people," and allowed a degree of criticism by the media. He flew to Cuba to embrace Castro, paid lip service to third world solidarity, rendered homage to Salvador Allende (the popularly elected socialist president of Chile), gave all peasants within reach a big *abrazo* in the countryside, and pressed the flesh of workers in whichever city he happened to be passing through. A man of the common folks, it seemed. At least that was the carefully created and orchestrated image.

During the Díaz Ordaz regime, Echeverría had often received CIA briefings, and he was the most senior civilian to sign off on the massacre of students at Tlatelolco. So, was his later leftist posture no more than a disguise? That might appear to be the case because when things went a bit too far, it was repression time as usual for the Echeverría regime. Shortly after Echeverría's inauguration on June 10, 1971, eleven students were killed by Mexico City police dressed like workers at the first protest march since Tlatelolco. Later, 25,000 troops were dispatched to crush a peasant rebellion organized by rural schoolteacher Lucio Cabañas. Yet the image of Don Luís the people's president, tailor-made by the media, was paraded about as if he were the world's favorite populist. In the end, however, the sand castle came tumbling down. Economic chaos and an overvalued peso led to the first devaluation in twenty-two years when he left office. Now it was López Portillo's turn, and after him came de la Madrid and the business school graduates. The rhythms now ceased taking their supple, elegant swings. They become tentative, swerving just enough to keep things from going too far astray. The big-time PRI band was now marching along a broad causeway without the customary twists and turns.

One of the chief disruptions of this theme occurred on September 19, 1985, when the most devastating earthquake in recent times hit Mexico City. According to government figures, 10,000 people died, but nongovernment estimates had it that the number of victims went as high as 30,000. The world's heartstrings went out to the Mexican people, while millions of World Bank dollars went into the country as aid. Much of the money mysteriously disappeared and very little was accomplished in favor of the earthquake's victims. Inactivity on the part of the government brought about a series of self-help efforts on the part of the general community that became the greatest force for social change since the 1960s. This has all the qualities of grassroots self-organization. The people literally took things into their own hands, disregarding the lumbering giant that called itself the revolutionary government. Meanwhile, back in the presidential palace, a request was issued that all citizens should remain in their homes and do nothing until further instructions. The government was caught completely off guard. It became paralyzed with its hands in the cookie jar. The patriarchs of the Revolutionary Family had apparently lost contact with their stepchildren.

The people had defied the government, and they began helping one another by the hundreds, then the thousands, then the tens of thousands. They poured into the streets with a wave of enthusiasm and energy unknown to a country that had grown apathetic since the 1960s. Now there was little protest of negative bent, but rather protest in the form of small armies of volunteers set upon helping people help themselves. Many of the organizers of the brigades were of leftist political orientation, leaders of community organizations who were not acting on their own initiative. There were hardly any store windows crashed, no slurs spouted out at the police, no antigovernment marches. There was just positive activism.

Volunteer brigades moved tons of rubble to save lives, built temporary shelters for the destitute, and provided food for the homeless. A local folk hero emerged, *Superbarrio* ("Superghetto"). Dressed like the masked cartoon strip wrestling champion, El Santo ("The Saint"), *Superbarrio* acted as mediator between the people and the government, taking their complaints to the local politicians: all this in spite of government inactivity. This was genuine solidarity, a spontaneously emerging community sense of interconnection. It had always existed as a latent force within the Mexican people. Now, in a time of crisis, it surfaced. The people themselves took power from the government as they never could in 1968 in spite of all the unrest. In a sense, the people themselves became their own government. They had a greater sense of national pride and civic spirit than anyone had imagined. Before, it was the *calle*, street life, where everybody was out for what he could get in a cruel world where only the fittest survive. Crawling like ants over and into the rubble, the people had become a community, a family. It was as if they all dwelled under a roofless *casa*. They were one.

How could the government have possibly reacted? The people were engaging in their own bootstrap operation as a protest against the corrupt do-nothing politicians who remained ensconced in their plush homes in the San Angel district that had been barely affected by the earth's tremors. The people weren't marching against the presidential palace; they weren't creating violence in the name of protest. This was a new form of activism against which the president was helpless. Something new, something different was underfoot. Popularization of this new political view can be attributed primarily to reporter and social critic Carlos Monsiváis. In a series of newspaper and magazine articles later collected in a volume, *Entrada libre: Crónicas de la sociedad que se organiza* (Free Admission: A Chronicle About a Self-Organizing Society) (1987), Monsiváis interpreted the people's response to the earthquake and the government's lethargy as a new force for social change and a new form of political protest: civic action.

When Mexico City shook on September 19, "all the old idols fell from their altars and were shattered. Mexico was ready for a new movement and, equally important, for a new way of thinking about and describing that movement" (La Botz 1995, 72). Meanwhile, the politicians stared blankly at themselves. And what did they see? Pale reflections of outmoded ideas dressed up in their Ivy League best.

Pomp and Politics

Almost a decade later, another burp occurred in the Mexican social-economic-political milieu. I refer to New Year 1994, NAFTA, and the EZLN rebellion. The Zapatistas' cry for indigenous autonomy and a struggle against neoliberalism brought out the tear-jerking best in human rights groups and intellectuals the world over. Marcos the mad-faxer proved adept at beating torpid politicians at their own game of rhetoric and endearing himself with the media. Over 100,000 sympathetic demonstrators filled the *Zócalo* (central plaza) of Mexico City thrice in a display of mass support. The defiant slogan *Todos somos Marcos* ("We are all Marcos") was directed at Marcos's supposed unmasking to assert that the Subcomandante's identity was of no consequence, for they were all one in mind and spirit.

Money fled Mexico and the gross domestic product slid; the peso had been devalued and interest rates and inflation exploded; wages fell to new lows while cynicism over Mexico's new line of *técnicos* brought nothing but howls. As already noted, NAFTA spelled quick death to the people's *fayuca* industry—smuggled or cheaply bought defective goods from the United States sold on the streets and in neighborhood markets. Since many U.S. products could now be brought across the border without charge, big business caused thousands of small family-owned businesses to close their doors. It quickly became apparent that "free trade" was less freedom in trade than the powerful flexing their muscles and the weak either bowing down or going under. Freedom is the colonizer doing what it wishes with the colonized, the *hegemonic* state exercising its will on its satellites, big bucks ripping off small-time capitalism in order to ensure its perpetuity. Free trade opened Mexican markets to wild speculation that gave the advantage to those who had the experience, the connections, and the financial wherewithal. A few Mexicans enriched themselves, but above all multinational corporations from the United States raked in the money. Free trade offered a huge pool of cheap labor at the doorstep of many of the biggest manufacturing concerns in the world. The factories that pushed their way through the desert floor like mushrooms along hiking trails in a temperate rain forest provided few benefits and poor working conditions, and they dumped intoxicants by the hundreds of gallons per day. What happened was inevitable: in the short run, a union of two nations so disparate in power and wealth could not be anything but crushing for the weaker of the two, leading to a radical diminishing of its sovereignty.

When the Mexican meltdown of 1994 occurred, President Bill Clinton offered a $40 billion loan guarantee, but it didn't get past the U.S. Congress. Then he took $20 billion from the Exchange Stabilization Fund, an action that didn't need congressional approval, and convinced the International Monetary Fund to chip in $17.5 billion. In order to acquire this support, President Zedillo promised greater foreign control of Mexican banks and privatization of transportation and telecommunications, all of which Salinas had refused to do. At one point, around 80 percent of North

Americans opposed the bailout, and most Mexicans were against their nation's loss of its sovereignty to the United States. The industrial giants in Mexico opposed the move, and money lenders in the United States were wary. Riordan Roett, Mexican expert advising the Chase Manhattan Bank, observed that the Mexican government would "need to eliminate the Zapatistas to demonstrate their effective control of the national territory and security policy" (Warnock 1995, 273). Nevertheless, it was damn the torpedoes and full speed ahead. The new lean and mean Revolutionary Family with their slick suits pushed on.

In sum, the pendulum effect of the Mexican political machine, as illustrated in Figure 14.1, had stripped a pinion gear and suffered a broken axle. Mexican politics was previously qualified in pragmatic fixing-what-needs-to-be-fixed terms. By the 1980s, in contrast, presidents could be labeled "leftist" or "rightist," but the words had lost their substance:

> Echeverría was considered a radical, yet he tamed the domestic Left and did nothing to hurt the private sector; López Portillo was seen as pro-business, but he took over the country's banks at the end of his term; and De la Madrid began conservatively but did not reduce the state's role in the economy. Thus, the pendulum does swing—not to the left and right, but in all directions—and its purpose is to correct a political imbalance even if in the process a new imbalance is created. (Riding 1984, 70)

From the more or less orderly rhythms that emerged out of the revolution, disorder set in. The disorder verged toward chaos, now in a somewhat orderly direction, now teetering precariously while trying to keep up the balancing act, now in the act of ephemerally establishing some semblance of order. And so it went in Mexico, land of magic, miracles, and *maquiladoras*.

Or Perhaps Virtual Mexico?

Politics to the left and to the right and oscillation in between. Economics with the Mexican miracle or the Mexican malaise. Society of Imaginary

Mexico and México Profundo, of the haves and the have-nots. The verdict is usually: Mexico is a land of contrasts. Contrasts? The very idea suggests a morass of contradictions, oppositions, polar conflicts.

But this is not the case at all. When pairs of opposite forces exist, the common assumption is that they exist in either the one end or the other of the polarities. There can hardly be any alternatives. What there is, there is, and when it comes in a two-way choice, you make your choice and take your chances. However, Mexico has never been a land of either this or that as two roads promising a definite goal at the end. Mexico has hardly been a land of real opportunities on the order of the North American myth dictating "Go west, young man!" You carve out your niche in the world and make fame and fortune by the sweat of your brow. Mexico was never "real" in this sense. Since the very beginning, the Spaniards, upon entering Tenochtitlán, in Bernal Díaz del Castillo's words, felt they were in an enchanted land. Mexico has ever since been tinged with *enchantment*. Indeed, if there can be a virtual land, a virtual nation, a virtual polity, a virtual economy, a virtual culture, Mexico surely fills the bill.

Mexico has always been an experiment. Cortés in an enchanted New World constantly improvised, since at every step of the way in the march of conquest, new situations never ceased to arise. The establishment of a colonial empire was a great experiment, an attempt to create a City of God in this New World. Bartolomé de las Casas's struggle for a forerunner to modern human rights movements and Father Vasco de Quiroga's grand utopian dreams are shining examples of the experimental nature of this New World as virtuality. Criollo independence was a return to the past and a look to an indeterminate future with an eye toward constructing an entirely new society. Nineteenth-century Mexican liberalism from Benito Juárez to the end of the Porfirio Díaz dictatorship, with its positivist overtones, was a throwback to those age-old Western ways of blueprinting how a nation should work. Here we have the first monolithic departure from Mexico as the virtuality of innumerable possibilities in favor of an authoritarian "this is the right way and the way it's got to be, because it's the Western way to modernization!"

Then came the revolution. A feast of virtualities. Every move brought on a host of indeterminables, and any one of them could lead to nobody knew where. The most progressive constitution in the West at the time was written. Then there was land reform evoking pre-Hispanic times, muralists creating art for the people, a political party created for particular Mexican cultural characteristics: everything was an experiment, a groping in the dark for elusive hand- and footholds. After problems erupted in 1968 and afterward, there was neoliberalism. Like nineteenth-century liberalism, it was more an imported doctrine than an experimental creation, more a question of Imaginary Mexico's wanting to be something it never was and will never be than México Profundo's genuine self-expression. It was more *maquiladora* and "Made in America" Mexico than Magical Mexico. It was more the best of the West and to hell with the rest than the Other Mexico. (As the story went from Imaginary Mexico, the Other Mexico could never carry its share of the load, and therefore Imaginary Mexico had to take on the "lighter man's burden," if not exactly the "white man's burden.")

Mexico was never simply an *either-or* choice. This is revealed in the first of the novels of the Mexican Revolution, Mariano Azuela's *The Underdogs* (1996). Demetrio Macías, peasant leader of a local band of revolutionaries with hardly any awareness of the overall picture, engages in a personal struggle against landowner Don Mónico. Demetri's small peasant group enters into a few important battles but otherwise roams the countryside, looting and destroying. Thus far we have clear conflict between Amerindian peasants and criollo and mestizo landlords. Early in the novel we read about a medical student from Mexico City, Luis Cervantes, who leaves for the countryside to engage in an idealistic fight to end tyranny, injustice, and dictatorial governments once and for all. Luis's abstract platitudes fall on deaf ears, however. Macías's peasants will have no truck with his sweeping generalities. They desire a piece of land they can call their own and the concrete affairs of everyday life. Another character, Alberto Solís, briefly enters the narrative to present a cynical view of the revolution that complements Luis's idealism after a battle:

How beautiful the revolution! Even in its most barbarous aspect it is beautiful. . . . A pity what remains to do won't be as beautiful! We must wait a while, until there are no men left to fight on either side, until no sound of shot rings through the air save from the mob as carrion-like it falls upon the booty; we must wait until the psychology of our race, condensed into two words, shines clear and luminous as a drop of water: *Robbery! Murder!* What a colossal failure we would make of it, friend, if we, who offer our enthusiasm and lives to crush a wretched tyrant, become the builders of a monstrous edifice holding one hundred or two hundred thousand monsters of exactly the same sort. (Azuela 1996, 81)

And so it is becoming. According to many observing the Mexican scene today, neoliberal Mexico is a "monstrous edifice" holding "monsters of the same sort" as the monsters of nineteenth-century liberalism.

But this is not the end of the tale. Luis Cervantes's idealism mixed with Alberto Solís's cynicism to make a concoction of *neither* hope *nor* despair, *neither* tunnel-minded revolutionary zeal *nor* imitation of the West, *neither* carefully trimmed hair and an expensive suit and a laptop computer in hand and two private secretaries in the office *nor* an Amerindian peasant subsisting on a few acres of eroded land, but something else. What is that something else? Is it a corporate state? No. That had been present in Mexico since colonial times. Is it a paternalistic, patriarchal, society of patronage and favors granted for favors received and the "old boys club"? No. There was always a matriarchal side of Mexican society, in part derived from non-Aztec pre-Hispanic cultures, and in part the woman's powerful influence in the *casa* as a counterpart to the male, macho world of the *calle*. What, then, is that something else?

Mexican society is in a very real sense more than multiethnic and more than pluralistic, and more than a juxtaposition of cultural artifacts and traditions and proclivities. It is, in our now familiar word, *hybrid*. It is *neither* the one cultural manifestation *nor* the other, but rather something *emergent*. Imitating a monolithic model in order to make Mexico something other than what it is would be insufficient, as are pairs of oppositions or contradictions that force a choice between *either* the one extreme *or* the other. Mexico is Other, an Other that is always becoming something Other than what it was becoming. The fluid *interdependent interrelations* between classes and ethnicities and genders and ages and cultural trends gives them the appearance not of things but of process. Process is a time and a place where a story is being told. The staging of the story is no stage in the ordinary sense but, like the canals of ancient Tenochtitlán, it slowly flows, and the actors do a walk-on-water syncopated dance along the surface, changing their countenance with every pirouetting maneuver.

The flow and the dance were in process long before the conquest. The dance flowed during the Bourbon reforms, when there was an attempt to impose foreign models on the Hispanic-criollo-mestizo-Amerindian-African Mexican emergent cultural hybrid, which culminated in the movement for independence. It flowed until the liberal reforms of Juárez and took a bizarre turn in the Porfirio Díaz era. That imitation of things foreign ended in part during and after the Mexican Revolution. It flowed again. The flow went its way, with syncopated hiccups and a few violent eruptions, yet it continued along its undulating channel. Then there was neoliberalism. Once again the Hispanic-criollo-mestizo-Amerindian-African Mexican tradition was shaken violently. A fissure appeared and widened, and Subcomandante Marcos and EZLN revealed the alien neoliberal model for what it was, at least with respect to the Mexican condition: an empty shell. What will the next move be?

A New-Style Caudillo?

There was a sparkle in the eyes of many Mexicans after the 2000 presidential elections, for they believed the next move had begun. This sparkle was lit by Vicente Fox Quesada of the National Action Party (PAN), president elect.

Born in 1942 in the provincial city of León, Guanajuato, educated in Jesuit schools, including the Iberoamerican University, and holding a degree from Harvard University, Vicente Fox began working for Coca-Cola in 1964 and eventually became Director of the Mexican branch. After he was appointed PAN candidate for the presidency, he caught the eye of news correspondents in the United States. *Time* magazine touted him as "Big Hat, Big Man." At a "swaggering 6 ft. 5 in.," he "satisfies the Mexican hankering for a caudillo—a strong man. He's built like an ideal candidate: tall enough so everyone in a crowded zócalo can get a good look at the 'Marlboro Man' of Mexican politics" (McGirk 2000, 42). After the elections, *Newsweek* dubbed him "Soda Pop to *Vox Populi*," the "Coca-Cola man" who did the impossible: he beat up on the PRI. However, as Alan Zarembo of *Newsweek* was quick to point out,

> Delivering soda pop is child's play compared to managing a nation in which a largely corrupt, age-old power structure has just been razed and everybody is scrambling for influence. There are business moguls who dominate the Mexican economy in no small part because of their ties to the PRI. There are drug traffickers who have bribed police and politicians to help them move billions of dollars worth of cocaine into the U.S. each year. Most important, there are millions of poor voters counting on Fox, 58, to make economic growth trickle down to them. (Zarembo 2000, 36)

Yet the *Newsweek* correspondent conceded that

> In his first week as president-elect, Fox did everything right. He didn't gloat. He calmed investors by vowing to work closely with the outgoing government during the five-month transition. . . . But . . . the honeymoon will not last long. (Zarembo 2000, 36)

Still, Fox has a lot going for him. The price of oil, Mexico's chief export (Mexico ranks fifth in the world as an exporter), has been high. The economy has seen five years of sustained growth for the first time in decades, and the GNP increase was expected to be around 4.5 percent for 2000. Inflation is under 10 percent, the lowest in recent memory, and the same can be said of the interest rate at 13 percent (Danell Sánchez 2000).

How does Fox think he can accomplish what a year earlier would have been virtually inconceivable? He plans to increase the growth of the economy up to 7 percent to make sure 1,350,000 new jobs are created each year. He realizes there are huge differences in salaries between Mexico and the United States. On the Mexican side, a worker makes about $5 a day; on the U.S. side the same work would bring in about $60. In an attempt to reduce that gap and eliminate the differences as much as possible, Fox is taking a long-term look at the problem. His proposal is to move to a second phase of NAFTA according to which the border will be open to the free flow of people, workers, and transit, which is now occurring with products, services, and merchandise. He is looking toward a common market like the one in Europe that raised the standard of living in Greece, Spain, and Portugal to a level approaching that in other European countries.

With respect to political changes, Fox envisions a cabinet that will be integrated plurally, selected from the best men and women available. Talent, experience, delivery of results, honesty, accountability, and moral fiber will be the key, rather than nepotism and old-boy tactics as was common every six years during PRI rule. Fox wants one real democracy including three genuine branches of power with ample checks and balances. Ethical values and moral fiber are of utmost importance, he believes, to reduce the corruption that has been rampant over the past years. Fox promises much and even talks about compromise with the Zapatistas— although at the end of 2002 the talks bore little fruit.

Can the president-elect pull it off? Who knows? Whatever the future holds, as always, Mexico, radically PC and HC Mexico, "illogically logical" Mexico, perpetually enchanting and enchanted Mexico, will have an intriguing story to tell.

Further Reading

Agosín 1989, Baddeley and Fraser 1989, Bernal and Knight 1993, Castañeda 1995, Davies 1986, Dunn 1996, Gómez-Peña 1996, Gómez-Quiñones 1990, Heusinkveld 1994, Kandell 1988, Katzenberger 1995, Maciel and Herera-Sobek 1998, Maril 1992, Martínez 1994, Monroy 1990, Moore and Pachón 1985, Mora 1990, Padilla 1985, Rangel 1987, Rouffignac 1985, Sánchez 1993, Sayers 1991, Schaefer 1992, Steele 1992, Suro 1999, Vélez-Ibáñez 1996, Vigil 1988, 1998, Warnock 1995. Fiction and documentary: Conover 1987, Glantz 1991.

Mexican Presidents Since the Revolution

Francisco I. Madero..1911–1913

Victoriano Huerta 1913–1914

Venustiano Carranza..1915–1920

Álvaro Obregón...1920–1924

Plutarco Elias Calles 1924–1928

Emilio Portes Gil 1928–1930

Pascual Ortíz Rubio...1930–1932

Abelardo Rodríguez 1932–1934

Lázaro Cárdenas 1934–1940

Manuel Ávila Camacho 1940–1946

Miguel Alemán Valdés......................................1946–1952

Adolfo Ruíz Cortines.......................................1952–1958

Adolfo López Mateos..1958–1964

Gustavo Díaz Ordaz 1964–1970

Luis Echeverría Álvarez....................................1970–1976

José López Portillo 1976–1982

Miguel de la Madrid Hurtado 1982–1988

Carlos Salinas de Gortari 1988–1994

Ernesto Zedillo..1994–2000

Vicente Fox Quesada..2000–2006

Glossary

Aguantar The verb means to endure, tolerate, resist, have patience, put up with. Earl Shorris (1992, 106) uses the term in reference to Latino attitudes in the United States. When the Anglos first contacted Mexicans in what is now the U.S. Southwest, they judged from the Mexicans' willingness to endure that they were docile and easily managed. As a result of this judgment, the Anglos, indoctrinated with a more aggressive, competitive spirit, began imposing their will on their neighbors. Consequently, Shorris writes, the Mexicans lost out in labor negotiations, education, housing, and every aspect of life in the United States.

American The term customarily attached to citizens of the United States of America. Mexico's full name is the United States of Mexico, and the same can be said of many other Latin American nations. This offers food for thought. Mexico is "American," Bolivia is "American," Argentina is "American." Would not Colombians, or the citizens of any other Latin American nation, also have the right to call their country the "United States of America" if they so desired? Americans have, in a certain sense, a country without a name they can call their own. In this volume I use the terms "North America" and "United States" when referring to our country.

Amerindian A Native American. This term, more economical than "Native American" or "Native American Indian," is now commonly used in Latin American scholarship.

Biculturalism This term qualifies a person who knows a second language and a second culture. But in today's world, the idea of pure biculturalism is questionable. Even those who know two languages and two cultures are aware of words and expressions and gestures from people who speak many other languages. In everyday life, and through the media, people are exposed to bits and pieces of many foreign cultures.

Black Legend   The tradition that points a finger at Spain and the misconduct of the conquerors. It was chiefly the creation of English writers attempting to denigrate and denounce Spain's role in the Americas. Their early source of ammunition was the writings of Bartolomé de las Casas and his vitriolic works criticizing the Spaniards' destruction of Amerindians and their cultures. The Black Legend has thrived wherever there has been a need, as in English-speaking nations and modern Spanish America, to criticize Spain and her colonial history.

Bourbon Reforms   The Habsburgs of Austria ruled Spain from the time of Ferdinand and Isabella until 1700, when the French Bourbons occupied the Spanish throne, extending the influence of France and French ideas. The Bourbon reforms, which included practices inspired by Enlightenment thought, reached their zenith under Charles III (1759–1788). Charles III centralized authority, brought greater unity between the Crown and the colonies, and injected the colonial economy with more efficient and capitalistic practices. When Charles III died in 1788, he left the throne to his son, Charles IV, who was weak and vacillating. Subsequently Charles IV undid much of what his father had accomplished, eliciting a general sense of ill will that eventually erupted in a movement for independence.

Cacique   Derived from Taino-Arawak, a dialect from the Caribbean, it means "chief" or "boss." During the twentieth century, the term "cacique," at times carrying pejorative connotations, has been put to use to designate someone who exercises local dominance.

Caudillo   Derived from an Arabic term meaning "leader." The Latin American caudillo is a charismatic, physically impressive, strong-willed, domineering individual, often of military background, whose rule is usually marked by populist tactics. Caudillos of diverse sorts dominated much of Latin America for the greater part of the nineteenth century, and in some countries even into the second half of the twentieth century.

Científicos   The group of advisers under Porfirio Díaz who were indoctrinated in the positivist doctrine of French philosopher Auguste Comte. They attempted to apply Comte's abstract metaphysics to Mexican social reality.

Compadre   Literally, a "godfather," who in the Latin community is considered the protector and benefactor of the child he sponsors. In popular speech and customs, the term also indicates an intimate friend, companion, buddy, pal, or person of close bonding. The complementary term *comadre* is used of female companions.

Contact Zone   Understanding a culture, subcultures within one's own culture, or the culture of other people implies a "contact zone." Outside the zone there are hardly any cultural differences capable of identifying what is more important and what is less important within each of the two or more cultures or subcultures in question. Within the contact zone there is conflict and struggle and sometimes violence, and hopefully some negotiation and a little bit of comprehension. In the contact zone there is an ongoing process of confrontation and conflict, complementation and accommodation, and hopefully comprehension.

Contradictory Complementarity   The cultural model propagated in this volume, in contrast to dualist philosophies. Contradictory complementarity involves hybridization (which produces rich cultural settings), and it brings about the emergence of cultural practices that conflict on some points. Cultural practices are replete with tensions that can erupt in conflict and violence unless they are mediated by dialogue. It can run the gamut from confrontation to soothing and exuding good will. In this sense, contradictions, rather than all-or-nothing, either-or binary oppositions, are actually complementary: they are contradictorily complementary, caught up in an intimate liquid embrace in which the one merges into the other and neither can exist without taking in some of the other.

Corporatism   A political system in which the principal economic functions (business, industry, labor, peasants, bureaucracy, professionals) are organized as collective bodies or *sectors* that address themselves directly to the person or corporate body in power, which in the case of Mexico has traditionally been the president. In Mexico, the demands of influential groups are channeled toward the president, who acts as the ultimate arbiter and ideally sees that no one group becomes predominant.

Criollo(a)   A person born of Spanish parents in the Americas, in contrast to the *peninsular*, who is a Spaniard born in Europe.

Cultural Pluralism   Replaces the "melting pot" idea, which was never a reality in the United States, though Mexico and Latin America approach the ideal of a racial and ethnic "melting pot" in certain respects. Ideally, members of a pluralistic culture recognize the contributions each group makes to the common society and encourage the creation of diverse lifestyles, languages, and convictions. Of equal importance is a commitment among the different groups in a pluralistic culture to cooperate toward common concerns in such a manner that the entire collection of cultures and subcultures may develop in the most harmonious possible way.

Culture   Edward T. Hall (1983, 230–231) specifies three levels of culture: *primary*, *secondary*, and *explicit* or *manifest*. Primary level culture "is that variety of culture in which the rules are: known to all, obeyed by all, but seldom if ever stated. Its rules are implicit, they are taken for granted, almost impossible for the average person to state as a system, and generally out of awareness. Secondary level culture, though in full awareness, is normally hidden from outsiders. Secondary level culture is as regular and binding as any other level of culture, possibly even more so. It is that level of culture which the Pueblo Indians of New Mexico keep from white people. But it can also be the special culture of virtually any group or society. Tertiary or explicit, manifest culture is what we all see and share in each other. It is the façade presented to the world at large. Because it is so easily manipulated, it is the least stable and least dependable for purposes of decision making." In short, a culture is a complete form of life, a composite of an entire community's ways of living. It includes values, beliefs, esthetic standards, linguistic expressions, patterns of thinking, behavioral norms, and styles of communication that a group of people has developed to ensure its survival in a particular physical and human environment. Cultures are the sum of all the propensities and proclivities, the belief patterns and the attitudes, and the responses of the entire group of human beings to the valid and particular needs of their members.

Dedazo   Indicative of the centralized power of the Mexican government. The *dedazo* is incorporated in the procedures of the official party, now going by the name of the Institutionalized Revolutionary Party (PRI). Mexican presidents traditionally have power to "point the finger *(dedo)* and give a favorable nod" to the person who, it is immediately assumed, will be next in line.

Ejido   Communal land among the Amerindians. The *ejido* system was instituted during pre-Hispanic times. The Amerindians were granted the privilege of working the communal property, though there was no concept of private ownership because all the land was considered property of the community. The *ejidos* were reinstituted principally during President Lázaro Cárdenas's land reform (1934–1940).

Encomienda   During colonial times, a grant of land and authority over the Amerindians residing on the land. The *encomienda* carried obligations to Christianize and protect the Amerindians in exchange for their labor and tribute. In the beginning, *encomiendas* were given as a reward to the Spanish conquerors. The owner of an *encomienda* is an *encomendero*.

Ethnicity   Identification of the people within a particular community in terms of national or cultural characteristics, and, often unfortunately and erroneously, as a consequence of race. Ethnic group membership is determined at birth, but it is gradually acquired as the individual is assimilated into and accommodates himself to the community. Ethnicity is commonly conceived as that which distinguishes one subgroup from another subgroup within a larger, usually heterogeneous society.

Guadalupana   A cult of the Virgin Mary, specifically the Virgin of Guadalupe, who appeared to Amerindian Juan Diego in 1531. Guadalupe has over the years contributed to a sense of Mexican national heritage and identity.

Habsburg   The Austrian ruling family in Spain from the time of Ferdinand and Isabella to 1700, when the French Bourbons occupied the throne.

Hacienda   A large ranch, or plantation, owned by a *hacendado*, who obliged landless peasants to work the land while maintaining control over their services in the form of debt peonage.

HC Culture–LC Culture   Edward T. Hall (1966) places language use along a continuous spectrum from "low-context" (LC) cultures to "high-context" (HC) cultures. In communication that tends toward HC, the focus of information is either in the physical context or is internalized in the speakers and listeners. If the focus of information lies chiefly in the physical context, there is less need for explicit and exclusively linguistic meanings: the meaning is in the entire context, including the situation that prevails, the conditions present, and nonverbal gestures and body language displayed by the interlocutors. If the focus of information is primarily internalized in the body and mind of the interlocutors, they have expectations as a result of past experience that certain meanings will be forthcoming, and their ability to communicate (or not) is a matter of how effectively their expectations merge and interact with one another. If LC is the tendency, information is forthcoming chiefly by way of explicit linguistic ways and means of expression.

Hegemony   The result of dynamic interaction between state and citizens. Italian intellectual Antonio Gramsci viewed both the state and the citizenry as dynamic processes flowing within the stream of history. In this manner, there is neither absolute dominance nor absolute subservience, but rather perpetual flows of power give-and-take such that the people bring pressure to bear on the state and act as agents of change, and the state is forced to devise ever newer means of reexercising its dominance as a result of its interaction with the people. Unfortunately, the term *hegemony* is occasionally—and erroneously—considered in the order of a static, intransigent two-way conflict between the center of power on the one hand and the people on the other hand.

Hidalguismo   Considered the right of nobility to which virtually all Spaniards aspired during the precolonial and early colonial period in Spain and America. Under certain circumstances the prestige accrued through becoming a *hidalgo* could be purchased.

Hybridity   The fusion of cultural practices and their implied norms and conventions into something new that, according to the perspective, can be perceived and conceived as *both* one practice *and* another practice or *neither* exactly one practice *nor* the other practice but something different. This entails the emergence of new transcultural forms within the contact zone, the in-betweenness where cultures meet. Hybridity, according to the term's use in this book, should not be limited to "cross-cultural exchange." There is no "cross-culture," for two or more cultural practices have merged into one another to give birth to something other than what could be qualified as *either* the one *or* the other. And there is no "exchange," since what was of one cultural practice is now of the other practice, and vice versa. The *mutual interpenetration* of *interdependent, interrelated, interactive* cultural practices gives rise to the emergence of something generically new.

Interactive   See Interdependence.

Interdependence   Related to *interactiveness* and *interrelatedness*. One of the major thrusts of this present volume is that Mexican, Latin American, and indeed all cultures the world over, are composed of multiple interrelatedness between people, events, and things. This interrelatedness is qualified by the ongoing process of interactivity as a result of the interdependency of everything with everything else in such a way that nothing happens without that happening bringing about some alteration, however minute, within the interrelated whole of culture.

Interrelated   See Interdependence.

Latinos   People of Hispanic origin whose heritage may also be liberally sprinkled with Amerindian, African American, and some Oriental, Italian, Germanic, and Anglo roots. A single noun that qualifies any and all "Latinos" does not exist. In the U.S. census and for legal purposes, Hispanic is most common. Geographically, Hispanic is usually preferred in the Southeast and in much of Texas, although in certain parts of New Mexico and California, Spanish is considered "more refined." In the Southwest one may occasionally hear *Mexican* used as a blanket noun, but this usage is becoming less common with the influx of Central Americans and Caribbean immigrants. During the 1960s, militant citizens and immigrants chiefly of Mexican origin began referring to themselves as *Chicanos* (after *Mexicas* ["Meshicas"], the ancient Aztecs), but that term has been used less and less with the passage of time.

Legitimacy Vacuum   The political vacuum that remained after independence in Mexico and Spanish America, when legitimacy no longer commanded the image of a sovereign King, endowed with authority by the divine grace of God. Elected officials usually failed adequately to fit the bill, that is, unless they were of sufficient charisma—caudillo types—and could captivate the people to the extent that they became inspired to place an unwritten stamp of legitimacy on their leader.

Logic (classical) Based on the Aristotelian principles of *identity* (*A* is *A* and nothing else), *noncontradiction* (if *A* is the case, then it cannot be the case that *Not-A* is the case at the same time), and *excluded-middle* (either *A* or *Not-A* [or either *A* or *B*] is the case, and there can be no alternatives). The chief characteristics of this logic are *linearity* (if *A* implies *B* and *B* implies *C*, then *A* implies *C*) and *binarism* (only two values are possible, truth or falsity, positive or negative, *A* or *Not-A*, *A* or *B*). Linearity falls in line with cause-and-effect sequences, and binarism gives credibility to common cultural values, such as male/female, good/evil, we/they, aristocracy/masses, developed/undeveloped, that have led to justification of many ethnocentric biases throughout history.

Machismo A concept of manliness in Mexico and throughout Latin America. It involves physical strength, braggadocio, sexual virility, self-confident boldness and brashness, a will to dominate (especially women), and a readiness to demonstrate all of these characteristics at a moment's notice. In regard to Mexican machismo, this self-assertion is often displayed through verbal prowess.

Malinchista A person who has taken a liking to foreign things and customs and criticizes and shuns Mexican things and customs, that is, "betrays" the Mexican cultural heritage. *Malinchista* is derived from the Amerindian name Malintzín or Malinche (later with the baptism name of "doña Marina"), the woman who was given to Hernán Cortés shortly after he arrived on the Gulf Coast in 1519. Malinche subsequently played an important role as an interpreter and adviser to the Spaniards, which helped Cortés in his effort to conquer the Aztecs. Thus she "betrayed" her people.

Mestizo The offspring of an Amerindian mother and a Spanish father, but the inverse was and is occasionally the case as well.

Monoculturalism Qualifies a person who knows one language and one culture and no more. However, in today's world, even someone who does not know a second language cannot help becoming aware of words and expressions and gestures from people who speak another language. Even someone who has not navigated through another culture, in everyday life and by way of the media, cannot help picking up bits and pieces of various foreign cultures. Thus the idea of pure monoculturalism is debatable.

Mulatto The offspring usually of a European father and an African mother, but the inverse is occasionally the case as well.

Multicultural Awareness Possessed by one who understands, accepts, and has a sense of and an appreciation for various cultures. Multicultural awareness entails acknowledgment of (1) socioeconomic interrelationships (urban, rural, age-groups, worker, middle and upper classes), (2) professional interrelationships (doctors, lawyers, businesspeople, teachers, and professors), and (3) interrelationships at work, church, school, places of recreation, and between families and friends. A multiculturally aware person has a profound sense of the differences between all the above between one culture and another culture.

Nonverbal Communication An essential characteristic of all human cultures. Verbal communication composes only a small portion—E. T. Hall estimates 10–15 percent—of the communication that goes on within a given culture. Of more importance is the silent, nonverbal communication of which we are at best only partly aware (i.e., primary and secondary culture). Millions of people cross paths daily in New York, Tokyo, São Paulo, and Mexico City. They pass nonverbal cues to one another with such facility that it seems well-nigh incomprehensible. A nod of the head, a wave, a glance, a thumbs-up sign, a hand held out indicating "halt," a smile or grimace, a shrug, a slap on the back or a hug: there is an endless number of signs, most existing on relatively nonconscious or tacit levels. These tacit signs are of a subtlety too complex for words. It is these shared, often unarticulated, and occasionally unarticulable and nonconscious patterns of perception, conception, communication, and behavior that make up most of what is known as "culture."

Other Entails the state of being Other or different or distinct. The popular cultural Other is usually considered subordinate to the Other of the Other, the dominant culture. As such, the popular cultural Other can present alternatives to the patterns, norms, and standards of the dominant culture of which the Other is Otherness.

Paternalism The practice of treating or governing people in a patriarchal manner, especially by providing for their needs while allowing them a minimum of responsibility and expecting their loyalty in return.

Patronage Support, aid, or a helping hand extended to someone of lower social status by someone of higher social status, a *patrón* ("patron"). This is usually done in a patronizing manner, and it entails the prior distribution of individuals along the political, bureaucratic, social, and cultural hierarchy in order that paternalistic lines of interrelations and interaction may be carried out.

PC Time–MC Time Edward T. Hall (1966) places "monochronic time" (MC) at one end of a cultural time spectrum and at the other end he places "polychronic time." MC cultures stress activities on a one-thing-at-a-time basis. PC cultures are immersed in a mix of activities. Time in predominantly MC cultures is relatively *linear*; time in cultures leaning toward PC time is relatively *nonlinear*.

Personalismo   The nature of Mexican concrete, personal, interrelational ties as a natural outgrowth of a paternalistic culture. *Personalismo* exists in contrast to the relatively abstract, institutional, systematic ties more typical of Anglo-American culture.

Populism   Political tactics directed toward the masses, usually advocating a more equitable distribution of wealth and power, although sometimes with a tinge of falsity or hypocrisy in an effort to win the approval of the people.

Race   A term of questionable value and use. With respect to culture, race usually implies a human community identified by a shared set of distinctive hereditary physical characteristics. However, racial identification can be used as an all-too-convenient distinction between one community and the culture it contains and another community for the purpose of maintaining privileges and biases.

Repartimiento   The allocation of an Amerindian leader and his people to a Spaniard landowner to provide labor. Replacing many of the land grants called *encomiendas*, the *repartimientos* were an essential form of forced labor.

Subaltern   A term adopted by Italian intellectual Antonio Gramsci that literally means "of inferior rank." Gramsci used the term in relation to those groups in society who are subject to the hegemony of the ruling classes. Subaltern groups may include peasants, workers, and other groups denied access to hegemonic power. In the spirit of Gramsci and in the conception of the term as it is used in this study, however, there is constant negotiation between those in power and the powerless, the haves and the have-nots, with the latter exercising cultural guerrilla tactics that tend to subvert the power of the hegemonic classes.

Syncretism   The combination or juxtaposition of two or more cultural artifacts or terms relating to distinct practices within different cultural norms and conventions into one practice. The problem with this concept is that it threatens to carry with it the observer's (anthropologist, sociologist, political scientist, cultural or literary critic, or philosopher) perception and conception of two or more distinct terms and their corresponding practices, whether the practitioners actually envisage them as distinct or otherwise distinguishable or not. As far as the cultural practitioners are concerned, their culture is a whole. It is the presumably objective observers and analysts who break it up into chiefly dualistic categories.

Tapado After an incumbent president has given the person of his choice within the ruling political party a *dedazo* (identifying him as his successor), his identity is not yet known to the public. He remains *tapado* ("hooded"). If this person's identity were made known, then the reigning president's virtually absolute authority could be in jeopardy. The future candidate hence remains *tapado*, and at the proper moment there is a *destape* ("unhooding" or "revealing") and the official election campaign begins in full swing.

Técnicos The new breed of economic advisers to the Mexican president beginning with Miguel de la Madrid (1982–1988). Many of the *técnicos* have degrees from Ivy League universities with training in neoliberal economics.

References

Agosín, Marjorie. 1989. *Women of Smoke: Latin American Women in Literature and Life*. Trenton, N.J.: Red Sea.

Aguilar Camín, Héctor, and Lorenzo Meyer. 1985. *The Mexican Revolution and the Anglo-American Powers*. La Jolla, Calif.: Center for U.S.-Mexican Studies.

Agustín, José. 1990. *Tragicomedia mexicana I*. México: Planeta.

Ainsa, Fernando. 1989. "The Invention of America: Imaginary Signs of the Discovery and Construction of Utopia." *Diogenes* 145: 98–111.

————. 1993. "Invención de la utopía y deconstrucción de la realidad." In L. Zea, ed., *Sentido y proyección de la conquista*. México: Fondo de Cultura Económica.

Alba, Victor. 1967. *The Mexicans: The Making of a Nation*. New York: Praeger.

————. 1969. *The Latin Americans*. New York: Praeger.

Aleramo, Sibila. 1990. *Una mujer*. Barcelona: Circe.

Alvar, Manuel. 1992. "Fantastic Tales and Chronicles of the Indies." In R. Jara and N. Spadaccini, eds., *American Images and the Legacy of Columbus*. Minneapolis: University of Minnesota Press.

Alvas, Abel A. 1996. *Brutality and Benevolence: Human Ethology, Culture, and the Birth of Mexico*. New York: Greenwood.

Anda, R. M. de, ed. 1996. *Chicanas and Chicanos in Contemporary Society*. Boston: Allyn & Bacon.

Anzaldúa, Gloria. 1987. *Borderlands/La Frontera: The New Mestiza*. San Francisco: Aunt Lute.

Arens, W. 1979. *The Man-Eating Myth: Anthropology and Anthropophagy*. Oxford: Oxford University Press.

Arrom, S. M. 1985. *The Women of Mexico City, 1790–1857*. Stanford: Stanford University Press.

Azuela, Arturo. 1985. *Shadows of Silence*. Notre Dame, Ind.: University of Notre Dame Press.

Azuela, Mariano. 1983. *The Flies, the Bosses*. Berkeley: University of California Press.

_____. 1996. *The Underdogs*. New York: Signet.

Baddeley, Oriana, and Valerie Fraser. 1989. *Drawing the Line: Art and Cultural Identity in Contemporary Latin America*. London: Verso.

Barkin, David. 1990. *Distorted Development: Mexico in the World Economy*. Boulder: Westview.

Barry, Tom. 1995. *Zapata's Revenge: Free Trade and the Farm Crisis in Mexico*. Boston: South End.

Bartra, Roger. 1992. *The Cage of Melancholy: Identity and Metamorphosis in the Mexican Character*. Translated by C. J. Hall. New Brunswick, N.J.: Rutgers University Press.

Baudet, Henri. 1965. *Paradise on Earth: Some Thoughts on European Images of Non-European Man*. Translated by E. Wentholt. New Haven: Yale University Press.

Bauer, K. J. 1974. *The Mexican War, 1846–1848*. New York: Macmillan.

Bazant, J. 1977. *A Concise History of Mexico: From Hidalgo to Cárdenas, 1805–1940*. Cambridge: Cambridge University Press.

Becker, Marjorie. 1996. *Setting the Virgin on Fire: Lázaro Cárdenas, Michoacán Peasants, and the Redemption of the Mexican Revolution*. Berkeley: University of California Press.

Benjamin, Thomas. 1996. *A Rich Land, a Poor People: Politics and Society in Modern Chiapas*. Rev. ed. Albuquerque: University of New Mexico Press.

Berger, Peter L., and Thomas Luckmann. 1966. *The Social Construction of Reality: A Treatise in the Sociology of Knowledge*. New York: Doubleday.

Berkhofer, Robert F. 1978. *The White Man's Indian: Images of the American Indian from Columbus to the Present*. New York: Knopf.

Berman, Morris, *The Re-Enchantment of the World*. Ithaca: Cornell Universtiy Press, 1981.

Bernal, M. E., and G. P. Knight, eds. 1993. *Ethnic Identity: Formation and Transmission Among Hispanic and Other Minorities*. Albany: State University of New York Press.

Bonfil Batalla, Guillermo. 1996. *México Profundo: Reclaiming a Civilization*. Translated by P. A. Dennis. Austin: University of Texas Press.

Bradford, Sax. 1962. *Spain in the World*. New York: D. van Nostrand.

Brading, David A. 1980. *Caudillo and Peasant in the Mexican Revolution*. Cambridge: Cambridge University Press.

_____. 1986. *Prophecy and Myth in Mexican History*. Cambridge: Cambridge University Press.

Brandenburg, Frank. 1964. *The Making of Modern Mexico*. Englewood Cliffs, N.J.: Prentice-Hall.

Brenan, Gerald. 1943. *The Spanish Labyrinth*. Cambridge: Cambridge University Press.

Brenner, Anita, and George R. Leighton. 1984. *The Wind That Swept Mexico: The History of the Mexican Revolution of 1910–1942*. Austin: University of Texas Press.

Brislin, Richard W. 1993. *Understanding Culture's Influence on Behavior*. New York: Harcourt Brace Jovanovich.

Britton, John A. 1995. *Revolutionary Ideology: Images of the Mexican Revolution in the United States*. Lexington: University Press of Kentucky.

Bruhn, Kathleen. 1996. *Taking on Goliath: The Emergence of a New Left and the Struggle for Democracy in Mexico*. College Park: Pennsylvania State University Press.

Brusco, Elizabeth E. 1995. *The Reformation of Machismo: Evangelical Conversion and Gender in Colombia*. Austin: University of Texas Press.

Burkholder, Mark A., and Lyman J. Johnson. 1994. *Colonial Latin America*. New York: Oxford University Press.

Burns, E. Bradford. 1980. *The Poverty of Progress: Latin America in the Nineteenth Century*. Berkeley: University of California Press.

Camp, Roderic Ai. 1989. *Politics in Mexico*. New York: Oxford University Press.

_____. 1993. *Who's Who in Mexico Today*. Boulder: Westview.

Campa, A. 1993. *Hispanic Culture in the Southwest*. Norman: University of Oklahoma Press.

Campobello, Nellie. 1988. *Cartucho: My Mother's Hands*. Austin: University of Texas Press.

Campos, Julieta. 1993. *She Has Reddish Hair and Her Name Is Sabina*. Athens: University of Georgia Press.

Carbaugh, David, ed. 1990. *Cultural Communication and Intercultural Contact*. Hillsdale, N.J.: Erlbaum.

Carr-Ruffino, Norma. 1996. *Managing Diversity: People Skills for a Multicultural Workplace*. Albany: International Thompson.

Carrasco, D. 1992. *Quetzalcoatl and the Irony of Empire: Myth and Prophecies in the Aztec Tradition*. Chicago: University of Chicago Press.

Carroll, P. J. 1991. *Blacks in Colonial Veracruz: Race, Ethnicity, and Regional Development*. Austin: University of Texas Press.

Castañeda, Jorge G. 1993. *Utopia Unarmed: The Latin American Left After the Cold War*. New York: Vintage.

———. 1995. *The Mexican Shock: Its Meaning for the U.S.* New York: New Press.

Castellanos, Rosario. 1992. *The Nine Guardians*. New York: Readers International.

———. 1998. *The Book of Lamentations*. New York: Penguin.

Castillo, Ana. 1994. *Massacre of the Dreamers*. New York: Penguin.

Chance, K. 1978. *Race and Class in Colonial Oaxaca*. Stanford: Stanford University Press.

Cline, Howard F. 1963. *Mexico: Revolution to Evolution, 1940–1960*. Oxford: Oxford University Press.

Cockcroft, James D. 1968. *Intellectual Precursors of the Mexican Revolution, 1900–1913*. Austin: University of Texas Press.

———. 1990. *Mexico: Class Formation, Capital Accumulation, and the State*. New York: Monthly Review Press.

———. 1991. *Diego Rivera*. New York: Chelsea House.

Coe, Michael. 1994. *Mexico: From the Olmecs to the Aztecs*. New York: Thames & Hudson.

Collier, G., and E. L. Quaratiello. 1994. *Basta! Land and the Zapatista Rebellion in Chiapas*. Oakland: Institute for Food and Development Policy.

Condon, John C., and Fathi Yousef. 1975. *An Introduction to Intercultural Communication*. Indianapolis: Bobbs-Merrill.

Conover, Ted. 1987. *Coyotes: A Journey Through the Secret World of America's Illegal Aliens*. New York: Random House.

Cottam, Martha L. 1994. *Images and Interventions: U.S. Politics in Latin America*. Pittsburgh: University of Pittsburgh Press.

Crow, John A. 1985. *Spain: The Root and the Flower*. Berkeley: University of California Press.

Cruz, Barbara C. 1998. *José Clemente Orozco*. New York: Enslaw.

Cumberland, Charles C. 1968. *Mexico: The Struggle for Modernity*. Oxford: Oxford University Press.

Cypess, Sandra Messinger. 1991. *La Malinche in Mexican Literature: From History to Myth*. Austin: University of Texas Press.

DaMatta, Roberto A. 1991. *Carnivals, Rogues, and Heroes*. Notre Dame, Ind.: University of Notre Dame Press.

Danell Sánchez, Juan, and Pedro Mentado. 2000. "No cambiar el rumbo econóico." *Época*, September 20, pp. 1–8.

Davies, Miranda. 1986. *The Latin American Women's Movement*. Rome: Isis International.

De Aragón, Ray John. 1980. *The Legend of La Llorona*. Las Vegas: Pan American.

De Mente, Boyé Lafayette. 1996. *There's a Word for It in Mexico: The Complete Guide to Mexican Thought and Culture*. Chicago: NTC.

Dealy, Glen Caudill. 1992. *The Latin Americans: Spirit and Ethos*. Boulder: Westview.

Degler, Carl N. 1971. *Neither Black nor White: Slavery and Race Relations in Brazil and the United States*. New York: Macmillan.

Díaz del Castillo, Bernal. 1963. *Conquest of New Spain*. New York: Viking.

Díaz-Guerrero, Rogelio. 1975. *Psychology of the Mexican*. Austin: University of Texas Press.

Díaz-Guerrero, Rogelio, and Lorand B. Szalay. 1991. *Understanding Mexicans and Americans: Cultural Perspectives in Conflict*. New York: Plenum.

Dobbs, B. J. T. 1975. *The Foundations of Newton's Alchemy*. Cambridge: Cambridge University Press.

Draper, Theodore. 1965. *Castroism: Theory and Practice*. New York: Praeger.

Drucker, Malka. 1991. *Frida Kahlo: Torment and Triumph in Her Life and Art*. New York: Bantam.

Dunn, Timothy J. 1996. *The Militarization of the U.S.-Mexico Border, 1978–1992*. Austin: University of Texas Press.

Eddy, Robert, ed. 1996. *Reflections on Multiculturalism*. Yarmouth, Me.: Intercultural.

Elliott, J. H. 1989. *Spain and Its World, 1500–1700*. New Haven: Yale University Press.

Esquivel, Laura. 1994. *Like Water for Chocolate*. New York: Anchor.

_____. 1997. *The Law of Love*. New York: Crown.

EZLN. 1994. "Versión de Propuesta del EZLN para que se inicie el diálogo." *La Jornada,* January 11, p. 10.

_____. 1995. "Declaration from the Lacandon Jungle." In J. Beverley, M. Aronna, and J. Oviedo, eds., *The Postmodern Debate in Latin America*. Durham, N.C.: Duke University Press.

Ferraro, Gary P. 1990. *The Cultural Dimension of International Business*. Englewood Cliffs, N.J.: Prentice-Hall.

Finer, Samuel E. 1988. *The Man on Horseback: The Role of the Military in Politics*. Boulder: Westview.

Fischman, Dennis. 1996. "Getting It: Multiculturalism and the Politics of Understanding." In R. Eddy, ed., *Reflections on Multiculturalism*. Yarmouth, Me.: Intercultural.

Fiske, John. 1989. *Understanding Popular Culture*. New York: Routledge.

Florescano, Enrique. 1994. *Memory, Myth, and Time in Mexico: From the Aztecs to Independence*. Austin: University of Texas Press.

Folgarait, Leonard. 1987. *So Far from Heaven: David Alfaro Siqueiros: The March of Humanity and Mexican Revolutionary Politics*. Cambridge: Cambridge University Press.

————. 1998. *Mural Painting and Social Revolution in Mexico, 1920–1940*. Cambridge: Cambridge University Press.

Foster, David William. 1989. *From Mafalda to Los Supermachos: Latin American Graphic Humor as Popular Culture*. Boulder: L. Rienner.

Fowler-Salamini, H., and M. K. Vaughan, eds. 1994. *Women of the Mexican Countryside, 1850–1990: Creating Spaces, Shaping Transitions*. Tucson: University of Arizona Press.

Franco, Jean. 1991. *Plotting Women: Gender and Representation in Mexico*. New York: Columbia University Press.

Frank, Patrick. 1998. *Posada's Broadsheets*. Albuquerque: University of New Mexico Press.

Fuentes, Carlos. 1964. *The Death of Artemio Cruz*. New York: Noonday.

————. 1971a. *Where the Air Is Clear*. New York: Noonday.

————. 1971b. *Tiempo mexicano*. México: Joaquín Mortiz.

————. 1976. *Cervantes, o, La crítica de la letra*. México: Joaquín Mortiz.

————. 1978. *The Hydra Head*. New York: Farrar Straus & Giroux.

————. 1990. *Valiente mundo nuevo: Épica, utopía y mito en la novela hispanoamericana*. México: Fondo de Cultura Económica.

————. 1992. *The Buried Mirror: Reflections on Spain and the New World*. New York: Houghton Mifflin.

————. 1997a. *The Old Gringo*. New York: Noonday.

————. 1997b. *The Crystal Frontier*. New York: Farrar Straus & Giroux.

————. 1998. *The Diary of Frida Kahlo*. New York: Abradale.

Fuentes, Patricia de. 1993. *The Conquistadors: First-Person Account of the Conquest of Mexico*. Norman: Oklahoma University Press.

García Canclini, Néstor. 1993. *Transforming Modernity: Popular Culture in Mexico*. Translated by L. Lozano. Austin: University of Texas Press.

————. 1995. *Hybrid Cultures: Strategies for Entering and Leaving Modernity*. Translated by C. L. Chiappari and S. L. López. Minneapolis: University of Minnesota Press.

Garro, Elena. 1967. *Recollections of Things to Come*. Austin: University of Texas Press.

Gerbi, Antonello. 1985. *Nature in the New World: From Christopher Columbus to Gonzalo Fernández de Oviedo*. Translated by J. Moyle. Pittsburgh: University of Pittsburgh Press.

Gibson, Charles. 1964. *The Aztecs Under Spanish Rule*. Stanford: Stanford University Press.

_____. 1966. *Spain in America*. New York: Harper & Row.

Gil, Carlos B., ed. 1992. *Hope and Frustration: Interviews with Leaders of Mexico's Political Opposition*. Wilmington, Del.: Scholarly Resources.

Glantz, Margo. 1991. *My Family Tree*. London: Serpent's Tail.

_____. 1995. "La Malinche: La lengua en la mano." In E. Florescano, ed., *Mitos mexicanos*. México: Cal y Arena.

Goldwert, Marvin. 1980. *History as Neurosis: Paternalism and Machismo in Spanish America*. Lanham, Md.: University Press of America.

Gómez-Peña, Guillermo. 1996. *The New World Border*. San Francisco: City Lights.

Gómez-Quiñones, J. 1990. *Chicano Politics: Reality and Promise, 1940–1990*. Albuquerque: University of New Mexico Press.

González, Alberto, Marsha Houston, and Victoria Chen. 1997. *Our Voices: Essays in Culture, Ethnicity, and Communication: An Intercultural Anthology*. 2d ed. Los Angeles: Roxbury.

Gossen, Gary H., and Miguel León-Portilla, eds. 1993. *South and Meso-American Native Spirituality: From the Cult of the Feathered Serpent to the Theology of Liberation*. New York: Crossroad.

Graham, Richard, ed. 1990. *The Idea of Race in Latin America, 1870–1940*. Austin: University of Texas Press.

Grayson, George W. 1980. *The Politics of Mexican Oil*. Pittsburgh: University of Pittsburgh Press.

Grieder, Terence. 1983. *Origins of Pre-Columbian Art*. Austin: University of Texas Press.

Grisword del Castillo, R. 1990. *The Treaty of Guadalupe Hidalgo: A Legacy of Conflict*. Norman: University of Oklahoma Press.

Gudykunst, William B., and Stella Ting-Toomey. 1988. *Culture and Interpersonal Communication*. Thousand Oaks, Calif.: Sage.

Gudykunst, William B., Stella Ting-Toomey, and Tsukusa Nichida. 1996. *Communication in Personal Relationships Across Cultures*. Thousand Oaks, Calif.: Sage.

Guillermoprieto, Alma. 1994. *The Heart That Bleeds: Latin America Now*. New York: Vintage.

Gutiérrez, R. 1991. *When Jesus Came, the Corn Mothers Went Away*. Stanford: Stanford University Press.

Gutmann, Matthew C. 1996. *The Meanings of Macho: Being a Man in Mexico City*. Berkeley: University of California Press.

Guzmán, Martín Luis. 1965. *The Eagle and the Serpent*. Garden City, N.Y.: Dolphin.

Hale, Charles A. 1990. *The Transformation of Liberalism in Late 19th Century Mexico*. Princeton: Princeton University Press.

Hall, Edward T. 1959. *The Silent Language*. New York: Doubleday.

_____. 1966. *The Hidden Dimension*. New York: Doubleday.

_____. 1976. *Beyond Culture*. New York: Doubleday.

_____. 1983. *The Dance of Life: The Other Dimension of Time*. New York: Doubleday.

Hall, Edward T., and Mildred Reed Hall. 1990. *Understanding Cultural Differences: Germans, French, and Americans*. Yarmouth, Me.: Intercultural.

Hamill, Hugh M. 1992. *Caudillos: Dictators in Spanish America*. Norman: University of Oklahoma Press.

Handelman, Howard. 1996. *Mexican Politics: The Dynamics of Change*. New York: St. Martin's.

Hanke, Lewis. 1959. *Aristotle and the American Indians*. Chicago: University of Chicago Press.

_____. 1965. *The Spanish Struggle for Justice in the Conquest of America*. Boston: Little, Brown.

Haring, Clarence Henry. 1947. *The Spanish American Empire*. New York: Oxford University Press.

Harris, Philip R., and Robert T. Moran. 1987. *Managing Cultural Differences*. Houston: Gulf.

Harrison, Lawrence E. 1997. *The Pan-American Dream*. Boulder: Westview.

Hartlyn, Jonathan, and Lars Schoultz. 1992. *The United States and Latin America in the 1990s: Beyond the Cold War*. Chapel Hill: University of North Carolina Press.

Harvey, Neil. 1998. *The Chiapas Rebellion: The Struggle for Land and Democracy*. Durham, N.C.: Duke University Press.

Hellman, Judith A. 1988. *Mexico in Crisis*. New York: Holmes & Meier.

Herrera, Hayden. 1983. *Frida: A Biography of Frida Kahlo*. New York: Harper & Row.

Herrera-Sobek, María. 1990. *The Mexican Corrido: A Feminist Analysis*. Bloomington: Indiana University Press.

Heusinkveld, Paula. 1994. *Inside Mexico: Living, Traveling, and Doing Business in a Changing Society*. New York: Wiley.

Hinds, Harold E., Jr., and Charles M. Tatum. 1985. *Handbook of Latin American Popular Culture*. Westport: Greenwood.

Hodges, Donald C., and Ross Gandy. 1983. *Mexico 1910–1982: Reform or Revolution?* London: Zed.

Holland, Gini. 1997. *Diego Rivera*. Austin: University of Texas Press.

Hoyt-Goldsmith, Diane. 1994. *Day of the Dead*. New York: Holiday House.

Iglesias Prieto, Norma. 1997. *Beautiful Flowers of the Maquiladora: Life Histories of Women Workers in Tijuana*. Translated by M. Stone and G. Winkler. Austin: University of Texas Press.

Ingham, J. M. 1986. *Mary, Michael, and Lucifer: Folk Catholicism in Central Mexico*. Austin: University of Texas Press.

Israel, J. I. 1975. *Race, Class, and Politics in Colonial Mexico*. London: Oxford University Press.

Jara, René, and Nicholas Spadaccini. 1992. *Amerindian Images and the Legacy of Columbus*. Minneapolis: University of Minnesota Press.

Johns, Christina Jacqueline. 1995. *The Origins of Violence in Mexican Society*. New York: Praeger.

Johnson, H. L. 1980. "The Virgin of Guadalupe in Mexican Culture." In L. C. Brown and W. F. Cooper, eds., *Religion in Latin American Life and Literature*. Waco, Tex.: Markham.

Johnson, John J. 1958. *Political Change in Latin America: The Emergence of the Middle Sectors*. Stanford: Stanford University Press.

Johnson, Julie Greer. 1983. *Women in Colonial Spanish American Literature*. Westport, Conn.: Greenwood.

Kandell, Jonathan. 1988. *La Capital: Biography of Mexico City*. New York: Holt.

Katz, Friedrich. 1998. *The Life and Times of Pancho Villa*. Stanford: Stanford University Press.

Katzenberger, Elaine, ed. 1995. *First World, Ha Ha Ha! The Zapatista Challenge*. San Francisco: City Lights.

Keen, Benjamin. 1971. *The Aztec Image in Western Thought*. New Brunswick, N.J.: Rutgers University Press.

Kicza, John E. 1983. *Colonial Entrepreneurs: Families and Business in Bourbon Mexico City*. Albuquerque: University of New Mexico Press.

Kicza, John E., ed. 1993. *The Indian in Latin American History: Resistance, Resilience, and Acculturation*. Wilmington, Del.: Scholarly Resources.

Kohls, L. Robert, and John M. Knight. 1994. *Developing Intercultural Awareness*. Yarmouth, Me.: Intercultural.

Krause, Enrique. 1998. *Mexico: Biography of Power*. New York: HarperCollins.

Kryzanek, Michael J. 1990. *U.S.-Latin American Relations*. New York: Praeger.

La Botz, Dan. 1992. *Mask of Democracy*. Boston: South End.

_____. 1995. *Democracy in Mexico: Peasant Rebellion and Political Reform*. Boston: South End.

Ladd, Doris M. 1978. *Mexican Women in Anahuac and New Spain*. Austin: University of Texas Press.

Lafaye, Jacques. 1976. *Quetzalcóatl and Guadalupe: The Formation of Mexican National Consciousness, 1531–1813*. Chicago: University of Chicago Press.

Lasky, Kathryn. 1994. *Days of the Dead*. New York: Hyperion.

Laurin, Asunción. 1978. *Latin American Women: Historical Perspectives*. Westport, Conn.: Greenwood.

Lawrence, D. H. 1951. *The Plumed Serpent*. New York: Vintage.

Lee, Dorothy. 1959. *Freedom and Culture*. Englewood Cliffs, N.J.: Prentice-Hall.

León-Portilla, Miguel. 1962. *Broken Spears: The Aztec Account of the Conquest of Mexico*. Boston: Beacon.

_____. 1990. *Aztec Thought and Culture*. Translated by J. Emory. Norman: Oklahoma University Press.

Leonard, Irving A. 1964. *Books of the Brave: Being an Account of Books and of Men in the Spanish Conquest and Settlement of the Sixteenth Century New World*. New York: Gordian.

_____. 1966. *Baroque Times in Old Mexico*. Ann Arbor: University of Michigan Press.

Levy, Daniel, and Gabriel Szekely. 1983. *Mexico: Paradoxes of Stability and Change*. Boulder: Westview.

Lewis, Oscar. 1951. *Life in a Mexican Village*. Champaign: University of Illinois Press.

_____. 1959. *Five Families*. New York: Basic.

_____. 1961. *The Children of Sánchez*. New York: Random House.

_____. 1964. *Pedro Martínez: A Mexican Peasant and His Family*. New York: Random House.

_____. 1966. *La Vida*. New York: Random House.

_____. 1969. *Death in the Sánchez Family*. New York: Random House.

Lieuwen, Edwin. 1965. *Arms and Politics in Latin America*. New York: Praeger.

Livermore, A. A. 1969. *The War with Mexico*. New York: Arno.

Lockhart, J. 1992. *The Nahuas After the Conquest: A Social and Cultural History of the Indians of Central Mexico, Sixteenth through Eighteenth Centuries*. Stanford: Stanford University Press.

Lomnitz, Claudio. 2001. *Deep Mexico, Silent Mexico: An Anthropology of Nationalism*. Minneapolis: University of Minnesota Press.

Lowry, Malcolm. 1965. *Under the Volcano*. New York: Signet.

Lu, Min-Zhan. 1996. "Representing and Negotiating Differences in the Contact Zone." In R. Eddy, ed., *Reflections on Multiculturalism*. Yarmouth, Me.: Intercultural.

Luce, Louise. 1992. *The Spanish-Speaking World: An Anthology of Cross-Cultural Perspectives*. Lincolnwood, Ill.: NTC.

Lugones, María. 1994. "Purity, Impurity, and Separation." *Signs* 19, no. 2: 458–477.

Lustig, Myron, and Jolene Koester. 1993. *Intercultural Competence: Interpersonal Communication across Cultures*. New York: HarperCollins.

Lynch, John. 1992. *Caudillos in Spanish America, 1800–1850*. New York: Oxford University Press.

Macías, A. 1982. *Against All Odds: The Feminist Movement in Mexico to 1940*. Westport, Conn.: Greenwood.

Maciel, David R., and María Herera-Sobek, eds. 1998. *Culture Across Borders: Mexican Immigration and Popular Culture*. Tucson: University of Arizona Press.

MacLachlan, Colin M., and Jaime E. Rodríguez. 1980. *The Forging of the Cosmic Race: A Reinterpretation of Colonial Mexico*. Berkeley: University of California Press.

Madariaga, Salvador de. 1947. *The Rise of the Spanish American Empire*. New York: Macmillan.

Maril, Robert Lee. 1992. *Living on the Edge of America: At Home on the Texas-Mexico Border*. College Station: Texas A&M University Press.

Martínez, Oscar J. 1994. *Border People: Life and Society in the U.S.-Mexico Borderlands*. Tucson: University of Arizona Press.

Mazón, M. 1983. *The Zoot-Suit Riots: The Psychology of Symbolic Annihilation*. Austin: University of Texas Press.

McGirk, Tim. 2000. "The Bionic Candidate." *Time*, July 3, pp. 39–41.

Meier, M. S., and F. Ribera. 1993. *The Chicanos: A History of Mexican Americans*. New York: Hill & Wang.

Menéndez Pidal, Ramón. 1957. *España y su historia*. Madrid: Minotauro.

merrell, floyd. 2002. *Learning Living, Living Learning: Signs, Between East and West*. Ottawa: Legas.

Meyer, Michael C. 1972. *Huerta: A Political Portrait*. Lincoln: University of Nebraska Press.

Michener, James A. 1969. *Iberia*. New York: Fawcett.

Mirandé, A., and E. Enríquez. 1979. *La Chicana*. Chicago: University of Chicago Press.

Monroy, D. 1990. *Thrown Among Strangers: The Making of Mexican Culture in Frontier California*. Berkeley: University of California Press.

Monsiváis, Carlos. 1987. *Entrada Libre: Crónicas de una sociedad que se organiza.* México: Era.

_____. 1997. *Mexican Postcards.* London: Verso.

Moore, J., and H. Pachón. 1985. *Hispanics in the United States.* Englewood Cliffs, N.J.: Prentice-Hall.

Mora, Carl J. 1990. *Mexican Cinema: Reflections of a Society/1896–1988.* Berkeley: University of California Press.

Moraga, Cherrié. 1983. *Loving in the War Years: Lo que nunca pasó por sus labios.* Latham, N.Y.: South End.

Mörner, Magnus. 1967. *Race Mixture in the History of Latin America.* Boston: Little, Brown.

Morse, Richard M. 1989. *New World Soundings: Culture and Ideology in the Americas.* Baltimore: Johns Hopkins University Press.

Naggar, Carole, and Fred Ritchin, eds. 1996. *Mexico Through Foreign Eyes.* New York: Norton.

Nelson, Cynthia. 1971. *The Waiting Village: Social Change in Rural Mexico.* Boston: Little, Brown.

Nicholson, Henry B., and Eloise Quiñones Keber. 1983. *Art of Aztec Mexico: Treasures of Tenochtitlan.* Washington, D.C.: National Gallery of Art.

Nuñez Cabeza de Vaca, Alvar. 1961. *Cabeza de Vaca's Adventures in the Unknown Interior of America.* Albuquerque: University of New Mexico Press.

Oboler, S. 1995. *Ethnic Labels, Latino Lives: Identity and the Politics of (Re)Presentation in the United States.* Minneapolis: University of Minnesota Press.

O'Gorman, Edmundo. 1961. *The Invention of America: An Inquiry into the Historical Nature of the New World and the Meaning of Its History.* Bloomington: Indiana University Press.

O'Malley, Ilene V. 1986. *The Myth of the Revolution: Hero Cults and the Institutionalization of the Mexican State, 1920–1940.* New York: Greenwood.

Oppenheimer, Andrés. 1998. *Bordering on Chaos: Mexico's Roller-Coaster Journey to Prosperity.* Boston: Little, Brown.

Orme, William A., Jr. 1993. *Continental Shift: Free Trade and the New North America.* Washington, D.C.: Washington Post Co.

_____. 1996a. *Understanding NAFTA: Mexico, Free Trade, and the New North America.* Austin: University of Texas Press.

Orme, William A., Jr., ed. 1996b. *A Culture of Collusion: An Inside Look at the Mexican Press.* Miami: University of Miami Press.

Ortega y Gasset, José. 1957. *Man and People.* Translated by W. R. Trask. New York: Norton.

Oster, Patrick. 1989. *The Mexicans: A Personal Portrait of a People.* New York: William Morrow.

Otero, Gerardo, ed. 1996. *Neoliberalism Revisited: Economic Restructuring and Mexico's Political Future.* Boulder: Westview.

Padilla, Félix M. 1985. *Latino Ethnic Consciousness: The Case of Mexican Americans and Puerto Ricans in Chicago.* Notre Dame, Ind.: University of Notre Dame Press.

Paz, Octavio. 1961. *The Labyrinth of Solitude: Life and Thought in Mexico.* Translated by L. Kemp. New York: Grove.

————. 1970. *The Other Mexico: Critique of the Pyramid.* Translated by L. Kemp. New York: Grove.

————. 1979. "Mexico and the United States." *New Yorker*, September 17, pp. 136–153.

————. 1988. *Sor Juana: Or, the Trope of Faith.* Cambridge: Belknap.

————. 1991. *Children of the Mire.* Cambridge: Harvard University Press.

Peña, Devon Gerardo. 1997. *The Terror of the Machine: Technology, Work, Gender, and Ecology on the U.S.-Mexico Border.* Austin: University of Texas Press.

————. 1998. *Chicano Culture, Ecology, Politics: Subversive Kin.* Tucson: University of Arizona Press.

Pike, Fredrick B. 1992. *The United States and Latin America: Myths and Stereotypes of Civilization and Nature.* Austin: University of Texas Press.

Pitt-Rivers, J. A. 1961. *The People of the Sierra.* Chicago: University of Chicago Press.

Poniatowska, Elena. 1992. *Massacre in Mexico.* Translated by H. R. Lane. New York: Thames & Hudson.

————. 1995. *Nothing, Nobody.* Philadelphia: Temple University Press.

Pratt, Mary Louise. 1991. "Arts of the Contact Zone." *Profession*, pp. 33–40.

Price, John A. 1973. *Tijuana: Urbanization in a Border Culture.* Notre Dame, Ind.: Notre Dame University Press.

Pritchett, V. S. 1965. *The Spanish Temper.* New York: Harper & Row.

Raat, W. Dirk. 1992. *Mexico and the United States: Ambivalent Vistas.* Athens: University of Georgia Press.

Rabasa, José. 1993. *Inventing A-M-E-R-I-C-A: Spanish Historiography and the Formation of Eurocentrism.* Norman: University of Oklahoma Press.

Ramírez Berg, Charles. 1992. *Cinema of Solitude: A Critical Study of Mexican Film, 1967–1983.* Austin: University of Texas Press.

Ramos, Samuel. 1962. *Profile of Man and Culture in Mexico.* Translated by P. G. Earle. Austin: University of Texas Press.

Rangel, Carlos. 1987. *The Latin Americans: Their Love-Hate Relationship with the United States.* New Brunswick, N.J.: Transaction.

Reed, John. 1969. *Insurgent Mexico.* New York: International Publishers.

Revueltas, José. 1990. *Human Mourning.* Minneapolis: University of Minnesota Press.

Reyes, Alfonso. 1952. *La X en la frente.* México: Porrúa y Obregón.

Reyes Nevares, Salvador. 1970. "El Machismo en México." *Mundo Nuevo* 46: 14–19.

Ricard, R. 1966. *The Spiritual Conquest of Mexico.* Berkeley: University of California Press.

Ricks, David A. 1983. *Big Business Blunders: Mistakes in Multinational Marketing.* Homewood, Ill.: Dow Jones-Irwin.

Riding, Alan. 1984. *Distant Neighbors: A Portrait of the Mexicans.* New York: Vintage.

Rodríguez, Antonio. 1969. *A History of Mexican Mural Painting.* London: Thames & Hudson.

Rodríguez, Jeanette. 1994. *Our Lady of Guadalupe.* Austin: University of Texas Press.

Rodríguez, Victoria Elizabeth. 1997. *Decentralization in Mexico.* Boulder: Westview.

———. 1998. *Women's Participation in Mexican Political Life.* Boulder: Westview.

Rodríguez O., James E., ed. 1989. *Mexican and Mexican American Experience in the 19th Century.* Tempe: Bilingual Press/Editorial Bilingüe.

———. 1997. *Common Border, Uncommon Paths: Race, Culture, and National Identity in U.S.-Mexican Relations.* Yarmouth, Me.: Scholarly Resources.

Romero, José Rubén. 1967. *The Futile Life of Pito Pérez.* Englewood Cliffs, N.J.: Prentice-Hall.

Rosaldo, Renato. 1995. Foreword to Néstor García Canclini, *Hybrid Cultures: Strategies for Entering and Leaving Modernity.* Minneapolis: University of Minnesota Press.

Rosenfeld, Lawrence B., and Jean Civikly. 1976. *With Words Unspoken: The Nonverbal Experience.* New York: Holt, Rinehart & Winston.

Ross, John. 1998. *The Annexation of Mexico.* Monroe, Minn.: Common Courage.

Ross, Stanley R. 1955. *Francisco Madero: Apostle of Mexican Democracy.* New York: Columbia University Press.

Rotella, Sebastián. 1998. *Twilight on the Line: Underworlds and Politics at the U.S.-Mexican Border.* New York: Norton.

Rouffignac, A. L. de. 1985. *The Contemporary Peasantry in Mexico: A Class Analysis.* New York: Praeger.

Rowe, William, and Vivian Schelling. 1991. *Memory and Modernity: Popular Culture in Latin America.* London: Verso.

Rubenstein, Anne. 1998. *Bad Language, Naked Ladies, and Other Threats to the Nation: A Political History of Comic Books in Mexico*. Durham, N.C.: Duke University Press.

Rubert de Ventos, Xavier. 1991. *The Hispanic Labyrinth: Tradition and Modernity in the Colonization of the Americas*. New Brunswick, N.J.: Transaction.

Ruiz, Ramón Eduardo. 1998. *On the Rim of Mexico: Encounters of the Rich and Poor*. Boulder: Westview.

Ruiz, V. L., and S. Tiano. 1987. *Women on the U.S.-Mexico Border*. Boston: Allen & Unwin.

Rulfo, Juan. 1971. *The Burning Plain*. Austin: University of Texas Press.

———. 1994. *Pedro Páramo*. New York: Grove.

Salas, Elizabeth. 1990. *Soldaderas in the Mexican Military: Myth and History*. Austin: University of Texas Press.

Sale, Kirkpatrick. 1990. *The Conquest of Paradise: Christopher Columbus and the Columbian Legacy*. New York: Knopf.

Samora, J. 1971. *Los Mojados: The Wetback Story*. Notre Dame, Ind.: University of Notre Dame Press.

Samora, J., and P. V. Simon. 1977. *A History of the Mexican American People*. New York: Norton.

Sánchez, G. J. 1993. *Becoming Mexican American: Ethnicity, Culture, and Identity in Chicano Los Angeles, 1900–1945*. Oxford: Oxford University Press.

Sanderson, Susan R. Walsh. 1984. *Land Reform in Mexico, 1910–1980*. New York: Academic.

Sayers Peden, Margaret. 1991. *Out of the Volcano: Portraits of Contemporary Mexican Artists*. Washington: Smithsonian Institution Press.

Schaefer, Claudia. 1992. *Textured Lives: Women, Art, and Representation in Modern Mexico*. Tucson: University of Arizona Press.

Schroeder, Susan, ed. 1997. *Indian Women in Early Mexico*. Norman: University of Oklahoma Press.

Schurz, William Lyle. 1964. *This New World*. New York: Dutton.

Seelye, H. Ned, ed. 1996. *Experiential Activities for Intercultural Learning*. Vol. 1. Yarmouth, Me.: Intercultural.

Seelye, H. Ned, and Alan Seelye-James. 1995. *Culture Clash: Managing in a Multicultural World*. Lincolnwood, Ill.: NTC.

Seelye, H. Ned, and Jacqueline Howell Wasilewski. 1996. *Between Cultures: Developing Self-Identity in a World of Diversity*. Lincolnwood, Ill.: NTC.

Shorris, Earl. 1992. *Latinos: A Biography of the People*. New York: Avon.

Simpson, Lesley Byrd. 1967. *Many Mexicos*. Berkeley: University of California Press.

Smith, J. B. 1983. *The Image of Guadalupe: Myth or Miracle?* New York: Doubleday.

Smith, Michael E. 1998. *The Aztecs.* London: Blackwell.

Sokolov, Raymond. 1991. *Why We Eat What We Eat: How the Encounter Between the New World and the Old World Changed the Way Everyone on the Planet Eats.* New York: Summit.

Soto, Shirlene Ann. 1990. *Emergence of the Modern Mexican Woman.* New York: Arden.

Souchère, Elena de la. 1964. *Explanation of Spain.* New York: Random House.

Soustelle, Jacques. 1961. *Daily Life of the Aztecs.* Stanford: Stanford University Press.

Spota, Luis. 1957. *The Wounds of Hunger.* Boston: Houghton Mifflin.

_____. 1963. *Almost Paradise.* Garden City, N.Y.: Doubleday.

Staudt, Kathleen A. 1998. *Free Trade: Informal Economics at the U.S.-Mexican Border.* Philadelphia: Temple University Press.

Stavans, Ilan. 1990. *The Riddle of Cantinflas: Essays on Hispanic Popular Culture.* Albuquerque: University of New Mexico Press.

_____. 1995. *The Hispanic Condition: Reflections on Culture and Identity in America.* New York: HarperCollins.

Steele, Cynthia. 1992. *Politics, Gender, and the Mexican Novel, 1968–88: Beyond the Pyramid.* Austin: University of Texas Press.

Stein, Philip. 1994. *Siqueiros: His Life and His Works.* New York: International.

Stevens, Evelyn. 1973. "Marianismo: The Other Face of Machismo in Latin America." In A. Pescatello, ed., *Female and Male in Latin America.* Philadelphia: University of Pennsylvania Press.

Stone, Samuel Z. 1990. *The Heritage of the Conquistadors.* Lincoln: University of Nebraska Press.

Storti, Craig. 1990. *The Art of Crossing Cultures.* Yarmouth, Me.: Intercultural.

Suchlicki, Jaime. 1996. *Mexico: From Montezuma to Nafta, Chiapas, and Beyond.* New York: Brasseys.

Suro, Roberto. 1998. *Strangers Among Us: Latino Lives in a Changing America.* New York: Random House.

Szanto, George. 1997. *Inside the Statues of Saints: Mexico Writers on Culture and Corruption, Politics and Daily Life.* New York: Vehicle.

Taibo, Paco Ignacio, II. 1994. *Four Hands.* New York: St. Martin's.

_____. 1996. *Return to the Same City.* New York: Mysterious.

Tangeman, Michael. 1995. *Mexico at the Crossroads: Politics, the Church, and the Poor.* Maryknoll, N.Y.: Orbis.

Tannen, Deborah. 1990. *You Just Don't Understand: Women and Men in Conversation.* New York: Ballantine.

Taylor, W. B. 1987. "The Virgin of Guadalupe in New Spain: An Inquiry into the Social History of Marian Devotion." *American Ethnologist* 14, no. 1: 9–33.

Teichman, Judith A. 1988. *Policymaking in Mexico: From Boom to Crisis*. Boston: Allen & Unwin.

Thomas, Hugh. 1995. *Conquest: Moctezuma, Cortes, and the Fall of Old Mexico*. New York: Touchstone.

Todorov, Tzvetan. 1984. *The Conquest of America*. New York: Harper & Row.

Traven, B. 1963. *The Treasure of Sierra Madre*. Boston: Hill & Wang.

_____. 1969. *The Cotton-Pickers*. New York: Allison & Busby.

Trompenaars, Fons, and Charles Hampden-Turner. 1998. *Riding the Waves of Culture: Understanding Diversity in Global Business*. 2d ed. New York: McGraw-Hill.

Turner, F. C. 1968. *The Dynamic of Mexican Nationalism*. Chapel Hill: University of North Carolina Press.

Usigli, Rodolfo. 1937. *El Gesticulador*. México: Stylo.

_____. 1971. *The Crown of Light; One of These Days*. Carbondale: Southern Illinois University Press.

Vallens, V. M. 1978. *Working Women in Mexico During the Porfiriato, 1880–1910*. San Francisco: R. & E. Research Associates.

Varner, John G., and Veannette J. Varner. 1983. *Dogs of the Conquest*. Norman: University of Oklahoma Press.

Vázquez, Josefina Zoraida, and Lorenzo Meyer. 1985. *The United States and Mexico*. Chicago: University of Chicago Press.

Velázquez, Fidel. 1987. "The Most Powerful Man in Mexico." *Washington Post*, p. D8a.

Vélez-Ibáñez, Carlos G. 1996. *Border Visions: Mexican Cultures of the Southwest United States*. Tucson: University of Arizona Press.

Vigil, James D. 1988. *Barrio Gangs: Street Life and Identity in Southern California*. Austin: University of Texas Press.

_____. 1998. *From Indians to Chicanos: The Dynamics of Mexican-American Culture*. Rev. ed. Prospect Heights, Ill.: Waveland.

Wagner, Roy. 1975. *The Invention of Culture*. Chicago: University of Chicago Press.

Warnock, John W. 1987. *The Politics of Hunger*. London: Methuen.

_____. 1995. *The Other Mexico: The North American Triangle Completed*. Montréal: Black Rose.

Weaver, Gary R., ed. 1998. *Culture, Communication, and Conflict: Readings in Intercultural Relations*. 2d ed. Needham Heights, Mass.: Ginn.

Weber, D. J. 1973. *Foreigners in Their Native Land*. Albuquerque: University of New Mexico Press.

Weber, Max. 1958. *The Protestant Ethic and the Spirit of Capitalism*. Translated by T. Parsons. New York: Scribner.

Whitaker, Arthur P. 1961. *Latin America and the Enlightenment*. Ithaca: Cornell University Press.

_____. 1962. *The United States and the Independence of Latin America*. New York: Russell & Russell.

Wilkie, James W., and Albert I. Michaels. 1984. *Revolution in Mexico: Years of Upheaval, 1910–1940*. Tucson: University of Arizona Press.

Wise, Carol. 1998. *The Post-Nafta Political Economy: Mexico and the Western Hemisphere*. University Park: Penn State University Press.

Wolf, Eric Robert. 1959. *Sons of the Shaking Earth*. Chicago: University of Chicago Press.

_____. 1972. "The Virgin of Guadalupe: A Mexican National Symbol." In W. A. Lessa and E. Z. Vogt, eds., *Reader in Comparative Religion: An Anthropological Approach*. New York: Harper & Row.

Wolfe, Bertram D. 1963. *The Fabulous Life of Diego Rivera*. New York: Stein & Day.

Womack, John. 1970. *Zapata and the Mexican Revolution*. New York: Vintage.

Yáñez, Agustín. 1971. *At the Edge of the Storm*. Austin: University of Texas Press.

Zamora, Margarita. 1993. *Reading Columbus*. Berkeley: University of California Press.

Zarembo, Alan. 2000. "Soda Pop to *Vox Populi*." *Newsweek,* July 17, p. 36.

Zavala, Silvio Arturo. 1955. *Sir Thomas More in New Spain: A Utopian Adventure of the Renaissance*. London: Hispanic and Luso-Brazilian Councils.

Zea, Leopoldo. 1969. *Latin America and the World*. Norman: University of Oklahoma Press.

_____. 1992. *The Role of the Americas in History*. Lanham, Md.: Rowman & Littlefield.

Zorita, Alonso de. 1963. *Life and Labor in Ancient Mexico*. Translated by B. Keen. New Brunswick, N.J.: Rutgers University Press.

Index